7/18/2

Susan + Dan
you are two of
my favorite people!
Read about Jake
Gotlieb on Page 69!
He saved my life +
I loved him!
        Best
            Jack 8-

LET THERE BE LIGHT

By Jack Zukerman

My Life Among Giants, Monarchs & Mobsters
In the World of Architectural Lighting

With contributions from Randy Burkett, Barbara Horton, Mike Gehring, Paul Gregory, Charles Stone, David Singer, Craig Roberts, Charles (Chip) Israel, Gary Steffy and Ray Grenald

WorldLit Publishing
Los Angeles, California

Let There Be Light
by Jack Zukerman

Published by: WorldLit Publishing
Address: 18375 Ventura Blvd. #655
                  Tarzana, CA 91356
Telephone: 866-547-0298
Fax: 818-230-7993
Website: www.worldlitpublishing.com
E-mail: jackzukerman@gmail.com

ISBN: 978-0-9830646-0-2
Library of Congress Control Number: 2010940765
First Edition. Printed in the United States of America
10 9 8 7 6 5 4 3 2 1

Cover Design by Keith Johnson
Page Design by One-On-One Book Production,
West Hills, California

DEDICATION

To Roz, who has always been there through thick and thin.

To four of the greatest kids any man could love and respect as his children:
Marti, Steve, Jeff and Mike.

To all twelve of the grandkids, who follow in the footsteps of their parents:
Jamie, Julia, Max, Niki, Kate, Rachel, Marielle,
Lynn, Brad, Sara, Jake and Molly.

ACKNOWLEDGMENTS

"Acknowledgments" isn't nearly a strong enough word to express the gratitude I owe to all those who helped make this book possible.

Directly involved were all the wonderful people that have crossed my path from Moline to New York to Los Angeles. There were monarchs, poets and mobsters.

Sherwood Kiraly, my editor, provided the kind of guidance that honors his profession and performed this difficult task with gentleness and humor. Many times he said, "Jack are you sure you want to say that?" and usually he was correct, and I rewrote it. I am grateful for this new friend.

Michael Guinzburg, who provided me with the title of this book, is a master of his trade, and I shall always be indebted to him.

It is impossible to acknowledge my wife Roz enough for her contribution to this book because she was my toughest critic. As in all things in my life, it is impossible to tell where she begins and I leave off.

To all the wonderful lighting designers who wrote articles for this book, I shall forever be grateful.

Candy Potter has been my office wife for over ten years and my right arm; words alone could never express my feelings for this wonderful, talented lady.

Finally, Cooper Industries, a giant among giants, has shown me for the last six years the way a Fortune 500 company works.

TABLE OF CONTENTS

INTRODUCTION

One night in 1942 I walked down into the basement of my dad's Blue Ribbon Market in Moline, Illinois, to find my big brother Bill working on a big new gadget. Bill was ten years older than me and very good with his hands; he had a real understanding of mechanical and electrical products.

"Whatcha doing?" I asked.

"Take a look at this," he said, plugging in a cord. "It's called fluorescent light."

The radiance produced by the gizmo was brilliant, amazing, almost blinding, like nothing I'd ever seen.

Right then, at that moment … .

No. I will not say it. I *can't* say "I saw the light." For one thing it's unforgivable, and for another, it's not really true. I didn't see my future life's work shining in my face. I *remember* that moment, yes, and I remember I was impressed, but I wasn't all that interested in fluorescent light. I mean, come on, I was 12. I liked football, Hank Greenberg, Joe Louis, Gary Cooper, Humphrey Bogart and *Captain Midnight*.

I only got into the lighting industry after college, and then only because my father had died and my brother needed help. I was just pitching in, I thought. I had no intention of making a life and career of it.

But, as time went on, I began to see what light could do – in office buildings, shopping centers, hotels, museums, restaurants and residences. I learned that it can transform our surroundings as well as illuminate them.

There are hundreds of art books available but I haven't seen any books on architectural lighting, which is a shameful deficiency. It's a relatively new field, but it touches everyone's life and combines art and utility in a way that few crafts can.

Architectural lighting has its roots in theatrical lighting, which owes its compositional emphasis to painting. The architectural lighting designer paints with light, creating ambience, mood, and comfort, a stage for us to live in. A designer can be said to be a poet, a sculptor, a magician. Lighting design is, in my opinion, the ultimate marriage of art and science, and stands on its own as one of the highest and most powerful of all the arts.

In a lifetime in the field, I've been lucky enough to meet the best designers – pioneer visionaries, such as Abe Feder, of whom *The New Yorker* said, "Feder plays with light as a composer plays with sound." Abe was truly a magician, an inspiring man to know; his favorite saying was, "Push back the darkness!"

He also said light was a material that "can fill space without actually filling it" and that it had phantasmagorical possibilities. "Lighting – especially lighting at night – can make you see things you've never seen before."

Another great lighting-design innovator, Lesley Wheel, was always willing to share her discoveries with the next generation of designers, explaining, "After you realize something remarkable you want to pass it on."

In this book, I'm going to take Lesley's advice and pass on what I've learned on my own American-dream journey. Over the years my work has matched me with industrial giants on projects as challenging as the John Hancock building in Chicago, the World Trade Centers in New York, and the Library of Congress in Washington, D.C. Along the way, I've encountered every kind of businessman and artist – from mobsters to poets in light.

On a personal note, I've also encountered just about every kind of attitude – from near-saintly good will and kindness to bigotry. As a member of one of only two Jewish families in Moline, I had to meet prejudice head-on while growing up, and it taught me a lot about the way we all look at each other. Although there's still plenty of work to be done, we've made great strides since my boyhood.

As my career expanded, my wife Roz and I eventually found our way to Beverly Hills, where our neighbors included Hollywood names such as Danny Thomas and Alfred Hitchcock (another lighting expert). Finally, a few years ago, I sold my company, RSA, to a Fortune 500 company, Cooper Lighting. I'm not the retiring type, though, so I still help run RSA under the Cooper banner.

I've come this far "on my own" because I had someone with me every step of the way: parents to give me a work ethic and ethics in general; siblings, teammates and classmates; kids and grandkids; most of all, Roz, whom I first saw in a photograph 61 years ago, and who still knocks me out; and, finally, by my colleagues, the friends I've made in a field which enriches all our lives by pushing back the darkness in vivid and innovative ways.

I'm still learning. Selling my company a few years ago introduced me to the Fortune 500 culture, which you'd think would mean the hard work is over. But, even at that height, it's easy to misstep. If you're not careful, your wildly successful Fortune 500 company can become remote from its own product, stop innovating and lose contact with its employees and customers – without whom, of course, you've got no company. At RSA we still do our best to stay ahead of the competition.

And it is a competitive business, in which others are quick to mimic any new wrinkle that works. For years, I've kept a piece of writing on my office wall to remind myself of the best way to protect against imitators. It's by Rudyard Kipling. He obviously wasn't talking about running a lighting company, but he describes the attitude successful innovators have always had in any field:

> *They copied and they copied and they copied,*
> *But they couldn't copy my mind,*
> *So I left 'em sweating and stealing*
> *A year and a half behind.*

We live in a time of economic anxiety. People don't have a lot of confidence. I grew up in a time when people were also worried, the economy was in disarray, jobs were scarce, and money was tight. I don't know if my story will offer an example for today's would-be entrepreneurs picking their way among the business pitfalls, but, even if it doesn't provide a guaranteed roadmap to success, it will introduce you to a fascinating, underappreciated field – and that should be illuminating.

BOOK ONE

CHAPTER I

MOM, MOE, MOLINE & ME

"Whaddya mean I killed Jesus? I didn't even know him!"

The gang of kids became more intense. For me, the eight-year-old they called "Zook," it was another in a series of fights – this one was against Keith Anderson – that I had while growing up in small-town Moline, Illinois.

Keith and I stood there pushing and punching, for no reason I could see. I didn't understand why a bunch of rabid third and fourth graders were calling me a "Jesus killer." How could they think I did it, eight years old and living in Moline the whole time?

I couldn't understand why they were calling me "dirty" Jew either, but I knew I didn't like it and I had to do something about it. I was a tough kid because I had to be. America in 1938 was infected with bigotry.

When I got home that day – bruised, bloody, knuckles skinned, clothing torn – I had one question for my mother: "Why?"

She sat me down and looked me in the eye.

"Jack, you can't fight back."

Then she added, "If you're Jewish, you have to be gold to be silver."

That stayed with me. There was something about Jewishness that made it mandatory to try harder. To be respected, I had to be twice as good. Sound advice. Actually, if you want to do good work, it's sound advice for anybody.

But "You can't fight back" – well, to me that was Mom talk, not practical talk. Moms thought if they all got together and said don't fight, maybe boys would stop fighting all over the world.

I wasn't about to take any crap from anybody.

✿   ✿   ✿   ✿

To New Yorkers and Californians, "Moline" sounds like the name of a girl in an old Chuck Berry song, but it's really from the old French word, "Moulin," meaning mill. My Moline is a blue-collar town on the bluffs of the Mississippi River, 180 miles west of Chicago. It's part of the area called the Quad-Cities, which include Moline and Rock Island on the Illinois side and Davenport and Bettendorf, Iowa. When I was a kid, before the war, Bettendorf was smaller and the area was called the Tri-Cities.

Coastal people also think nothing ever happens in Moline since they've never heard of anything happening there. But before the Zukermans even arrived, my home turf hosted the Black Hawk Indian War, the agricultural revolution and a big step toward glory for Abe Lincoln.

Before the whites moved in, the area was home to the Sauk and Fox tribes. At one time 5,000 Native Americans lived there in elm bark lodges, planting corn, pumpkins, beans and other crops, fishing in the river and hunting fowl on its banks. It was the largest Indian village on the Upper Mississippi, a true home; but in the winter months, in keeping with their nomadic traditions, the Sauk would move west, across the river, to hunt on the snowy Iowa prairies.

During their wars against the whites, the Sauk and Fox were led by the great warrior Chief Black Hawk (1767-1838), an inspirational leader and brilliant military tactician. He might have won the Black Hawk War of 1832, but he never got the help he hoped for from the British in Canada, so eventually he and the Sauk and Fox ended up in Iowa year-round.

A Vermont blacksmith named John Deere set up shop in the area in 1848 and revolutionized farming by developing and marketing the world's first commercially successful, self-scouring steel plow. Deere's plow (made cost-effective by the utilization of cheap, available Pittsburgh steel) tamed the prairie and made the Tri-Cities area the farm-implement capital of the world.

In 1856, a steamboat owned by a man named John Hurd smashed into the railroad bridge spanning the river. The boat burned down and the bridge was destroyed. Hurd sued the Rock Island Railroad, owners of the bridge, and the owners engaged a Springfield trial lawyer, Abraham Lincoln, to defend them. Lincoln was an expert on railroad law and had experience splitting the rails besides. The trial was national news, pitting the old (the steamboats and the agrarian past) against the new (the railroads and the industrial future). Lincoln skillfully defended the railroad's interests and the case was thrown out. *Hurd v. Rock Island Railroad Company* was a pivotal case in Lincoln's career and solidified his reputation as a great trial lawyer.

Rock Island, Moline's sister city, sits on 946 acres in the middle of the Mississippi and is the site of the Rock Island Arsenal, maker of toys of war. It's the largest government-owned and operated arsenal in the U.S., the second biggest employer in the area after John Deere. During the Civil War, the Union housed nearly 13,000 Confederate prisoners on Rock Island. More than a thousand of them died in captivity and were buried there.

In World War II, Rock Island hosted Italian POWs, much to the delight of some lonely local gals who'd draw a line on the back of their legs with a ballpoint pen to approximate the hemline of a stocking and then head on over to the arsenal for some Italian-accented romance.

Life in Moline was life on the Mississippi. Samuel Clemens grew up not too far south, watching the moon shine on the same water that had passed by Moline. A town connected to Black Hawk, Abe Lincoln, Mark Twain and John Deere is about as heartland as it gets.

✿   ✿   ✿   ✿

I was born on May 5, 1930, and the Moline of my boyhood was 98 percent white.

The inhabitants were mostly Swedish, Belgian and German immigrants who had been enticed to the area, recruited to work for John Deere. There were only two Jewish families in all of Moline, or "John Deere Town," as it was sometimes called: the Brotmans, who owned the local movie theater, and the Zukermans. I never met the Brotmans until I was about 12 years old, so as far as I knew, I was the only Jewish kid in town.

In the war movies we saw growing up, the American GI platoons were usually made up of what Hollywood considered a healthy melting-pot mix: an Italian, a Latino, a black kid, a Jewish kid, a Filipino or a Chinese and Van Johnson. This was to reflect the diversity of cities like Chicago and New York, with their large, varied ethnic populations.

At school in Moline, I was the diversity.

I don't want to overstate it. Kids will find ways to tell each other apart even when they're all of the same background: the fat kid, the smart kid, the rich kid, the slow kid, the funny kid, the mean kid. I was just the one who was *officially* different.

Jews just weren't the norm in small-town America. Most Jewish immigrants at the beginning of the 20th century settled in cities like New York and Chicago, where they lived in their own communities, spoke their own languages, and did their best to recreate their neighborhoods in the old country.

My father, Moe Zukerman, came to America in 1913, all by himself at the age of 18, from Vaslouie, Romania. There had been eight Zukerman siblings, but only two besides Moe made the arduous journey from Vaslouie to America: older brother Julius, who settled in Chicago, and older sister Dora, who married a man named Sam Moskowitz and moved to Davenport, Iowa. The brothers and sisters who stayed behind would later be wiped out by the Nazis during Hitler's insane quest to rid the world of the Jews.

Moe came to the Tri-Cities because his older sister did, and he met my mother at a Rock Island social in 1919 – the men on one side of the room, the women on the other, everyone in their best clothes, standing around until the men got up the nerve to ask the cute women to dance. That aspect of the mating ritual seems eternal; the faces and dances change, but each generation of young men has to work up the same nerve.

Once Moe took on a family man's responsibilities, he never set them down. Like most boys, I got my image of what it meant to be a man from watching my dad – so, to me, a man was somebody who worked. Hard. To Moe, it was all about making good in America, creating something solid for the family: my mother Anna, my brother Bill, ten years my senior, my sister Frances, eight years older, and me, Jack, the baby of the family, the all-American kid who was crazy for sports.

The odds were stacked against Moe hitting it big. Sure, he had heart, energy and guts, as well as tons of integrity and smarts, but he'd had no real formal education.

Moe was an immensely strong man, 5-10 and 175 pounds of pure muscle, and as nice a guy as you'd ever want to meet. Like many immigrants of the time, he tried his hand at a variety of things to make a living – including a less-than-successful stint at running a diner – but the banks weren't keen on lending to Jews with no equity, so when he wanted to start his own business he turned to the Oxie, a private loan association run by a group of Jewish businessmen in the Tri-Cities area, including my father's friend, chicken farmer Louis B. Rich – whose name still graces a whole line of turkey products in the supermarket.

The Oxie worked like this: when you joined you put five dollars into a "savings account" – as did all the participants, regardless of need. When you wanted to borrow money you went to the board of directors; they'd loan you $5,000 and you'd pay back $100 a week for 50 weeks, no interest. The Oxie also functioned as a social club where hard-working men could play cards and have a few drinks and laughs after a long day – a place to share and compare their dreams, struggles and triumphs.

With the loan from the Oxie, Moe established his dream: the Blue

Ribbon Market in Moline. The Blue Ribbon building included three smaller stores – Dad's tenants – and a vacant lot which stood between the Blue Ribbon and the phone company offices. The Blue Ribbon was a full-service grocery store, from soup to nuts, with a superb butcher shop to boot.

Unfortunately, he faced some monster competition. There were no supermarkets in the 1940s, just the A&P (the Atlantic and Pacific, the precursor to today's chains) – which stood across the street from the Blue Ribbon.

I hated the A&P. How could we compete with their prices? Their wholesalers always undercut our suppliers' price and we couldn't go to their guys – couldn't buy in the same volume. Despite the superior quality of our meats, Moe had to lower our prices to rock-bottom profit margins just to stay in the game.

He had managed to buy the Blue Ribbon building with just $1,000 down, the rest in monthly payments, so he was always looking for ways to cut costs. He bought his groceries from a company called Arsenal Foods, owned by two friends, John and Herb Gellerman, who extended him credit.

But with the A&P across the street, turning a profit was an uphill battle all the way. To make ends meet, Moe often resorted to borrowing cash from a local gentleman I knew as Mr. Curtis – who today would be called a "hard money lender," or, in less formal circles, a loan shark. Mr. Curtis charged a weekly "vigorish," an exorbitant interest rate.

So Moe worked endless hours, stocking shelves, running the register, working the butcher shop, smiling and joking with the customers, chatting about births and deaths and the weather, the price of eggs. "How do you make a Romanian omelet?" he'd joke. "First, steal two eggs."

But my dad was anything but a thief, and he inspired great loyalty in people. Mr. Campbell, a wonderful, dignified Southern gentleman from Mississippi whom I adored, was the real butcher (and my protector when I was in Dad's doghouse for getting into fights), but if anything needed doing in the Blue Ribbon, Moe got it done. And he was a good provider despite having to juggle to keep up with the bills.

The customers loved him. He had a great ear for languages. Self-taught in the school of life, Moe spoke English, Swedish, Italian, Greek from his days in the restaurant business, and a few other languages (although whenever he wanted to tell a secret he spoke in Romanian or Yiddish, which I learned to understand, too). He knew what it felt like to fall behind on bills, worry over every penny, budget and plan and then re-plan, so he extended credit to the customers, whatever their ethnicity. He called them "charge accounts" because it sounded more dignified.

Many Saturday nights he'd take the whole family to the classiest joint in town, the Manhattan restaurant, for big thick delicious steaks. The Manhattan's owners shopped at the Blue Ribbon and didn't have enough money to pay their bills, so Moe would take us there for a big night and then tear up all their outstanding debts. And we loved every minute of it: the great slabs of steak and the steaming baked potatoes with hot pools of butter and cool wedges of cream cheese, the professional waiters in their fancy suits and bow ties making a big deal out of us all, Moe playing the big shot – this was living!

My father was what they now call a workaholic and he didn't like to leave the store for long, so it was always memorable when we hopped in the car and motored somewhere special on a vacation. One time we drove to Excelsior Springs, Missouri, a popular spa at the time. We also went to South Haven, Michigan – a Jewish resort known as the "Catskills of the Midwest." This was at a time when many hotel newspaper advertisements assured Gentile vacationers of their "restricted clientele," meaning "No Hebrews entertained." But South Haven was a magical place, fun-filled, with activities galore. That's where I met my first crush. Her name was Gloria. She was from Cleveland and "an older woman" of 12. I was 11 and had to go home. I'll always remember her, though.

✧   ✧   ✧   ✧

My mother, Anna Esrick, stood 5-4 and weighed in at 130 pounds of dynamic life force. She lived to the age of 97, with all her marbles.

Anna came to America in 1903, at the tender age of two, from Russia. Her mother had died giving birth to her, and Anna never got over it. To her dying day, she regretted not knowing her real mother: "I never even had a picture of her."

Once in America, Max Esrick, her father, remarried, giving Anna a mother, a lovely lady called Hanna, and four brothers. But Max himself was not an easy man to deal with. He had minimal education, earned his living as a blue-collar worker, and he was old school – he made my mother quit her studies at 15 and go to work to help support the rest of the family. But my mother was truly a renaissance woman; despite her lack of formal education, she would later become an accomplished public speaker, utilizing her speaking and organizational skills as the President of the national Jewish women's organization, Pioneer Women, and was also on the national board of City of Hope.

Max settled in Rock Island because of its higher concentration of Jewish people. There were at least 400 Jews in their own self-defined ghetto. The house my mother grew up in was on 9th Street, around the corner from the shul where the Orthodox Jews prayed – the women upstairs and the men downstairs. Max went there every morning and night to ask God to forgive him for his sins. His religion was no more easygoing than he was. Christians acknowledge ten biblical commandments; Orthodox Judaic tradition acknowledges 613.

About two blocks away sat the black Holy Rollers church, where they prayed by singing and rocking on the floor in a joyous frenzy of religious zeal. I was fascinated by the exotic sounds and sights of their worship. There weren't many blacks in the Tri-Cities area.

My mother loved her stepmother Hanna, and she adored and cherished her four brothers: Herman (the champion golfer), Ruben (her favorite, her "Ruby"), Joe, the second oldest, and Ben, the oldest, wisest and most caring of all. I knew Ruby better than the others since he lived in

Rock Island his whole life. He was a kind, gentle man whom I dearly loved. He died on his 65th birthday. I still miss him.

My mother was the disciplinarian in the family. When I'd come home from one of my after-school brawls – I never did master the art of not fighting back – she'd chase me around the kitchen with a wooden cooking spoon.

"Wait till your father gets home!" she'd cry, trying to get a few licks in while we waited. But I was always her favorite, and I knew I could get away with almost anything.

When I needed a haircut, I'd tell her I needed a dollar. In reality it cost just 75 cents. With the leftover quarter I'd buy four mini-hamburgers and a Coke – those burgers were really small.

My major crimes weren't too serious, although I guess one or two of them could have been.

When I was 12, on Halloween, I threw a garbage can through a neighbor's front window. Mr. Glockoff called my mother and I caught hell.

Then there was the time I pulled the fire alarm on 15th Street and watched delightedly as the fire trucks arrived, the firemen swearing under their breaths at the false alarm. She never found out about that one.

I wasn't so lucky the night I snuck out of the house, stole my dad's truck with my pal, George Malcolm, Jr., took a joyride, and ended up crashing into a telephone pole and getting arrested. I was supposed to be studying.

"I got bored," I told my father.

He thought it was hilarious, but my mother wasn't laughing. I was banned from driving for two years – kind of a given since I was only 14 – and for six months, every Saturday, I washed police cars until they sparkled.

A lot of my misbehavior was more on the order of ill-advised experiments. For instance, my mother had the old-fashioned type of washing machine in the basement. One time I put my arm into the wringer before it could stop. My arm got mangled pretty badly; I still have scars and indentations as a reminder of my boyhood curiosity.

At this point you may be thinking, "This young man does not seem destined to light the nation." And looking back at the youngster I was I'd have to agree with you. All I can say in his favor is he does show a willingness to try new things, even if the results don't inspire confidence.

We lived at 2320 13th Street in Moline, a lovely neighborhood called Prospect Park, on a tranquil street of green trees and tidy lawns, home to doctors and lawyers and shop owners – small-town America at its manicured best. The house had been bought for $13,000 and was a typical Midwestern home, with a big screened porch in the front, two bedrooms upstairs and one downstairs. Our next-door neighbor was Mr. Lindblad, head of the chemistry department at Moline High School. I would take advantage of our friendship when I got old enough to be in his class. The lab was on the third floor, and we'd fill balloons with water and throw them out the window at kids. I goofed around a lot in high school.

The garage was in back of the house. The narrow driveway made it very difficult to navigate the car safely in and out. I had many narrow scrapes parking the car, as well as the truck from the store.

We might have been the poorest family in the neighborhood, but my father prided himself on his home and his new Buick Roadmaster. Sure, he had to work like a dog, but he'd given his family a beautiful castle to live in.

My sister, Frances, had her own bedroom upstairs. My bedroom was upstairs and in the front. The yard was full of lilacs and I can smell them now, scenting the night with magic. Even today, lilacs are my favorite flower. We had twin beds, one for me and one for my big brother Bill. I could climb out my bedroom window, jump down to the porch, sneak out at night, wander the neighborhood, listen to frogs and crickets and just enjoy the freedom.

Bill was quiet, an introvert who always wanted to belong, to be a part of something, but never quite fit in. He didn't express himself easily; he wasn't a people person. We shared a room for years until he moved away and got married. When I was old enough, he let me use his car; I never had a car until I got married. Bill was good to me as a kid.

My mother also employed domestics, immigrant girls she'd pay five dollars a week plus room and board. They lived in a converted room in the attic, and Mom was a tough task-mistress, making them clean and cook and scrub the floor on their hands and knees. Years later, when she lived with us in California, even after the advent of "advanced mop technology," my mother would admonish our wonderful housekeeper, Maria, to hit the deck and clean the floor the old-fashioned way.

"In my day you get on your hands and knees and scrub like this!" she'd say, making vigorous wiping motions. "When you work for me, you'll do it like I say!"

Maria would just smile and nod, try not to roll her eyes, and stick with the mop.

✿ ✿ ✿ ✿

Back then, for a kid, the way the world was set up made sense. I looked up to my father and mother, and we all looked up to the man in the White House.

Franklin Roosevelt was president all through my early childhood, from 1932 until his death in 1945. He was wildly popular in our house, loved by all Jewish Americans. He seemed like the great man of the time, whose bold social programs and leadership were rescuing the nation from the financial collapse of 1929 and the Great Depression. Later, though, we found out he didn't allow some ships carrying Jews fleeing Hitler to dock in the USA, and I lost all respect for him. It might seem harsh to judge a man on one bad deed when he did a lot of good things, but you hold a hero to a high standard. That's why he's a hero.

The bigotry I'd encountered earlier worsened as America was drawn into the war.

I attended Garfield Elementary School, seven blocks from home, and after school some of the guys and I would head over to Browning Field on 16th Street to play pickup baseball games. My friends weren't anti-Semitic, but it seemed I was always mixing it up with some jerky kid or other who had a remark to make. The bigotry was literally in the air – the radio airwaves sizzled with the hate speech of the lunatic Father Coughlin, and the German-American Bund, an American Nazi group, which drew 20,000 nuts to Madison Square Garden in New York. That bunch even had its own Fuehrer. Anti-Semitism was an airborne virus.

So I'd end up toe-to-toe with some jackass – sock 'em in the nose, punch 'em in the face, that's how we settled things back then, with our fists, no guns or hand-held rocket launchers like they have today.

And I became tougher. Eventually that toughness would translate perfectly to the football field.

That bigotry was the one dark cloud over an otherwise happy kid's head – a cloud from a storm that was breaking out all over Europe.

I hadn't understood as a little boy why other kids would call me "Christ-killer" when I hadn't done it. But in a lot of ways I was lucky to be growing up where I was. In Europe the Nazis were rounding up six million people who hadn't done it either.

CHAPTER 2

FRIDAY NIGHT LIGHTS

Movies, music and radio glued us together in the late '30s and '40s, turning America into one giant audience for a few studios and a couple of networks.

We all loved the movies. The local movie house was called The Paradise. It was owned by the other Jewish family in Moline, the Brotmans. I was crazy about Gary Cooper, William (Hopalong Cassidy) Boyd, Ingrid Bergman, Humphrey Bogart, Lauren Bacall, and Cary Grant (a real gentleman; years later I would meet him at my tailor's in Beverly Hills). Judy Garland, Myrna Loy and Jean Arthur were other favorite stars. My favorite films of the time were *Arsenic and Old Lace, Casablanca, Citizen Kane, Destination Tokyo, The Philadelphia Story, The Maltese Falcon, The Postman Always Rings Twice, The Great Dictator, Thirty Seconds Over Tokyo,* and *Yankee Doodle Dandy.*

Next door to the Paradise was a music store run by an Italian immigrant family, four brothers and their parents. That's where I met the great Louie Belson, a friend of the family, who became one of the three greatest drummers of the time, along with Gene Krupa and Buddy Rich. Louie was of Italian heritage and married the great African-American singer Pearl Bailey, proving once again that true love and true talent are blind to bigotry – even though, sadly, his family didn't agree.

At night our family would gather around the radio and listen to *Amos 'n' Andy, The Adventures of the Thin Man,* Bing Crosby's *Kraft Music Hall, Captain Midnight, Duffy's Tavern* (written by a man who later became a good friend of mine, Bob Schiller, who also wrote *I Love Lucy* and *Maude*),

Edgar Bergen and Charlie McCarthy, Fibber McGee and Molly, The Glenn Miller Show, The Green Hornet and *The Whistler*. Long before TV, radio was "the electric fireplace."

On Sunday, December 7th, 1941, my buddies and I were downtown at a Tarzan movie when we heard the Japanese had bombed Pearl Harbor. I rushed home to find the whole family huddled around the Philco, in a state beyond shock, absorbing the news.

It was "a day that will live in infamy," as FDR famously said, and over the next two years, gasoline, candy and meat (anything the government considered essential) were all subject to strict rationing. (In those days, a carton of cigarettes and a few silk stockings could buy a mature man almost anything, but I was a kid and had no clue about such things.)

In order for Dad to get meat from the wholesaler, he had to give them ration stamps. He was always being approached by people who wanted to buy meat without stamps, but Dad rejected their overtures. His integrity wasn't for sale; the customer wasn't "always right."

At a certain point in 1943, though, with America deep into the war, gas and meat rationed and the Blue Ribbon struggling, Moe had to do something bold. So he sold the vacant lot between the Blue Ribbon and the phone company, shaking hands with his good friend Dr. Ben Williamson on an offer of $35,000.

While Dr. Ben's lawyers were drawing up the papers, Moe received a visit from a vice president of Illinois Bell phone company next door. Always curious, I listened in from just outside the ten-by-six-foot office at the back of the store.

"As your neighbor," the phone company executive said, "I'd like to discuss purchasing your vacant lot. Illinois Bell is prepared to offer you $60,000."

I couldn't believe my ears. That kind of money was a fortune in those days.

There was a brief pause, and then I *really* couldn't believe my ears.

"Can't do it," my father said. "I've already sold it to Dr. Williamson."

After the man left, I reminded my father that he hadn't yet signed anything with Dr. Ben. He looked at me with compassion and pity.

"I gave my word to Dr. Williamson," he said slowly and clearly, looking me in the eye to make sure I got it. "And if my word isn't any good, neither am I."

That was my dad. What a lesson to learn at 13.

✧   ✧   ✧   ✧

As I got older I started helping out at the Blue Ribbon. At 14, I was big enough to do a man's work, but delivering hundred-pound sacks of potatoes, one over each shoulder, up three flights of stairs to the Masonic temple wasn't exactly my idea of a good time – it felt just like exercise, which I have always hated. But I did love selling Christmas trees. It fit my personality. I was outgoing, good-humored, quick with a smile and a joke – a natural. And although I didn't know it, it was good training for the tougher customers I'd be running into in the years ahead.

"Thanks, Mr. Anderson," I'd say, winking at his son Keith, my old after-school bigoted brawling buddy who was now silent, even shamed, as I took his father's money in return for a tree. "Merry Christmas!"

I went to John Deere Junior High for seventh through ninth grades, a couple blocks from my home. It was there I first played organized football, on the 7th grade team, and I loved it. It was a way for me to express myself … on defense, by delivering a jolting tackle (I relished the crashing of bodies), and on offense, by creating something beautiful – catching a pass, stiff-arming an opponent, scoring a touchdown. Glory!

I played with two great black kids, Willie and David McAdams, brothers. Willie was older, David was in my class. We played together in junior high and in high school – in fact, both Willie and David were captains of Moline High's football team at different times.

While I was playing football in junior high, my parents enrolled me in Hebrew School in Rock Island, so three times a week I'd run ten blocks from football practice to catch the bus that took me to another bus that took me to my ancient roots – an hour of travel each way. This routine continued well into 8th grade, until I was Bar Mitzvahed.

My biggest heroes were athletes. There was Barney Ross, the great boxing champ, a Jew from Chicago … . Joe Louis, the Brown Bomber, the heavyweight champion of the world, a man of color – we'd listen to his fights on the radio with the rest of the nation, mesmerized by this likable and lethal boxing champ who dispatched his opponents (the "bum-of-the-month club," they were called) with grace and ease … . Hammerin' Hank Greenberg, the slugging first baseman for the Detroit Tigers, who had almost eclipsed Babe Ruth's home run record and who had to put up with terrible anti-Semitism in the major leagues. And there was Dolph Schayes, the great Jewish basketball player out of Brooklyn who played for the Syracuse Nationals … and many others, great heroes, from all the tribes that made up America.

Sports was a way out of poverty, the great equalizer, and at its best – witness Hank Greenberg, Joe Louis, Barney Ross, and Jackie Robinson after the war – it broke down barriers of prejudice and helped America grow up. Athletes of the time made the best role models a kid could have: proud champions who rose above poverty and bigotry to show that America really could be the land of inclusion and opportunity.

Browning Field, where I would play high school football, had a baseball field that was used by the Three-I League Moline Plows, the local minor league club. Now, the players on the Plows would never be confused with the athletic heroes of America – they were Class B ballplayers, part of the Chicago Cubs farm system, most of them destined never to get even a cup of coffee in the "big show," but they sure interested me. I wasn't much of a baseball player but I loved the team atmosphere, and the fact that they were being paid to play a kid's game. So I hung around, so much that they asked me to be their batboy – you know, the kid who picks up the bats, fills the water bucket, runs errands, the kid who's the butt of loving insults and practical jokes … .

One day one of the players gave me a dollar and said, "Hey, Zook, be a good guy and go buy some pigeon milk."

"Go on," said the first baseman, pounding his mitt. "It's good for oiling the glove, softens the leather right up."

So off I went in search of this magical elixir that softened baseball gloves, thinking, "Boy, how many pigeons does a guy have to milk to fill a bottle?"

I went to about ten different grocery stores. I was stared at, laughed at, told to get lost – even informed by one straight-faced joker that they were fresh out: "Darn it, I just sold the last quart!"

Tail between my legs, I went back to Browning Field, admitted my failure to find even a single drop of pigeon milk, and gave the guy back his buck. And then they started laughing. At me. Oh, I get it. Hahaha. The joke was on Zook. I felt like a dope, but I got over it.

Also, during high school, I was an usher for the Tri-Cities Blackhawks, then of the NBL (National Basketball League) and soon to be one of the original NBA teams. They played in Wharton Field House, adjacent to Browning Field. They later moved to Milwaukee, changed their name to the Hawks, and went on to Atlanta where they still are today. The team was once coached by Red Auerbach and actually drafted the great guard Bob Cousy. Cousy demanded a salary of $10,000 when the team was only offering $6,000. He didn't want to play in a small market, so both coach and star ended up as cornerstones of the Boston Celtics, the most successful pro basketball team in history.

But I saw them all when they came to Moline: Dolph Schayes, George Mikan, the first great NBA "big man" who starred on the Minneapolis Lakers, and many others. It was a great experience to interact with these top athletes. Pro basketball in those days was rough and the pay was abysmal by present-day standards, yet these giants exhibited a class and sportsmanship you rarely see among today's multimillionaires.

I grew up during a Depression, a global war and a post-war period during which the world seemed about to destroy itself, but those who survived it all would see some amazing things. The Chinese have a saying: "May you live in interesting times." It's meant to be a curse, but I count it as a blessing. During the span of my life I've witnessed advances in science, health, communications, travel and space exploration. America has gone from radio to Internet, from *Fibber McGee* to email and eBay, from a nation consumed by a virulent bigotry (that found me fighting all the time, that saw Japanese-Americans thrown into internment camps during the war and blacks suffering despicable examples of racism) to the election in 2008 of a black president.

I think our best quality has always been our determination, despite our shortcomings, to make things better … and make better things.

In the midst of my wartime boyhood, I went down in the basement of the Blue Ribbon one night and saw Bill working on some fluorescent lights. To me, a 12-year-old who was crazy about football, they made a dazzling but brief impression. I saw them and set them aside. But Bill was ten years older, thinking ahead.

Bill was not in the war. When he graduated from high school, he went to work at Moe's. Then he opened his own grocery store, which didn't work out, so he wound up back at the Blue Ribbon Market, working for our father. He also got married, to Ethel Edelman, a girl from Chicago.

Many years later, Ethel and Bill's older son, Gary, was tragically killed in an auto accident. He was about 50 years old. Their other son, Morrie, is today a lighting representative in Los Angeles.

The truth is, Bill would never be much of a businessman, but he was sharp enough to know a good thing when he saw it shine, and he would become a pioneer in the lighting field, making some of the first fluorescent fixtures in America. He sold the units to local merchants and installed them. Soon these long bulbs would revolutionize the lighting of public spaces: stores, markets, offices, restaurants, hospitals and schools. But the industry was only in its infancy. Bill was learning the business –

you might say inventing the business, like many others across America – with a friend of his, a wizard of an electrical engineer named Glen Olsen.

Bill and Glen lived across the street from each other after Bill got married and moved out of the house. They'd fabricate the metal, buy the sockets and the ballasts, assemble them, and then Bill would take them and install them in local stores. Their first lights were primitive 200 miliamp fluorescent strips, eight feet long.

Bill convinced my dad to go into the business, and B&M (Bill and Moe) Lighting was born. Among their first customers was a good friend of my father, Mr. Medd, who owned Dairy Queen, the national chain of ice cream stores. They were building Dairy Queens all over the country; they went from 100 stores in 1947 to almost 1500 in 1950 – Bill and Moe were fabricating and shipping fluorescent lights as fast as they could make them – the first national account!

As for me … well, the future was calling when I saw those lights in the basement, but it would have to call back later. For now I had more important things on my mind. I was in high school.

My three years at Moline High were a happy time, a time of plenty. Plenty of friends, plenty of great sports moments as a top football player, and plenty, let me repeat that, plenty of fun – unaided, strange as it may seem, by drugs or alcohol, at least among my cadre of pals. World War II was over and the economy was booming. These truly were "the best years of our lives."

I had a crush on a girl named Pat Tilburg. She was our homecoming queen, immensely popular and very nice. She could have been snobby but wasn't. Her father was a Lutheran minister and never approved of me. I didn't know if he was biased, but she wasn't. She ended up marrying the president of the University of Minnesota.

As I was writing this book, I felt extremely nostalgic and wanted to talk to Pat. I went to the University of Minnesota web site and looked for her last name, now that she was married to the President of the University.

I stared at the web site, not believing what I was reading, Pat had died a few months before. I sat at my computer, and my tears came without even realizing what had happened to me.

The kids at Moline High were super nice, the girls I was friends with were refreshingly clean-cut. It really was a gentler time – there was no pressure on kids to grow up too quickly.

But physically I had grown up in a hurry. I was 6-1 and 190 pounds – I guess toting bags of spuds up three flights of stairs to the Masons and all the years of clean living and Moe's quality meat were paying off.

My high school days were pretty free of the kind of bias I had encountered as a kid, but there would be a couple of memorable exceptions. One involved a kid called Dick Black who had been in the penitentiary. "Kid" makes him sound harmless; he was about 21 when the rest of us were 16, and he was big. I was big too, but this guy was a mammoth 6-3 and 240 pounds of farm boy/penitentiary toughness.

About 20 kids surrounded us one day as Dick Black beat the stuffing out of me. It was bad, but I never whimpered or cried. I'd made up my mind years before that they could beat the hell out of me, but I wouldn't let on.

My first high school coach, Jack Foley, was a man of steel who would go on to become the superintendent of schools in Rock Island and one of my best friends. After I'd been on the freshman football team two weeks, Coach Foley moved me up to the varsity and I never looked back.

I played end, on both defense and offense. Given a choice, I preferred offense – more glory. But back then you played both ways. I had good hands, I could catch a ball. I wasn't very fast, but no one big was very fast back then.

Football helped me grow in more than a physical way. Playing ball in high school and college really instilled the idea of team play, and I think it follows in life. You need individual initiative to fulfill your own potential, but I know now, working with a Fortune 500 company, that you have to be a team player if you're going to succeed in a corporate environment. An individualist just cannot succeed in that environment – he'll always be the odd man out.

I wore a facemask on the field because I had broken my nose a few times. The helmets then were a kind of plastic, but most players didn't wear anything in front of their faces and the pads were minimal. It was a tough sport. Everyone was big, everyone was strong. There were a lot of corn-fed, beef-brawny farm kids, most of them in better shape than I was – I hated to exercise. A lot of guys lifted weights. I didn't, I was too lazy; I did as little as possible.

I had to wrestle, though. It was mandatory for football players to join the Moline High wrestling team, the theory being that wrestling taught you how to move your hands and feet, how to use leverage. I was a heavyweight. I won three or four matches but that was about it. My coach was named Joe Vavrus. Joe was a great guy. He'd come from Northwestern University. (I didn't know much about Northwestern back then, but I'm an expert now; three of my kids ended up graduating from there and two of my grandkids go there too.)

Our team used the T formation. The quarterback was always right behind the center; he had the option to either run or pass. Our quarterback was a great kid named Don Henss. He went on to the University of Illinois and later became a football coach there.

If you get to be part of a strong, cohesive team when you're young, you retain affection for your teammates forever. The guys on that Moline High team really were special. We'd go out there every day in practice and just beat each other's heads in, day after day. I admit it doesn't *sound* like fun, and I wouldn't enjoy it right this minute, but it was fun then. We took pride in our toughness and there was a lot of mutual respect among the players.

One of my best friends during high school was Bill Mitton, who was captain of the team. Another good friend was Alan Shipley, probably the finest basketball player I ever knew and a delightful guy. He led the great Moline High team to the state finals, where we lost. He went off to the Korean War as a fighter pilot and got killed in the first few months. He was listed as MIA and was never found. We mourned him.

Henss, our quarterback, was another good friend, as was Kenny Harrison, who later went to work for John Deere. A lot of the guys did that; it was the hometown thing to do. John Williams was the center on the football team, a bright kid who became a doctor. Harvey Carrothers was a co-captain of the football team and became a fire chief. He died at a young age. Several of the guys I went to school with died young, but some, like Bill Mitton and Ralph Medd (son of the Mr. Medd who owned Dairy Queen), are my friends to this day.

Even back then, it was easy to spot the winners, the future leaders. Tom Railsback became a U.S. congressman; my son, Jeff, later worked for him in Washington. Bud Crampton became a judge. Don Frazier became an executive with John Deere. The class of '48 had a lot to be proud of.

All of us on those high-school teams got a taste of what it was like to perform under pressure, because the crowds at our games were intense. Unless you've lived in a small town, you cannot fathom the level of hysteria and emotion caused by high school football and basketball. The whole town shows up for the game on Friday night. Every game is life or death. It really is like the popular TV show *Friday Night Lights,* set in Texas. The coaches and the players are part of the social fabric of the community and the games are a kind of ritual.

There was a vicious sports rivalry between Moline and Rock Island. We hated Rock Island like poison, to the point where a bunch of teammates and I would drive over there during the week and look for trouble – four or five of us cruising in cars, wearing our letter sweaters, looking to get into beefs with our cross-town rivals. Often it never escalated to fisticuffs, just ended with a lot of taunting and screaming and teasing. And once on the field, both teams shared a very sportsmanlike brutality, a healthy kind of hate, if such a thing is possible.

My father was a regular at most of my games, and it was a big day for the family in my senior year, when Moline played Rock Island and my picture was on the front page of the Rock Island newspaper. I remember the opening kickoff – I had never caught a kickoff in my life, but this time they kicked it straight to me! Nine or ten of them gang-tackled me, just pounded the hell out of me. There were a lot of Jewish people from Rock Island at that game and they were cheering for me because I was "the Jew from Moline" the Rock Islanders wanted to nail. But it was all in good, head-banging fun, part and parcel of the high school football ritual.

I also played basketball back then and did some traveling through the AZA, an inter-city Jewish social organization that hosted conventions for Jewish kids from all over. The conventions included basketball tournaments – we had a regular Jewish basketball team. My best friend was Benny Halpern, who played on that team with me; we got as far as a district championship in Minneapolis.

But football was my main game. I was an all-state honorable mention selection, an honest-to-goodness star, one of four Moline players recognized by the Moline/Champaign *Gazette*, and the bigotry I had grown up with seemed to have disappeared from my life.

But one freezing cold night, as my friends and I were hanging around the Rec (the high school recreation center), the whole stupid business reappeared like an ugly boil.

Some guy I knew only casually came up to me in front of all my friends and made a dirty crack about Jews, then baited me to come outside and fight.

I was really sick of this crap. But if I didn't go, I knew I'd lose my friends' respect and probably my own. So I went outside. It was about ten degrees out there, the middle of winter, snow everywhere.

Now, this kid was Bob McKinzie, the Illinois high school state heavyweight wrestling champ. I remembered what my mother had said about being twice as good, and I knew that to beat a monster like McKinzie I really would have to be twice as good – twice as tough, twice as determined, twice as right. And maybe twice as lucky.

And I was all that. I hit him first and I hit him hard. Then I hit him again. I felt his lip split, felt his nose crack – the blood spurted. I heard a grunt, and then I tripped him. He slipped on the ice or I'd have never gotten him down, but once he was down I just kept pounding him until he said he'd had enough. Every time I saw him after that, he walked the other way.

As we matured and headed toward graduation there were a lot of proms. One time I took a Jewish girl from Rock Island and one time I took Pat Tilburg. I really did like her a lot, but she was more of a friend than a girlfriend. She came from a very moral background, minister's daughter and all that.

It was 1948. We were dancing to the some of the last pre-rock-'n'-roll hits: *Buttons and Bows,* sung by Dinah Shore (who later became a friend – years later we played golf together at Hillcrest Country Club in Los Angeles, where Dinah was one of the first female members), *Nature Boy* sung by Nat King Cole, *It's Magic* by Doris Day, *The Twelfth Street Rag* by Pee Wee Hunt. Gasoline cost 20 cents a gallon, bread was 14 cents a loaf, a brand-new Buick set you back $1,550, a U.S. postage stamp was three cents, the minimum wage was 40 cents an hour … and I, the kid called Zook, was graduating high school! Not only that, but my coach had written a letter on my behalf to Depauw University in Greencastle, Indiana, and they'd accepted me on a full football scholarship. I was growing up, moving out – becoming a man.

The graduation ceremony was wonderful. My parents were there, a proud moment for them. And all my friends. And where was the ceremony held? I couldn't have picked a better place to say goodbye to my childhood if I'd planned it myself; I graduated right where I'd enjoyed so many great moments as a kid – from pick-up baseball to pigeon milk to Moline High School football glory. I graduated at Browning Field.

CHAPTER 3

THE KNOCKOUT

College is a self-contained world of magnified fun and magnified feelings, hijinks mixed with angst. I went in one school a jock and left another a married man with no career, having found the love of my life, and having lost a parent.

DePauw University, in Greencastle, Indiana – 45 miles west of Indianapolis – is a highly rated liberal arts college with a longstanding reputation as a party school for rich kids. I didn't find this out until I went there, in the autumn of 1948, on a football scholarship.

I reported before the start of school, for football practice. It was August and the temperatures soared into the high 90s daily. We had practice twice a day. The mornings were bearable, but the afternoons were pure torture. The humidity was above 95 percent. The men returning from the armed forces couldn't handle it.

Bob Winslow had played for Michigan State before he was drafted, but now here he was, defeated by the heat, washed up at 24. Bob didn't have the stamina anymore; the soldier's life of beer drinking and cigarettes didn't mix with our brutal regimen of two-a-day workouts in the relentless Indiana heat. He just said, "The hell with it, this isn't for me anymore."

I had excellent practices, made some spectacular plays and delivered some crushing tackles, so the coaches bumped me from the freshman team to the varsity, something rarely done in college athletics at the time.

There were no black players on the team. Integration was slow in coming to the college game. In the years since college football's inaugural game in 1869, there had been a number of blacks suiting up for predominantly white colleges, but none of them had an easy time. Such standouts as Fritz Pollard of Brown (the first African-American to play in the Rose Bowl) and Paul Robeson of Rutgers, who went on to fame as an actor, singer, orator and civil-rights activist, faced horrible racism.

To make matters worse, the southern universities refused to play northern schools with black players on their teams – the exception being when the northern coaches lived by a "gentleman's agreement" not to put their black athletes in the game.

Though times were changing in the nation, with long-overdue civil rights legislation passed in the 1960s, racism shackled college football in the south until the early '70s. In 1970, Bear Bryant of Alabama, realizing a change was necessary, scheduled and played USC, which had a number of black players. Bryant's all-white team was a national powerhouse, but USC, with running back Sam "The Bam" Cunningham and coached by John McKay, shellacked the Crimson Tide, 42-21, in front of 78,000 stunned white fans in Birmingham. (The black people had to watch the game from a hillside outside the stadium.)

This was a watershed moment in the integration movement. The southern universities, smarting from the spanking, learned that to compete they would have to field integrated squads. Bryant's strategy paid off and he was able to recruit black players. Soon everyone else did, too.

✧   ✧   ✧   ✧

"What frat are you going to pledge, Jack?" asked Barbara Nutt, a girl I knew from Moline. Like many kids at DePauw, she came from money – her dad was an industrialist. Apparently, fraternity and sorority life was a big part of the DePauw experience, and where you ended up could determine the rest of your life.

"Beta Theta Pi," I answered.

Beta Theta Pi was the top jock fraternity on campus and my friends on the football team had suggested I pledge there.

When you go through Rush Week, if they really want you, they sit you with the president of the fraternity and the seniors, the big shots; but Beta Theta Pi had me sitting with the lowly sophomores. The message was clear: they were giving me the brush-off.

I moved on. I knew some of the guys from the football team didn't like me; maybe they had hard feelings – after all, I was a freshman playing on the varsity. Or maybe it was something else. Could it have been my old nemesis anti-Semitism rearing its ugly head in this beautiful all-American setting? I didn't want to think it.

Still, at every frat I pledged, I kept encountering the same frosty reception. I finally got to a place called Sigma Nu, and a friend I played football with told me: "Our charters prohibit anybody Jewish from joining."

Ultimately, the only fraternity that would accept me was Delta Kappa Epsilon – the Dekes, known as the drunks on campus, the richest of the rich kids, a bunch of real goof-offs.

There weren't any other Jews in the fraternity and I didn't feel like I fit in. I was a jock, a Jew, and I didn't drink. I kept asking myself, "What am I doing with these kids who've had everything handed to them?"

I did enjoy participating in one major pledge effort. One of the other fraternities, the Sigma Chi's, had a tradition. They guarded the bell at University Church. Every other frat on campus tried to find a way to outsmart them and ring that bell. If you succeeded in ringing it, you were a big hero and automatically infuriated the Sigma Chi's.

My Deke pledge class decided to take on that challenge; we'd find a way to beat their security set-up and ring that bell. We drew up a plan to divert the guards' attention and gain access to the bell tower.

We strategized like generals, carried out the plan with the precision of a Marine commando unit, and one night we rang that bell loud and clear, like the Hunchback of Notre Dame on steroids and Starbucks. Then, whooping with glee, we scattered to the four winds.

There aren't many more intimidating sights than a horde of giant, enraged Sigma Chis who've had their bell rung. They were like angry bulls. They tracked down the malefactors, one by one, and shaved their heads – all except mine. When I saw a pal being tackled by a pair of beefy frat boys outside one of the houses, I flagged down a passing car, jumped in, and said, "Drive." I wasn't about to get my head shaved.

My fellow Dekes weren't too happy that I emerged from the incident as the only pledge with a full head of hair, but what were they going to do, shave me themselves? Come to think of it, they were almost that crazy.

✧   ✧   ✧   ✧

While I was feeling trapped in an animal house and wishing I hadn't joined up, an old acquaintance from Moline was trying to get into a fraternity as if his life depended on it.

Porter Skinner had been editor-in-chief of the Moline High School newspaper the year before, a big fish in a small pond. Skinner's uncle was Warren Giles, who'd gone from president of the Moline Plows to president and general manager of the Cincinnati Reds to Commissioner of the National League from 1951 to 1969. Porter was a very wealthy kid, good-looking, with an air of superiority, and he hadn't been friendly with me in high school; as a Jewish kid whose father was a grocer and butcher, I was beneath his notice.

During Rush Week at DePauw, he was a "legacy," which meant that people in his family had been members of a particular fraternity – usually that was enough to be accepted by a frat. But the frat guys didn't like him. They weren't impressed by him, or maybe his attitude put them off. He didn't get rushed at all – by any fraternity.

Porter Skinner grew more and more depressed. I'd see him around the campus. No longer the young prince, he walked like a defeated soldier, like the air had been taken out of him.

We'd come from the same town, so I befriended him, tried to cheer him up. I actually felt bad for Porter Skinner, which is something I'd never expected to feel.

He was hurting worse than I knew. I could see he was suffering but I didn't figure it could be any worse than I'd felt, making the rounds of the fraternities and getting rejected myself.

The reaction most of us have to rejection is hurt, followed by anger ("Who the hell are they, anyway? What do they know?"), whereupon we move on, maybe with added determination to prove whoever rejected us was wrong. "I'll show them" is the motivator of half our later accomplishments.

But some kids take college to be the world. If they're rebuffed by their peers there, it seems like a judgment.

The acceptance and deference Porter took for granted in Moline disappeared at DePauw. And maybe because he had no experience in dealing with rejection, when it happened to him he couldn't cope with it.

The sixth or seventh week of school, Porter sat in his dorm room, pondered his life and his future, took a .38 caliber snub-nosed revolver out of his drawer, put it in his mouth, and pulled the trigger.

The DePauw college community was shocked. The city of Moline mourned the young man's death.

I've heard others talk about the guilt they felt when someone they knew committed suicide – that feeling that there might have been something they could have done to prevent it. I felt that way about Porter Skinner. It had never occurred to me that someone who had seemed so self-assured could succumb to despair so quickly.

The day afterward, I went over to where he lived, gathered up his belongings and sent them back to his family with a letter of condolence. No one seemed to know why he'd taken his life. It seems like a vast over-simplification to say he did it because he couldn't get into a fraternity – but in a way it was true.

DePauw University was a good school, and I did well there. I wasn't gung-ho for studying, but I loved playing football. It was the great passion of my youth. And my teammates were all dedicated athletes. But the drinking in the fraternity was too much for me. These frat members got just sopping drunk every week, on beer and whiskey. That wasn't my style at all. There was no drinking in my family. My father might have had a beer occasionally, my mother too, but I'd never gotten drunk in my life – I didn't socialize like that. So after five months of living with these raging boozers, I said goodbye to "Greek life" at DePauw and moved into the residence halls for the rest of the school year.

✧   ✧   ✧   ✧

At least once in our lives we take some seemingly trivial action that turns out to be a huge turning point – the kind where you look back and say, "If I hadn't gone out to celebrate the night they tore down the Berlin Wall I never would have met Doris, and little Katie and Claude would never have been born." What I did was take a train ride.

On a steamy June day that summer, with $20 in my pocket and a year of college behind me, I took the Rock Island "Zephyr" to Chicago, where I connected with a train to Cincinnati. Thirty-four miles beyond that lay my final destination, a children's summer camp in Aurora, Indiana, called Camp Shor, where I had secured a job as a counselor.

I was enjoying the trip. Twenty bucks is chickenfeed now, but back then you could buy something with it. Lunch on the train cost just 75 cents, dinner a dollar. Trains were a safe, pleasant, leisurely way to travel, and a bargain.

As the Cincinnati train pulled out of Chicago, I noticed a thin, dapper, middle-aged gentleman sitting nearby. We smiled at one another, an instant rapport, as urban Chicago gave way to small towns and rolling green fields.

The man naturally commanded respect. He had an impressive elegance, but his eyes had a friendly twinkle and he was very outgoing.

"I'm Jack Zukerman," I introduced myself.

"I'm very happy to meet you, Jack." He had a melodious, cultured voice – a trace of an accent. "I am Joseph Liebenson."

Dr. Liebenson was the educational director of the largest Hebrew school in Chicago and a successful writer of books for children. He was born in Lithuania and had come to America in 1920 at the age of 19.

"If my father had not passed away when I was 14, I might still be there."

His father had owned a thriving spinning-wheel factory in Lithuania, but in 1915, the factory caught fire and burned down. While attempting to extinguish the flames, Joseph's father was overcome with smoke inhalation and, not long after, tragically died.

"Getting here from Lithuania was not an easy feat," Dr. Liebenson related as the Illinois countryside rolled by outside the window – cows, red barns, green fields, blue skies, waving children. "I was now the man of the family, charged with bringing my mother and two sisters to the land where the streets were paved with gold. We were traveling steerage on a ship. We had $600 from the Hebrew Immigration Assistance Society. I was on deck one night and I overheard two Polish sailors plotting to throw the Jews overboard."

My eyes widened. I knew that in 1919, Europe was a recent battleground and hatred was always simmering over there, but I hadn't heard about sailors murdering their passengers. Dr. Liebenson explained that these particular sailors were drunk most of the time, which was why he'd been able to overhear them.

"You understood Polish?" I asked.

"Eight languages," he said, modestly.

The sailors boasted of having robbed passengers on previous trips and of raping some French women and throwing them overboard – not the kind of chatter you want to overhear from your courteous and friendly crew. On the other hand, it's better to hear it and be warned than not to hear it and be surprised later.

"So I made a decision then and there. We would leave the ship as soon as possible. And we did. We got off in Turkey. Constantinople."

In Constantinople (now Istanbul), Joseph sold newspapers and periodicals from a street kiosk, lived frugally, and saved enough money in a year to re-book passage for the family to complete the journey to America.

Dr. Liebenson's family were learned, cultured people, of a kind I had never encountered in my 19 years of football and fun. They had settled in Cleveland – his mother, his brother and four sisters.

As we chatted, I found Dr. Liebenson was headed to the same place I was, Camp Shor, where he was the educational director.

"That's a coincidence," I said. "I'm going to be a counselor there!"

"There are no coincidences," Dr. Liebenson said.

He told me about his two daughters – one, Jeannie, eight years old, and one my age. He pulled out his wallet to show me the older daughter's picture. His first comment was how smart she was.

My first observation, which I kept to myself, was what a knockout she was.

"She's in her second year at the University of Illinois, a straight A student."

Joseph's wife, Sarah, and cute little Jeannie showed up from where they were sitting. Sarah was a tiny lady, about five feet tall, very pretty and reserved. She might have been shy but I could also tell she was being careful – unlike her talkative husband, who'd speak with anyone anywhere, she wasn't about to bestow friendship on some young stranger on a train until she'd had a chance to evaluate his character.

She had come to America from Russia in 1923, at 16, with her mother and two brothers. Her father Louis was typical of his generation, a true family man. He had arrived in the USA in 1914, to find and feather a nest for his family. However, World War I delayed their reunion – no one was emigrating during the war years – and it wasn't until 1923 that the family was united again, in Cleveland.

Louis was kind and gentle – someone you'd naturally call Grandpa – but when I met him later, this man, just five feet four, had a handshake like an iron vise. After I retrieved my squashed fingers, I could only imagine what those hands could have done to men who had crossed him.

In Cleveland, where he had cousins, he managed to open a small grocery store. Like my own father, he earned a decent living from it and put food on the table for his family.

His daughter, Sarah, grew up to be a careful woman who now regarded me politely but remained reserved. I wasn't sure if it was just natural, understandable parental caution, or if it was something about me.

I remained on my best behavior, there was something I really wanted to find out.

"So where's the college girl hiding?"

"She's with friends in Cincinnati," the little sister chimed in. But, I was told, the college girl would also be going to the camp as a counselor.

Joseph's wife and younger daughter returned to their seats.

"Excuse me," I said. "May I take another look at the picture of your older daughter?"

Joseph opened his wallet and showed me the snapshot. "Her name is Roz."

"Roz," I said. "I like the name."

We arrived in Cincinnati late in the afternoon and were met by camp staffers who drove us the 34 miles to our destination. Camp Shor, situated on 15 acres of woodland with a magnificent lake two miles across, was a perfect, tranquil setting for a co-ed summer camp. I was to be given the lofty title of "athletic director" and put in charge of the cabin where the youngest boys lived, the five-and-six-year-olds.

When you're 19 and arrive in a place like this, the first thing you evaluate is the female situation. For me, it was over before I got off the train. And when we got to the camp in the early evening and I met Joseph's daughter Roz, I couldn't take my eyes off her. Her beauty took my breath away.

There were ten male counselors and ten female counselors. Roz was my opposite number, in charge of the five-and-six-year-old girls. I taught swimming, and over the eight weeks of camp I tried to teach Roz. The five-year-olds learned how to swim – Roz did not.

We started dating, and it didn't take long for me to fall in love with this beautiful, bright, talented young lady. On our days off we'd go to Cincinnati and have dinner. During the evenings at camp, the counselors would break the lock on the master refrigerator and gorge on sardines with bread and peanut butter, and then Roz and I would spend the starry nights just talking. The eight weeks went by in a flash. It was a wonderful, magical summer.

✧   ✧   ✧   ✧

After the "Summer of Roz," I went back home to Moline. Moe needed help in the store, so that was the end of my DePauw experience. Football had been important to me, but family came first. I spent my sophomore year at Black Hawk College in Moline, as well as putting in a lot of hours at the Blue Ribbon.

Roz and I wrote back and forth on a daily basis – believe it or not, she still has the letters. We missed each other terribly, so sometimes I would sneak the car out of our narrow driveway and drive the 180 miles to visit her in Chicago.

My father didn't mind me using the car, but I never told him I was going to Chicago – he'd have said I was nuts, it was over 350 miles round trip.

One night I borrowed the car, left home at 6 p.m., drove to Chicago, had a late dinner with Roz, visited with her family, and drove back to Moline. I got home very late, about 3 a.m., and there was Moe, sitting on the porch. His mood can only be described as volcanic. Turns out he'd been spending a lot of time fuming while I drove back and forth to Chicago, speculating on what I might be up to.

"Where were you?" he asked. I could almost see the steam coming out of his ears. "You couldn't be up to anything good at this hour."

He leaped from the chair and charged at me, murder in his eyes. I ran.

And I kept running. With Moe chasing me, I ran the night streets of Moline, block after block, as fast as I could. I was in top condition and he wasn't, but you know what? He caught me! I tripped and fell, and he was on me.

"You think you can fool your old man?"

He shook me like a 220-pound rag doll. I didn't fight back, I couldn't. He was my father.

Finally, exhausted and embarrassed, I raised myself off the pavement and stood before this fierce, muscular man I loved so much.

"Was it worth it?" he demanded.

I looked him in the eye.

"Yes," I said. "I asked her father for his blessing. Roz and I are engaged."

What a night. Nothing but fathers. I drove across Illinois to get one's blessing and ran for my life through the streets of Moline while another one chased me down – fathers everywhere. Lucky for me they were good ones.

⚙   ⚙   ⚙   ⚙

September of 1951 found me in Champaign, at the University of Illinois – a junior. I'd decided to pursue a law degree, so I only needed one more year of undergraduate credits before entering the University of Illinois law school. Roz was there, too, as were many of my pals from Chicago, whom I'd met at AZA basketball tournaments over the years.

You may have noticed that my ambitions at this point had nothing to do with my actual future, and it's true; for the last time in my life,

I wasn't thinking about lighting. But the country was going through a change around me – a change which would lay the groundwork for a whole new industry, of which I would soon become a part.

America was experiencing a post-war economic boom. The Korean War was on; the Cold War was heating up. It was the beginning of the "jet age." New technologies were coming to the fore. Television was about to oust radio and take over the living room. But America was socially conservative, and education was, as always, prized as the avenue to success. The University of Illinois was chock full of ambitious, smart kids, many of whom became my lifelong friends. It was a great place. I jumped in with both feet.

One of my best pals in Chicago was Bill Brown, whom I had met at 13 when we'd been on opposing AZA teams. Our competition had been fierce, but we'd ended up forging a truly great friendship – which was the whole idea behind the AZA: fellowship, athletics, and "social networking" for young Jewish people. Bill, who in later life became one of the most successful entrepreneurs in the lighting business, would remain one of my dearest friends, even though he still carries the bruises from our basketball days. He would always be there for me.

Harry Graff, Selwyn Shkolnik and Arwin Zollar were all members of my new fraternity, Pi Lambda Phi. These three fraternity brothers became real brothers to me. Selwyn, who became a top physician in Beverly Hills, was my doctor till the day he passed away at 65. Harry also became a doctor and is still practicing psychiatry in Miami. We talk all the time. Arwin has retired after an excellent career as a lawyer in Chicago.

Our fraternity was predominantly Jewish – one of the few that didn't discriminate. Every race and creed was welcome. Although I was a junior, I joined as a pledge like everyone else, and later was elected president of our pledge class. We lived at 52 East Armory, Champaign, across an open field from the laboratory where critical experiments on the atomic bomb project had been carried out in the early '40s.

Our house mother was a lovely woman named Mrs. Adams. On Saturday night, when the boys were letting loose and rough-housing, we'd lock her in her room. We didn't want to disturb her.

Fraternity life in the early '50s was childishly brutal. Paddling was commonplace, and hazing could be pretty extreme. It was more of an era of the "practical joke" than it is today, and some of the jokes could be humiliating. I didn't participate in those; they made me uncomfortable and I'd be hesitant to tell my grandchildren about them. I'm glad that particular part of the good old days is gone.

Sometimes I look back amazed at the young men in Pi Lambda Phi and what they achieved in later life. At the time, who could predict that this rambunctious group would go on to live such fruitful lives and accomplish the things they have! We're talking about successful doctors, lawyers, judges, many men who became pillars of the business world.

Certainly the University of Illinois had its share of goof-offs, but the truth is the guys who were there just for the good times didn't last long. The university was vigilant: if you posted failing grades for two semesters, they bounced you. Irresponsibility was not tolerated. If you fouled up you were kicked to the curb. There was too much at stake, too many talented young men and women in post-war America to waste time on those who didn't appreciate the opportunity they'd been given. It was an extremely competitive environment which brought out the best, and sometimes the worst, in people.

Speaking of the best: Roz lived in the Lincoln Avenue Residence Hall – this independent-minded young woman didn't believe in sororities – and every evening after studying in the library, I'd walk her home. Curfew was at 10:30 on weekdays, midnight on Saturdays. One night I was visiting Roz and her roommate and the curfew bell rung; I was stuck in the dorm room and had to crawl under the bed to hide. I managed to sneak out after a few hours.

Everything was a lot stricter than it is now. Today's college arrangements, where boys and girls live on the same floors, use the same bathrooms, and share everything, would have been unthinkable in the 1950s. On Sunday nights, Roz and I made a habit of going to a drive-in called Steak and Shake to eat hamburgers and listen to *Our Miss Brooks* and *The Shadow* on the radio. We took pleasure from small things.

The night Roz and I got "pinned" is indelibly fixed in my memory. The pinning process was a public declaration to the college community and the world that a guy and gal were going steady – that they were, as they say today, a couple. The fraternity had a corny but sweet custom to commemorate the moment: When one of the members got pinned, all the frat brothers got together and serenaded the gal. Roz loved the song that we sang to her, but the tradition required payback – she was required to sing a song back to the fraternity – and she'd tell you she can't carry a tune. She responded beautifully, though; nobody hit a wrong note that night, least of all my Roz.

She and I studied together all the time. Needless to say, she was a much better student than I. We shared a science class with ten of my fraternity brothers, and when the final exam was given, Roz made sure all of us passed.

One day, on our way to class, we passed a shop selling taffy apples – you know, an apple covered with caramel and nuts. I bought one for Roz – a giant Washington apple glistening with caramel and studded with nuts. I was just being a gentleman, but Roz lit up with pleasure – she was really touched. Over the years of our marriage, "giving a taffy apple" has meant doing something nice for each other. And to this day, Roz's license plate has always read TAFYAPL.

"Grandma," our then 11-year-old grandson, Max, asked her not so long ago, "what does 'taffy apple' mean?"

"That's my stripper name," Roz told him. "From my dancing days. Vegas, Chicago, Miami – they all know me as Taffy Apple."

Max's eyes grew big as saucers. He bought it, for about a week.

The school year flew by and the moment Roz and I had long

anticipated finally arrived. On June 17th, 1951, we were married at the Sherman Hotel in Chicago. It was a glorious day. Roz looked as stunning as she always does. My whole family was there – mother, father, brother, sister, and Roz's family and friends, too, the wonderful Liebenson and Barkan clans. Plus the entire fraternity turned out, all my fellow Pi Lambda Phi's, as well as many other buddies. Fifty friends of the family and various relatives from Moline and elsewhere, and Roz's friends, too, convened to celebrate and wish us well.

After all the kisses, the tears, the cake and the toasts, Roz and I jumped in the first car I'd ever owned, a 1951 Plymouth, and we motored away on a two-month honeymoon.

Our first married night was spent at the Blackstone Hotel on Michigan Avenue. I surprised Roz with a dozen peonies in the hotel room; she loved them! But the next morning, we had the first disagreement of our marriage – I wouldn't let her take the peonies with us; I didn't want flower petals shedding all over the new car. To this day, Roz likes to say that if I were a car, I'd be in perfect shape. She thinks I take better care of my cars than I do of myself!

I had $500, which we'd received as wedding gifts – more money than I'd ever seen – so we drove east to Niagara Falls and then spent the summer sponging off of Roz's relatives, the Schofers and Gaylins in Cleveland, and at my sister's house in New York.

We were young, in love, and the world was not at war – we didn't have a care in the world.

September found us back at the University of Illinois. We found a small furnished apartment in Urbana, next to Champaign. The bathroom had been a closet and the kitchen a hallway, but we had each other. I was now in law school and Roz was finishing her BA. She graduated *summa cum laude*, in the top two percent of her class.

Roz took one course with me in law school – criminal law. It was taught by one of the most brilliant minds in the field, Dean Harno. He later left the Illinois law school and went to San Francisco to help establish UC Hastings Law School, now recognized as one of the best in the nation.

Law school was hard work, but a lot of fun. My friends were mostly from Chicago. Ronnie Miller ended up a very important lawyer, representing Hugh Hefner's Playboy empire for years. Sheldon Mitchell, a great friend and fraternity brother, evolved into a leading authority on supermarket law. Alan Grieman, another Pi Lambda Phi, became a federal judge. Alan Mendelsohn, a very bright man who had grown up in extreme poverty, blossomed into an elite law professor at Harvard.

Some of the top judges in Chicago also came from this class. Chicago judges? Maybe we shouldn't dwell on that subject. There was a little incident known as the "Greylord scandal," in which some of my classmates were involved. The allegations ranged from fixing drunken-driving cases to more serious felony charges. Nearly 100 people were indicted, and all but a handful were convicted. Of the 17 judges indicted, 15 were convicted and sent up the river. Others put behind bars included 50 lawyers, as well as court clerks, police officers and sheriff's deputies, for fixing traffic tickets and other minor-league shenanigans. Illinois was then, and still is, a hotbed of political corruption. Sure, we had Abraham Lincoln, but we also "boast" a rogues' gallery of some of the most crooked politicians in American history.

I was a happy young man … the happiest I'd ever been. Of course, when everything is going well, the one thing you can count on is that it's temporary.

It was during final exams in my second year of law school, April, when my mother called me and asked that I come home as soon as possible. The whole way back to Moline, three hours at high speed, I knew something was wrong – my mother never wanted me to leave school for any reason.

I arrived to find my father in the hospital. This strong, healthy hunk of a man, this powerhouse of vitality, was lying helpless. It was shocking, bewildering. I couldn't believe it.

"Why are you here?" he asked with a smile.

Dr. Gamburg, our family doctor, told me my dad didn't have much time left. This was before open-heart surgery. All you could do was pray. And pray I did, but as the saying goes, "We make plans and God laughs." Ten days later, Dad passed away. He was just 56 years old. I was shattered. I'd considered him immortal.

My mother didn't want him in a funeral home, so everything was done at home. I looked at my father lying there, cold to the touch, so quiet and peaceful. The one bearable thought, however, was that at last, this man who had worked so hard his whole life, would have some rest.

There were 500 people at Moe's funeral. It seemed like all of Moline and Rock Island turned out to mourn my father. To get from our house in Moline to the Jewish cemetery in Rock Island required a police escort. We were all in a state of deep shock and mourning. My mother, at the age of 49, was now a widow.

My fraternity brothers, future doctors Harry Graff and Selwyn Shkolnik, skipped their MCAT exams to be with me. I have always been grateful for their presence and solidarity in this most difficult time; it was friendship at its most giving. The dean of the medical school arranged a special make-up test for them.

With deep grief, I went back to the University of Illinois to finish the semester and take final exams.

My father's death was not the only stunning blow to strike during this period. One night not long afterward, we were making the trip home to Moline from Champaign, a bunch of us, in two cars. Ben Halpern, who'd joined a different fraternity, was in the first car. He was kind and gentle, a bashful and considerate person – we'd been teammates on an AZA tournament basketball team and best friends back in high school. The car he was in had an accident about 30 miles from Rock Island. Ben was ejected from the car; there weren't any seat belts then. Roz and I came upon the scene ten minutes after it happened.

A father and a best friend, both gone in one year. Grief and pain, to a depth I'd never known.

My college career was over. Roz helped me hold together. I returned to Moline, a grownup, ready or not.

FOUR KIDS, TWO COLONELS

When the '50s began I was a 20-year-old schoolboy. By the end of the decade I had a wife, four children and a company which had grown enough to bring me into contact with some of the most brilliant – and a couple of the scariest – businessmen in the country.

When I came back to Moline, my brother Bill was running B & M Electrical Distributing Company, now a three-person operation, selling electrical supplies and lighting fixtures from a building in Rock Island right across the street from the local brothel, Mill's Café.

Bill didn't know it, but he was going broke in a hurry. His abrasive, introverted personality didn't endear him to customers – the current ones disappeared and potential ones shied away.

I went to work in the warehouse at $75 a week. I had to reorganize everything – no problem – but dealing with Bill was one problem after another. It was hard to discuss things with him. He didn't always throw the ball back.

I started to learn the electrical business by studying the parts and supplies. It takes many electrical products to construct a building: wire, cable, conduit, electrical fittings, switch gear, outdoor lighting and indoor lighting, and more, and I learned all about them; but with a nearly nonexistent customer base, it was like feeding oats to a dead horse. So I decided to try doing the stuff Bill couldn't do: I began to make calls on the electrical contractors in the Quad-Cities area and beyond, going as far as Des Moines, Iowa, to muster up business. Somebody had to do it.

I got lucky. I got to know Dick Yeager of L&W Electric, one of the biggest electrical contractors in Rock Island. Dick became my mentor, my customer, and, over the years, my best friend. He was cold to most people, but to me he was always warm. His family became my family. I also built a fast and fine friendship with Chet Robbins of Moline, the biggest electrical contractor in the Midwest. Together we would do projects with the University of Iowa and John Deere.

At first, Roz and I stayed with my mother in her house. It was quite an adjustment for us. And it wasn't easy for my mother to be thrust into the role of young widow. But I wasn't home much. I spent long hours learning my new business, and Roz, after being told repeatedly she was "over-qualified" for various positions – a polite way of saying "No Jews Need Apply" – found a job at the Ramsey Advertising Agency in Davenport. She loved it.

At Ramsey, she was in charge of proofreading all the ads and publications for grammar, punctuation and spelling. Roz has always been a great reader, a habit she inherited from her father, who read voraciously. She had razor-sharp skills, and she has never lost them.

I was learning on the job, every day, absorbing the business from the ground up. At night, I'd put catalogs together; by day I'd call on customers while Bill worked in the office. Bill was the inside man, I was the outside man.

I was on the road most of the time – to Cedar Rapids, Des Moines, and points beyond, calling on all the electrical contractors, trying to sell products. It seemed like I was always in the car, driving the roads, eating in diners, grabbing donuts on the go and drinking hot tea so I wouldn't snooze behind the wheel – drumming up business wherever I could. You've got to be patient on those rural two-lanes. If you get stuck behind somebody on a hill or curve and you decide to take a chance and pass, you can get to the end of the road a lot sooner than you wanted to.

Eventually, after business improved, I took flying lessons. I thought it would be a better use of my time. I rented a plane and I would fly to different cities; business had gotten that good. But in 1958, Mike Todd, the film producer and husband of the movie star Elizabeth Taylor, was tragically killed in a plane crash. Roz was, predictably, upset – she didn't relish the idea of becoming a young widow with four kids – so I gave up flying and went back to the endless cups of tea and the never-ending road.

In those years, electrical engineers were responsible for all lighting design and specified the products for the projects. If you weren't a recognized electrical distributor for the top brands such as Holophane and Daybrite, you couldn't sell the projects – no product, no business. At first, the big product lines refused to sell to me directly, and the major wholesalers blocked me from buying from them. I was, in effect, frozen out. So I turned to some friends, electrical distributors in Chicago, and purchased products from them, at cost, plus a small percentage. Before long, the manufacturers' representatives in my territory realized I was taking their business away by buying from my Chicago connection – they were losing out on commission – and decided they would be better off joining me than fighting me. In time, all of the top manufacturers sold to me, and my competitors had lost their edge.

Eagle Foods was a chain of 30 supermarkets which merged with a larger group, owned by some friends of mine. Over the years, Eagle built up a chain of 300 stores before ultimately selling out to Lucky Supermarkets in California. Their stores were on the cutting edge of design and their lighting was state-of-the-art. The architect of the stores was Harold Dismer, a bright man and a true student of lighting. I learned so much from him. Harold taught me the art of supermarket lighting – how to light meat cases and make the highlighted products look attractive – and soon I was furnishing all the lighting for over 200 supermarkets.

Harold taught me a very valuable lesson. Eagle had just finished building a 1,500,000-square-foot warehouse – a distribution center – and he said:

"Jack, how much will it cost if you add another 83 of these lights?"

I figured I had him over a barrel, I could charge whatever I wanted. I gave him a price and he wrote it down, then called me a couple days later and said:

"You know those 83 fixtures I asked you about? Now you can take back 83 fixtures at the price you gave me for the add-on."

In later years, Harold would have more than his share of personal tragedy. His 16-year-old daughter took her own life, and Harold himself contracted Lou Gehrig's disease. I watched this 6-foot-5 paragon of health and vitality wither away, dying at the age of 49. I loved this man dearly. Sometimes I feel an empty sadness and realize that it's Harold I'm missing.

✧   ✧   ✧   ✧

After living in my mother's house for four months, Roz and I decided we needed a home of our own. Roz wanted to live in Rock Island because more Jewish families lived there and it was where the house of worship was located. So with a $5,000 loan from my mother, we took on a mortgage of $11,000 and bought our first home.

It was a modest two-bedroom house, two blocks from the Jewish cemetery on 30th Street, 15 blocks from Blackhawk State Park – a $16,000 home. My pay from my brother? Seventy-five dollars a week.

This was when the average income was $4,000 a year, a new car cost $1,650, a gallon of gas was 22 cents, milk 94 cents a gallon, a jar of pickles a quarter, bread 16 cents a loaf, and a pound of romaine lettuce a dime.

Our new house was small, with a tiny living room, a kitchen and a porch, totaling about 1,100 square feet. We loved it. We didn't know any better. When it was hot, we retreated to the air-conditioned bedroom – and before long we were expecting our first add-on.

Roz was at work at Ramsey Advertising Agency in Davenport when the first labor pangs came. I was hoping for a boy, someone I could play ball with, someone to be my buddy. In those days, of course, there was no test to determine gender.

At 6:15 a.m. on August 26, 1953, Dr. Balzer called me into the delivery room at St. Luke's in Davenport to let me know we were a family now. We named her Marti Jill Zukerman, she weighed in at eight pounds, four ounces, was 21 inches long, and was, from the moment I saw her, the apple of my eye. She was my little halfback, so cute, so helpless, lying there in the nursery with all the others who were new to this world.

Roz and I were thrilled. Marti was a delight. Memory gilds the past, but I'll say it anyway, she never cried, always had a smile. If you could write a recipe for a perfect daughter, the result would be Marti – brilliant, athletic, sweet, affectionate, beautiful and so inquisitive. She loved books; she read a book a day growing up, usually reading herself to sleep.

And she was my buddy. As she grew, I taught her to throw, and throw she did – a football, a hard ball – with accuracy and zing. Shoot a basketball? Dribble? Marti Jill Zukerman was a whiz, a natural athlete, graceful and always in control, highly coordinated and dedicated.

She really did exceptionally well at everything – except, perhaps, when she was graduating Edison Junior High School. She was unanimously chosen the most outstanding girl by the Daughters of the American Revolution, but at the last moment was caught chewing gum in school and was denied the honor!

Roz didn't like the DAR, anyway.

Once she got old enough, along with many of her friends, Marti went to camp for eight weeks every year at Camp Maccabee in Pelican Lake, Wisconsin. She took to it like a duck to water, spending ten young summers there – in fact, it was the water she took to the most. At camp, she was captain of the Blue Team in the annual color war, and as a teenager she started a swim school for kids in our neighborhood. At 16, she became the youngest Red Cross water safety instructor in the state of Illinois and was on the water ballet team at Rock Island High.

In high school, she was also a member of the tennis team, playing in the No. 3 slot. I was present at most of her matches and always tried to be as quiet as possible. She got nervous when I was there.

Marti was the editor of the high school newspaper, a member of the Young Democrats, and was inducted into the National Honor Society.

During these years, business was improving. The long hours and hard work were paying off and the company was beginning to grow – and a good thing too, because as it expanded, so did my family.

We started planning for the next addition two years after Marti was born, and in December of 1955 we were anticipating our Chanukah present – a happy time, although marred by our mourning for Roz's grandfather Louis, who had recently passed away.

Our first boy was born December 6th. We decided to name him after a man who had been universally respected and admired – so Steve became Louis Steven Zukerman. He weighed eight pounds one ounce, and from the moment I laid eyes on him I knew he had a good soul. How did I know? Hey, if you'd seen him, you'd have known it, too. L. Steven Zukerman was, and is, as sweet and kind a person as you will ever meet.

As a baby, Steve never crawled – he just stood up at the age of nine months and started running.

Marti and Steve were very close, and we used to remind her not to get too frisky with him because he would end up towering over her – which indeed he has; he's now 6-3 – so when Marti got annoyed with him she restrained herself.

Later, Steve would accompany me to the YMCA on Saturdays and just sit, read a book, and watch all the activity around him – always doing the right thing instinctively, a joy to be around.

It's a lucky dad who can admire his kids. What I admired about Steve was his serenity. You don't expect that in a child – they're helpless, what have they got to be serene about? – but he always had that quality, and it tended to make him the most respected one in his peer group.

When he was old enough, Steve spent the annual eight weeks in summer with Marti at Camp Maccabee in Pelican Lake. At age six and a half, he became the youngest camper to swim the mile-and-a-half lake obstacle.

I remember an incident at camp one visiting day when he was 10. Roz and I, watching from a distance, saw a bully start to push Steve. Steve wasn't the confrontational type. He told the kid to stop it about four times, but he wouldn't. Steve calmly walked over to a tree, put his glasses down, returned to the bully, punched him in the nose, and said, "I told you to stop." He then retrieved his glasses and put them back on. You see stuff like that in movies – not so much in life. But that was Steve.

Steve followed in Marti's footsteps as a great student and, like his sister before him, became editor-in-chief of the Rock Island high school newspaper, a Zukerman family tradition in the making.

Next up: Jeffrey David Zukerman. Jeff's worth a book in himself. He's so different from the other two. Jeff was born on June 5, 1957. Steve was just 18 months old. Jeff is a big man now and was a big baby, weighing in at nine pounds two ounces.

Of the kids, he had the most "street smarts"; I think he was born with them. Whenever Roz and I went out, we'd tell the babysitter to ask Jeff where things were. That was when he was four and his siblings were eight, six, and two. He was remarkably bright and intuitive, a good student, and was on the tennis and wrestling teams. He did it all with great zeal and gusto.

Jeff also went to Camp Maccabee, following Steve and Marti. He never liked rules or regimentation, so I don't think he took to camp like the older kids, but he actually was one of the most outstanding horseback riders in camp and received the ribbon for best rider in his group.

In one way he was just the same as Marti and Steve: Jeff became our third high school editor-in-chief.

The last of the Mohicans, Michael Jay Zukerman, was born October 23, 1959, seven pounds, 13 ounces and so sweet and peaceful that Roz called him her "Miltown," one of the early chemical tranquilizers. "Little Miltown" became her safety valve. Having four kids in six years made the house pretty lively at times, and when things got hectic for Roz, putting Mike on her lap always had a calming effect.

Mike, like Jeff, didn't take to regimentation and when he went away to Camp Maccabee I'm not sure he enjoyed it as much as Steve and Marti, but Roz always felt Mike had the greatest sense of humor and the most playful personality of them all.

Mike loved to research all areas in which he was interested, a quality which would serve him well in his later professional life. I remember he received an aquarium for his 10th birthday, and before long he became a tropical fish expert who made "house calls" on his friends as the neighborhood fish doctor. He then added a second aquarium to his room – containing a piranha! It was better than having a jewelry safe!

All four of the kids went to Hebrew school and were Bat or Bar-Mitzvahed.

You'll receive a later update on how these four great kids turned out. For now, I'll just say that if I hadn't already had enough incentive to learn my business, all I had to do by the end of the '50s was look around the dinner table.

As a young man in his 20s with a burgeoning family, I was always trying to brainstorm ways to take the business to the next level, so I targeted the biggest fish in the Quad-Cities area, a high-profile client whose business would give other major corporations confidence in us and imbue us with credibility. Could there be a better endorsement than from John Deere? Deere was the most influential employer in the entire Midwest, a powerful force in the local community and economy – a household name in America and worldwide.

So I drove over to John Deere's corporate offices and introduced myself and B&M Lighting to the purchasing agent, a man named Al Schickel.

Schickel shook his head. "I never heard of you."

He proceeded to tell me what I already knew, that they bought all their electrical products from the national distributors.

"You're not on our approved list," he said, dismissively. And that was it.

I left his office and drove for 20 minutes continuing the conversation by myself, the way you do after you've been shown the door. Then I said, "To hell with this," pulled a U-turn, drove back to John Deere and marched back into Schickel's office.

"My family," I told him, "has held John Deere stock for the last 40 years. And I don't think the board of directors is going to like the letter I'm going to write them one bit. I'll be telling them all about how you don't want to give a stockholder a fair opportunity to bid for electrical products."

I chose not to specify how much John Deere stock my family actually held, because it was not a substantial amount. Fortunately Schickel didn't ask. As I went on, his eyes took on a glazed, defeated look, and that day I was approved to sell to John Deere.

John Deere had an in-house engineering department – electrical engineers, mechanical engineers and design engineers. I started calling on the electrical design department, about 25 electrical engineers doing nothing but lighting design and power for all the John Deere facilities. It was the beginning of a long and fruitful association.

I made a lot of contacts back then, and was fortunate in most of the people I met. The fortunate choices helped the company prosper; we hired more people and increased our business from $400K to $5 million in three years.

In 1954, two brothers I knew from Iowa, Martin and Matthew Bucksbaum, who were in the supermarket business, started a company called General Growth Properties and built a shopping center in Cedar Rapids – the first of what Martin dubbed "the new downtowns." The Bucksbaums were down-to-earth men, good friends of mine and about to take their place among the biggest shopping center developers in the world.

I sold Martin and Matthew all the lighting for their first shopping centers. GGP grew to employ over 4,000 people and have part or full ownership of, or management responsibilities for, over 200 regional shopping malls across the USA, totaling a mind-boggling 200 million square feet of retail space. In 2009, however, the economy was so bad they went into a chapter proceeding – an unhappy end to a great company.

I also started calling on a number of other shopping center developers. The shopping center was a new concept in the 1950s. Americans had made an exodus from the cities and were spreading into the suburbs. America had become a car culture, and "strip centers" were sprouting up all over the nation, like mushrooms after a rain, to service the needs of mobile consumers. A strip center was a group of stores with a parking lot. They weren't mega-malls, but they were a huge new industry to tap.

In 1959, I met Mel Simon of Simon Properties – now the largest shopping center developers in the world. Mel became a close friend, as did his brother Herb. Born in Brooklyn and raised in the Bronx, Mel graduated from Bronx Science, the famous New York high school for brainy kids. The kid from the Bronx built Simon Properties into such a giant that, in 1983, Mel bought the Indiana Pacers basketball team. His company would go public in 1993, folding most of its properties into Simon Property Group and raising $1 billion, the largest stock offering ever at the time. The company merged with DeBartolo Realty in 1990 (the DeBartolo family owns the San Francisco 49ers football team) to form Simon DeBartolo, the nation's pre-eminent shopping center owner. In 1998, the company reverted to Simon Property Group and continues to be the No. 1 mall owner in America.

Thanks to meeting Mel in '50, I was on the ground floor, selling them shopping center lighting all over the country.

The man who runs Simon Properties today is David Simon, Mel's son. When David was a kid, I took him and my son Jeff to a football banquet every year in Chicago – I was involved with the Better Boys Foundation, which was sponsored by the NFL, and many NFL greats generously gave of their time and goodwill.

✿   ✿   ✿   ✿

You can't keep expanding your business without eventually bumping into someone who does business in an exotic way. As the decade ended, I ran into a *Godfather*-style negotiator – only he made me an offer I couldn't accept.

The job that ended up scaring me the most – the one I call "The Case of the Two Colonels" – started out normally enough.

I met Eugene Ferkauf, the founder of EJ Korvette, the first American discount department store, in 1958. He had already built the first 12 stores of his empire and was hungry to expand.

Ferkauf was the first person to use discounting, even though most discounting was outlawed at the time, through a federal law called the Robinson-Patman Act of 1936, or the Anti-Price Discrimination Act. Korvette used a membership program similar to those of the five-and-dime stores like Woolworth's or Kresge's – a key step in the evolution toward today's immensely popular mammoths such as Costco and Sam's Club. Korvette passed out membership cards to anyone who wanted to buy, thus creating a new dimension in retailing.

Korvette was very clever in avoiding the anti-discounting provisions of the Robinson-Patman Act and undercutting the suggested retail prices for expensive items such as appliances and jewelry. This was something the regular department stores couldn't do. The big department store chains such as Macy's and Gimbel's filed suit to stop Korvette from cutting prices, but to no avail – the writing was on the wall for their business model and the classic department stores took a long slow slide into ruin.

Korvette was also one of the first chains to stay open seven days a week, challenging state and local Sunday laws. Once these barriers were broken, many chains followed suit, revolutionizing the industry and the shopping habits of Americans.

I was in New York in the spring of 1959 and got a call from an electrical contractor, Seymour Mellon of the Mellon Electric Company. He wanted to know if I was interested in the new program Korvette was embarking on – building a series of stores across America, including five stores in Detroit and five in Chicago. These new stores were bigger than anything which had previously been imagined for this type of retailing operation – 200,000 square feet of consumer heaven. Did I want to light these huge stores? Needless to say, I was more than interested.

The next thing I knew, I was introduced to the general contractor, Goodnor Construction in Long Island City. Goodnor Construction issued me a contract to furnish all ten of these monster projects in the amount of $2.6 million.

The lighting in the stores was to be composed of four-by-four fluorescent recessed fixtures – thousands of them – and, of course, many other types of fixtures that dominated that era of lighting. After completing the first five stores in Detroit, I moved on to the five in Chicago.

There were no problems with the actual job, but collecting monies owed proved a challenge, to say the least.

I was in New York to get paid for the products we had shipped to the Chicago stores. When in New York I stayed at the Plaza Hotel on the southeast corner of Central Park South, a wonderful establishment that had charm and timeless elegance beyond a small-town kid's imagination. The Oak Bar was the perfect spot for entertaining customers, and the elegant Oak Room restaurant, where you were entertained by a formally dressed harpist while having dinner, was the ideal locale to seal the deal – great food and wonderful ambience. Since I was becoming a regular visitor, I got to know the assistant manager, Frank Wells, and when checking in, I'd slip him a twenty-dollar bill and Frank would graciously upgrade me to a suite at regular room rates.

Goodnor Construction owed me $1.5 million but was giving me the cold shoulder about payment, so I kept going out to Long Island City to see if I could get a check. I always made it a habit to befriend the man who wrote the checks, and the controller of Goodnor was a Colonel Jablonowski, a real gentleman who had been an officer in the Polish army before coming to America. The Colonel was great company and over the years introduced me to some of the most wonderful ethnic restaurants in New York.

After I'd been in New York a week this time and gotten nowhere in my attempt to collect the million and a half, the Colonel told me the company was sending a man to settle accounts. This was not the answer I wanted to hear.

It was a Thursday evening and I was sitting in my room at the Plaza when the call came up from the front desk. A man who identified himself as a representative of the general contractor wanted to see me.

About ten minutes later, there was a knock on my door. The man who entered my room was 5-9, thin, with high cheekbones, silver gray hair, and walked like an injured halfback. He was very well groomed but dressed like an undertaker, wearing a black suit and tie, black vest and black hat. He identified himself as Sam S.

I ordered a double scotch on the rocks for Sam and a Virgin Mary for me. I didn't want him or anyone else to think I didn't drink, so I always ordered Virgin Marys on the sly, so my guests would think I was drinking a Bloody Mary. We made small talk for about half an hour. He knew quite a bit about sports. He was a big fan of the New York Giants, and I, of course, loved the Chicago Bears. I learned later that Sam was also a professional gambler – no wonder he knew so much.

As the hour grew later, Sam brought up the subject of the monies I "claimed" I was owed for the lighting fixtures shipped to the Chicago projects. As I was stating my case, Sam leaned a little to his right on the couch he was sitting on, intentionally revealing a holstered gun under his right armpit.

Wow. I had seen this plenty of times in the movies, a guy with a gat – so often that on the screen it had become kind of a yawn. In real life, however, it was electrifying. Was I scared? You bet your life.

Sam proceeded to tell me that in the informed opinion of the general contractor, we had overcharged them on every single project we had completed.

"You're trying to gouge us. We're willing to give you half a million dollars," he said.

I was in a state of shock – they owed me *three times* that much. My mind was a complete blank except for one thought: I won't be able to pay my bills; we're out of business. Inside I was panicking, but outside I was playing poker with this slick gangster.

He continued jabbering. His theme was: take the money and run. Take it while the taking is good. Something is better than nothing.

My mind was a million miles away. I was imagining all the consequences, none of them good. Finally, I told Sam I'd think it over, but in the meantime, could he give me a telephone number where he could be reached. He was reluctant, but gave me his home number.

After he left, I sat there, devastated. How could we have overcharged? I'd submitted a competitive bid against legitimate competitors. That's how business operated. You made your bid, you were accepted or rejected; if accepted, you did the job and then you got paid. Simple as that – except that now it wasn't. I called Colonel Jablonowski and asked to see him right away. He came to the Plaza an hour later and we went to dinner at the Forum of the Twelve Caesars, his favorite restaurant in Manhattan. And, I might add, one of the most expensive. Whatever advice he would give me, I'd be paying for it.

We talked for about two hours and the Colonel insisted I had done nothing wrong. This was par for the course – standard operating procedure with this group. They had worked it this way with every one of their subcontractors. If I wanted *any* money, I would have to dance to their tune.

"If you get tough," he said, between healthy bites of prime rib washed down with red wine, "maybe you can squeeze a few bucks more out of them. But Jack, this guy was very close with Legs Diamond. Don't think of getting too tough."

Back to the Plaza, back to my room, back to my cold sweat, knowing that if I didn't collect what was owed, I'd be out of business. Then it hit me: Jake Gottlieb. Oh my God, could Jake Gottlieb help?

It was about midnight in New York, but earlier out West, so I placed the long-distance call ... .

Colonel Jake Gottlieb and I had become very good friends following my father's death. Colonel Jake was a real, live, honest-to-goodness millionaire back when a million dollars denoted big money. He owned Western Transportation Company in Chicago, but had lived in Moline. Since then, Jake had bought the famous Dunes Hotel in Las Vegas after it went belly-up. One of his pals was Jimmy Hoffa, the Teamster boss. It was alleged that the Teamsters union had lent Jake $5 million from their pension fund money to buy the hotel. How close were Jake and Jimmy? I didn't know.

Jake had no experience running a casino, so he sold a small interest to one Major A. Riddle – Major was his name, not a rank. He operated the hotel for Jake and had all the right connections in Las Vegas.

After four calls I got through to Jake – apparently he was in the middle of a high-stakes poker game, betting big hands while he talked to me.

Jake asked for the details, took them in, then told me to relax, stop worrying, go to bed, he would take care of it. I wondered what "take care of it" meant.

The next morning, a Friday, I sat around the room drinking hot tea and working on a new cold sweat until about noon, when the telephone rang. It was Jake. He told me to call Sam.

"Everything's taken care of," he said.

"What do you mean, Jake, taken care of?"

"Just that. You don't have to know anything else." With that, he hung up.

As instructed, I called Sam, who told me he would be at my hotel about three that afternoon.

At precisely three, Sam walked into my room, still in that all-black suit and vest and wearing the black hat – maybe he had a closet full of identical outfits.

"It looks like you've got the right connections," he said. "I had a telephone call, and you're all right, kid."

I nodded like I knew what he meant by "all right."

"I'm going to help you," he went on. "But it'll cost you fifty large."

"What do you mean, fifty large?"

"Fifty thousand dollars, in green."

I agreed.

He said, "See you on Monday," and left, shutting the door behind him.

I spent the next two days worrying about collecting all the money I had in the world. Most of it was owed to suppliers. Monday was coming at me like a train, but fast as it came, I still managed to age about 40 years before it arrived.

Sam called me on Monday morning and told me he would come to the hotel about two o'clock. Would I meet him in the Oak Bar?

He walked in at two on the button, and we sat at the bar, with my Virgin Mary and his double scotch. We made small talk until he reached into his inside coat pocket (he still wore the gun) and handed me a cashier's check in the amount of $1.5 million.

Wow, I thought, he did it. But my next thought was, that is one expensive collection agency.

I asked Sam what it had taken to get Goodnor to pay up in full. He told me he'd paid a visit to the guy at the top – Art S., whom I'd met once. Art was more than a little intimidating; he looked like a charter member of Sam's fraternity.

"I told Art, this kid is crazy, and he'll kill you if he doesn't get paid. If he kills you, I gotta kill him, and nobody wins."

Art told him: "Pay the kid and be done with it."

I took the check from Sam and requested that he come back the next day. I then phoned my banker, Mr. Lin Vinyard of the First Trust and Savings Bank of Davenport, Iowa, and asked him for his correspondent bank in New York.

"Let them know I'm coming in with a cashier's check in the amount of one million five hundred thousand dollars."

I went over to the Banker's Trust on Park Avenue and met with the vice president, Mr. Blanchard. He took the check and wired it to my bank, then told me to come back in three hours when he would have the 50K in cash ready for me.

I walked to a luggage store called T. Anthony on Park Avenue and bought a briefcase – a fine black briefcase to match Sam's wardrobe.

Sam appreciated the briefcase, and what was in it.

I went home. Everything had worked out. I was out $50,000, but I still had a business, and I still had a pulse.

CHAPTER 5

JOHN DEERE TO JOHN TISHMAN

In the early '60s, the great Finnish-American architect and designer Eero Saarinen was commissioned to design John Deere's new state-of-the-art corporate headquarters. Saarinen fell in love with the Illinois countryside, and his vision of the grandeur of the American heartland was realized in the design of the facility that Deere built about seven miles outside of Moline.

The head of the electrical engineering department took me to view the prototype building they were constructing out in the country. The site was in the middle of nowhere and had an armed security guard – it was all top secret. John Deere didn't want the details of their designs reaching the public before the grand opening.

One of the unique design features was a luminous ceiling with Houserman partitions – the whole ceiling was lit. The Houserman partitions allowed you to put a sliding door anywhere; the door slid right into the ceiling, thus creating a separate room – as many separate rooms as you wanted in a given space. It was a great idea. The lighting was designed by Columbia Lighting of Seattle.

So I called the president of Columbia Lighting, a man named Walter Tolle, whom I didn't know. I told Tolle I wanted to be the man he gave the right price to when it came time to bid the new Deere building. He gave me the cold shoulder, implied he didn't know me from Adam. "Sorry, I'm busy," he said, and hung up.

Some guys can fire you up by brushing you off.

I went to see John Freund, the head of the lighting department at

John Deere, and asked him if I could go back out to the prototype building and get a sample of the luminous ceiling.

The job was enormous. The new corporate headquarters was going to be huge—three buildings on a 1,400-acre site, with a pond – and the buildings would have an enormous square footage of luminous ceiling. John gave me a small sample of the ceiling and I sent it to a friend of mine in New York named Ed Manning who ran a company called Curtis Electro. I told Ed that if he could figure out how to build this, I would get him the project from John Deere. I had no doubt that Ed would come through.

The time for the bidding came and the bidders converged on the LeClaire Hotel in Moline. It was a dynamic atmosphere, a major event in the lighting industry. The hotel was buzzing, big shots everywhere, the air thick with tobacco smoke, tension and hope. There were five electrical contractors from around the country bidding.

The contract was too big for anyone locally, so I chose a contractor from Dallas, Ling-Oliver-O'Dwyer. I befriended one of the principals of the company, Luther Oliver – as fine a man as I ever knew in the lighting business.

Columbia came in with the inflated bid of $4 million. Eventually they came down to $3 million. I bid $2 million from the get-go. Luther asked how I could guarantee that we'd be approved for the project if he used my price. I picked up the phone and called John Deere.

"Talk to the head of the electrical department," I told Luther.

John Freund got on the line. I could hear him loud and clear.

"If Jack tells you it's approved, it's approved."

Ling-Oliver-O'Dwyer used my price. We got the project.

After that, we furnished all the lighting for John Deere's new buildings, and also for Ling-Oliver-O'Dwyer, one of the most ethical electrical contractors in the country, and the biggest one we ever dealt with. John Deere used Ling-Oliver-O'Dwyer to do most of the electrical work for its factories, and B&M ended up lighting most of them. (There was another big company in Dallas called Harmon Electric which also did work for John Deere. Dallas had some big electrical contractors.) Ling-Oliver-O'Dwyer was a great company to work with, and I ended up becoming close with all three principals.

Tom O'Dwyer was a really good friend, and I got a kick out of surprising him one time. He had a small farm and I talked John Deere into giving me a ridiculous price on a sample tractor. I had it flown to Dallas and stashed in a warehouse. Then I flew down to Dallas, got on the tractor, drove it to where Tom was waiting, and said: "Here's a present."

Jimmy Ling was the third partner at Ling-Oliver-O'Dwyer. Jimmy was a flamboyant entrepreneur, a high-stakes financial gambler with his fingers in many pies. Through shrewd decisions and gutsy gambles, this high-school dropout from Oklahoma built a tiny electrical-contracting business, founded in 1946, into a massive, far-reaching conglomerate called LTV – Ling-Temco-Vought, the 14th-largest company in the Fortune 500. He was a dealmaker, a moneymaker and a great innovator.

Jimmy Ling took his largest, most daring gamble in 1968 with the purchase of Jones & Laughlin Steel Corp. – the sixth biggest producer of steel in the country. He borrowed to the teeth and bought controlling interest, shelling out $85 a share. It turned into a nightmare. Jones & Laughlin stock took a nosedive to $12.75 a share. Jimmy had to sell off his controlling interests in National Car Rental, Wilson Sporting Goods, Staco, Inc., Whitehall Electronics, Allied Radio, some stock in the innovative Braniff Airlines, and large chunks of his holdings in that wide-open new gold field – computer technology. Jimmy Ling had invested every bit of his and his children's money in LTV stock. The Lings were wiped out.

Jimmy was gracious in defeat, philosophical, recalling what another ousted CEO told him he felt when his company was taken over – as if he'd lost his manhood.

"He's no longer the prominent man in his industry. He no longer calls the shots, and that's a terrible blow…".

But in the early '60s, Jimmy and Ling-Oliver-O'Dwyer were riding high, and the Saarinen building opened in 1964 to rave reviews. The groundbreaking, breathtaking luminous ceiling won us kudos nationwide.

In 1971, my relationship with John Deere deepened. I became friends with William Hewitt, the CEO, a San Franciscan who had married the great-great-granddaughter of John Deere, Tish Wyman. Bill Hewitt was a visionary corporate leader who brought design, culture and a new era to our small town which had been sleeping for so many quiet years.

Bill was the sixth president of John Deere, the last Deere family member to run the company. He stood 6-5, a handsome guy and a real sophisticate. He'd graduated from the University of California in Berkeley, where he'd had two roommates you might have heard of: Bill Hewlett of Hewlett-Packard and Bill Haas of Levi Strauss. I had the pleasure of having lunch with the three Bills at the exclusive California Club on Nob Hill when I went to San Francisco with Hewitt.

When Roz ran for the school board in Rock Island in 1970, Bill's wife, Tish, was one of her major supporters. One of Roz's core issues was the education of children with learning disabilities. Roz and Tish were fierce advocates for challenged kids before it became a national issue.

Bill I were very close. We spent many hours talking about life. I became his Jewish confidant regarding the outside world; he often asked me about Israel and the Jewish viewpoint on certain issues. Bill was a regular guy who didn't have many local friends, since people in the "company town" were afraid of the power he wielded. Their fear was unwarranted; he was a good man, without malice, and he didn't abuse his position.

Bill had a keen eye for art and exceptional architectural awareness. He personally selected Saarinen to design the Deere corporate headquarters.

Saarinen's buildings read like a "What's What" of great American architecture: the General Motors Technical Center in Warren, Michigan,

IBM's corporate headquarters, and CBS's famous Black Rock building in New York, as well as the fabled TWA flight center at Kennedy Airport. Washington's Dulles International Airport, Bell Labs in Holmdel, N.J., the Gateway Arch in St. Louis, and the Vivian Beaumont Theater at Lincoln Center in New York are just a few of his amazing creations – once viewed, they are unforgettable.

Saarinen was recognized around the world as the Renaissance man of design. His furniture was praised right alongside his architecture. Among other ventures, he teamed up with Knoll Furniture to design and manufacture the famous "Tulip" or pedestal group of tables and chairs. Roz and I owned many pieces of this line and truly admired his aesthetic.

Originally, it had been Bill's idea to build the new corporate headquarters on a plot of land on the Mississippi that John Deere owned. Hewitt thought a riverfront property would be the best way to represent the John Deere image.

Saarinen, Bill told me, arrived in Moline one autumn morning with two of his assistants to check out the job. Bill drove them over to the building site. Saarinen stood wordless, in deep contemplation, looking at the setting for about ten minutes, making notes on a legal pad. He then expressed a desire to take a drive into the countryside. Hewitt was a bit surprised, but they got back in the car and off they went, into the wonderfully rich Illinois farmland.

They drove for several hours, exploring the area. Saarinen then requested that Bill arrange for horses to be available the next day for his party. Bill rounded up the horses. After riding over the countryside for three hours, the design team returned to John Deere headquarters and Saarinen described his vision of the future office complex. It was to be in the country, not on the river. The beautiful land, Saarinen believed, was the perfect symbol for John Deere's historic association with the American soil.

Real estate brokers were hired and various locations inspected. John Deere ended up buying the 1,400-acre site and erecting the three buildings – a main office building, seven stories high, flanked by two buildings, with a lake in front. Hewitt commissioned the great sculptor Henry Moore to create a sculpture which was transported to the island in the middle of the lake by helicopter. The lake actually served as the air-conditioning water tower for the buildings.

Sadly, Eero Saarinen died in 1961 during an operation for a brain tumor before he could see his design completed and greeted with universal praise.

The one blemish on the finished work appeared later. This was the first building in the United States to be covered with Core Ten steel. Core Ten steel, sometimes called Cor-Ten, is a kind of steel which develops a rusted, weathered surface after a few years of exposure to the elements. The product wasn't exactly a world-beater, and the main building would later be nicknamed "The Rusty Palace."

☼　☼　☼　☼

In 1965, my brother and I got together with a good friend in Moline named Sam Sable, a jeweler from Finland – a charming man and a shrewd businessman. There was a lot of inexpensive land available out in his area, so we bought some. We brought in Al Rabiner, a friend of mine and a successful businessman who, among other things, had made a lot of money converting animal intestines into feed for animals. He'd just sold his company for five or six million, huge money in the mid-'60s, and he was looking for investments.

The four of us – my brother, Sam Sable, Al Rabiner and I – built a 32-lane bowling alley, Regal Lanes, in East Moline. We built it in about three months with another friend of mine who owned a company called All Steel. The Regal Lanes was a beautiful, state-of-the-art bowling alley.

To me, bowling had always been one step above motorcycle racing – a low-end, rough pastime, associated with saloons. But recently it had begun to flourish, nurtured by the Brunswick Company. By the '60s it was a huge industry in America and had become fashionable – the weekly

Pro Bowlers Tour show on ABC, hosted by Chris Schenkel, gave the sport national exposure and a huge shot in the arm publicity-wise.

We built Regal Lanes from the ground up and turned it into a gorgeous place, with state-of-the-art lighting and a nightclub. All of a sudden, I wanted to be a nightclub impresario. It was a lot of fun as a sideline. Marti used to come in when she was 11 or 12 and work the snack bar, serving hot dogs and soda pop. She loved it and we all came to love bowling; I even got good at it. It was a great place to spend time with the kids.

Later we sold our portion of Regal Lanes to Sam Sable, who then ran it. Down the line, the land where we'd built the bowling alley became very desirable. It was a fun interlude.

At a certain moment in the '60s, after drifting apart business-wise, my brother and I decided it was time to separate. We would stay in the same building, each hold stock in the other's company, but we would call it a day for working together. He'd run B&M and I would run my own company, which I had named Chain Store Lighting.

I had had it with the electrical distribution business, which had become dull and limited to me. An electrical distributor is basically a middleman for the manufacturers of electrical equipment; all he really does is arrange for product to be moved from a seller to a buyer. Not too fascinating. Lighting, on the other hand, was challenging, intriguing, and exciting. I moved upstairs with my people, and Bill stayed downstairs with his. It was the best thing to do.

Since I was already cultivating the chains as clients, I now targeted all the shopping center developers, not just the Buckbaums and Simons. I was carving out a new market, and it was a wide-open field. One company, Goodrich Construction in New York, owned by a man named Arthur Cohen, chose me to light every shopping center they built. Arthur's brother Richard later moved to Los Angeles and became a friend. He started another company called Macerich Properties, a major shopping center developer on the West Coast. One of our other great clients was Caffero, a big developer in Youngstown, Ohio, which was later bought out by Simon.

But to try to reach the true big time in the industry, I knew I had to take another trip to New York.

✧   ✧   ✧   ✧

It was 1962, and I was in the Big Apple, a hunter tackling the biggest game of all – the top commercial real estate construction firm in the United States, Tishman Realty and Construction. I was calling on John Tishman, the head of the company. Without an appointment.

I stood in front of 666 Fifth Avenue, a 45-story black skyscraper, corporate headquarters of Tishman. I took a deep breath as the New York pedestrians streamed by me like so many ants at a picnic. The energy in the city was terrific. I entered the massive lobby, which featured sculptures by Isamu Noguchi, including "Landscape of the Cloud," with its amazing floor-to-ceiling waterfall. I was in a cathedral of commerce.

I took the elevator to the 38th floor and announced myself, handing the secretary my card.

"I'm Jack Zukerman. I'm here to see Mr. Tishman."

It was like asking to see the Wizard of Oz. The secretary relayed my request into the inner sanctum, smiled, and promptly seemed to forget about me.

I sat in that outer office for two hours. I didn't stare at the ceiling, I didn't read magazines; I stayed focused on the mission at hand.

Finally, I was ushered into the largest private office I had ever seen. The room was full of replicas and models of completed Tishman buildings and projects in progress.

John Tishman was a gracious, kind, mild-mannered man who was curious to know why this stranger from the heartland wanted to see him.

I explained that my intention was to furnish lighting equipment to him for his projects on a direct basis.

He looked at me as if I were from Mars, then sat there, wordless, for what seemed like five minutes. I could picture the wheels spinning in his head like a fine Swiss watch. Finally he nodded decisively, stood up, and led me to the office of Charley Debeneditis, who was in charge of construction.

Charley agreed with the boss; this was an interesting idea. I could save them serious money by cutting out all the middleman costs. Since Tishman was the largest builder of office buildings in the United States – building both for its own portfolio and as construction manager – my proposal, if acted on, would result in substantial savings.

As a test, they gave me a set of blueprints so I could figure out the lighting costs. Ironically, the job was a men's dormitory, Bromley Hall, at my alma mater, the University of Illinois. I took the blueprints back to Rock Island, worked out the specs, submitted them, and was subsequently approved.

Thus began an association that would make me the largest supplier of lighting fixtures to a national account for the next 35 years.

As my relationship with Tishman solidified and evolved, I traveled to New York once a month to meet with different people in the organization. I quickly realized that the real action in the office-building world was the tenant improvement department. Furnishing the core building products was standard stuff, not exciting, but the tenant improvements were interesting and challenging. Each building, each unit, presented a fresh and unique challenge, from both an engineering and aesthetic perspective. Thinking outside the box was mandatory. The art of lighting design was in its infancy; there were only a few designers working then, such as Seymour Evans and Lesley Wheel. And Tishman, like the majority of builders, didn't use lighting designers; the company adhered to the industry norm and hired electrical engineering firms.

I entered into arrangements with the major lighting manufacturers,

Lightolier, Daybrite, and Holophane, to make fixtures with our company's name on them. These were the same big companies which had coldly snubbed me just a decade earlier.

I bought the housings from the lighting fixture makers and the lenses from Holophane. I purchased the ballasts from a brand-new company, Universal, in Paterson, N.J., owned by a true gentleman, Archie Sergi. We became good friends, and even though Lightolier, Daybrite, and other major players objected, I held firm and insisted on using Universal ballasts.

One of my first office buildings was 919 Third Avenue in New York, a massive skyscraper office complex, 47 floors high and 1.4 million square feet, built atop a famous bar and restaurant called P.J. Clarke's – where Ray Milland boozed in *The Lost Weekend*, and where Johnny Mercer wrote "One For My Baby" on a napkin at the bar. A fixture in the area since 1884, P.J. Clarke's was known for its hamburgers, martinis and swinging singles, and was then owned by the Levezzo brothers, who also owned the property next door that Tishman coveted. Big Dan Levezzo, a drinking buddy of famed saloonkeeper Toots Shor, played hardball, held out for a good deal, and then gave Tishman a 99-year lease. Everyone was happy. P.J. Clarke's stayed put and the building went up above it.

Later, we did the lighting for 100 Gold Street in the heart of Manhattan's financial district (the building later served as a rest and relief center for rescue workers after the World Trade Centers were attacked on 9/11), and the Conde Nast building, another Manhattan skyscraper. One of the most exciting projects we were involved in was the World Trade Centers. Talk about a challenge! Ten million square feet; begun in September 1967, finished in December of '72.

Tishman's operations were vast and far-reaching, building office complexes all over the country.

We furnished the lighting for a Henry Ford project in Detroit known as the Renaissance Center – the Ren Cen, a complex of four office buildings and two hotels which was intended to revitalize the Detroit economy, but didn't.

When Tishman moved into the Philadelphia territory, we did the Centre Square projects, 1500 and 1700 Market Street.

Meanwhile, the Tishman office in Los Angeles was getting very busy, and I headed west to meet the man in charge on the West Coast – Mr. Abe Bolsky, a Brooklyn-born and bred old-school construction man who had learned the business the hard way.

Abe was tough but charming and had acclimated beautifully to the Los Angeles business world, bidding on all the major projects. He and I had a great rapport and I became his lighting maven. I worked with Abe for many years and not once did we exchange a cross word. I loved the guy.

Among his accomplishments was the construction of the Century Plaza Towers, two 44-story buildings located at 2029 and 2049 Century Park East. We furnished all the lighting for these two great buildings, still the highest structures in Century City.

Also in the City of Angels, we provided the lighting for the Wells Fargo Tower and for California Plaza, massive skyscrapers in downtown LA.

We also lit the Westin Hotel at South Coast Plaza, the Hyatt Hotel at LAX and the Hotel Nikko in Beverly Hills. Tishman was the leader in office buildings and soon would become the premier hotel builder.

Abe Bolsky ran a very tight organization and was definitely a micro-manager, but he was also a valued member of the community. Abe was a major benefactor to the Duboff School for the deaf, because he had a daughter who suffered with that affliction. I joined him in that endeavor.

Those of us who worked with him knew he had heart trouble, so everyone tried to shield him from unnecessary anxiety. He had annual checkups and on his 65th birthday was taking a stress test on a treadmill when he suffered a heart attack and died. I mourned him for many years and miss him to this day.

✧   ✧   ✧   ✧

When I heard that Tishman had the contract to build the John Hancock Building in Chicago, the first 100-story building, I was intrigued; but when I inquired about the job I was told by people in the New York office that they couldn't give me the green light because the new VP of Tishman Chicago was an "independent man who answered to no one," not even John Tishman. So I went to Chicago and met Mr. Mike Oppenheim.

Sure enough, he was his own man. He didn't want anyone from New York butting in – he was a millionaire long before he began to build the John Hancock Building and he liked to rely on his own judgment.

Fortunately for me, Mike Oppenheim and I got along right from the get-go. He was by far the brightest man I ever met in the construction business. He took me by the hand to meet Skidmore, Owings and Merrill, the job architects.

On the way to meet them, Mike said: "Jack, I can't take you there with the name Chain Store Lighting, it's not sophisticated enough. Let's change the name to CSL!"

CSL it became, on the spot.

Then I met Bob Diamant, head of the architectural team for Skidmore, Owings and Merrill for the Hancock Building. Skidmore didn't like the idea of Tishman furnishing the lighting equipment, but Mike assured me he could handle their objections.

It was 1968, and there I was in the middle of the biggest commercial real estate project in the United States. But I still had to make it over several hurdles to end up with the job.

Besides needing Skidmore's approval, we had to deal with Bill Waddell, John Hancock's VP of construction for the project. He was a delightfully bright man who was on the job to protect Hancock's interests.

Also, prior to my getting the order, I had to match up our design against two competitors. The three companies all mocked up samples for the Hancock Building on the site, in a closed room on the 42nd floor of the iron skyscraper shell. The room was full of fixtures, so the architects could pick the product that best suited their design.

The day before the decision, I went to the Hancock Building. The elevator was reserved for workers, so I had to walk up the 42 flights with two lighting fixtures on my shoulders, like a Sherpa climbing an urban Everest.

It was the bleak dead of winter, with iron-gray skies above vast smoking Chicago, the wind whistling off Lake Michigan like a winter hawk, chilling me to the bone. I remembered those bags of spuds I'd lugged up the stairs of the Masonic Temple in Moline years before. I was going up a lot more stairs tonight – and for a lot more potatoes.

I made it, and left my equipment. When the architects came the next day to view the presentation, they picked mine.

But the job still was not secure. There were complications with political overtones – specifically an Illinois state senator named James Ryan, who was affiliated with one of the biggest electrical distributors in Chicago, EFF&G Electric, and also was a big buddy of the ultimate power broker, Mayor Richard Daley. Ryan made indignant noises about anything for the job being bought outside of Chicago. Of course, Ryan wanted EFF&G to provide all the lighting. His insistence led to a mandatory meeting with Richard Daley. Mike and Bill and I were summoned to His Honor's office.

Daley was a real presence, a force. The corruption in the city politics of those days has been documented, but no one ever brought any personal wrongdoing home to the mayor. He knew how his machine worked, of course, but if he was a crook, he was the paradoxical kind: a crook who never kept anything for himself.

One thing you couldn't help but notice about him: he always made it clear what he wanted, and he was accustomed to getting it.

"The people of the great city of Chicago," he told us, "would like to favor one of our hometown suppliers. EFF&G Electric is a company with deep roots in the community and nothing would please the people more than seeing this excellent company involved in the construction of this historic building which reflects the great character of our great city. The character and contribution of Jimmy Ryan and EFF&G to the city cannot be overlooked. There is great virtue in doing hometown business."

"Thank you, Your Honor," Mike said, standing.

"Thank you, Your Honor," we all said, shaking hands.

"The will of the people is great," said the Mayor.

"We'll get back to you," we said.

We took our leave and talked things over in a Rush Street saloon where Mike and Bill assured me I still had the inside track to the job.

"Look," Mike said. "The will of the people of Chicago may be great, but I'm still my own man."

It took guts, but Mike stuck to his guns even when dealing with His Honor and I stayed on board. But the saga wasn't quite over. We still had to get final approval to write the order from Bill Waddell of Hancock, and Bill was waiting for one final call from his boss.

As Mike and I sat in Bill Waddell's office, the phone rang. It was Clyde Gay, the president of John Hancock, calling with his decision. Apparently he'd just received a strongly worded request from the head of Thomas Industries, a lighting equipment manufacturer which Hancock insured – at the last moment they lobbied hard for the job. Too hard, it turned out; Waddell informed me that the president of Hancock didn't like being bullied. That sealed the deal; I got the approval for the lighting contract. It was 1968, and a $5 million contract was top of the world – a hundred-story deal.

I can't stress enough the importance of John Tishman in my life. He and his company made me a national player in architectural lighting. The day I stepped into that big black building in Manhattan, took the elevator to the 38th floor and walked into John Tishman's office with one idea and no appointment … that day was far and away the most important of my career.

Holophane was one of the leaders in the lighting field in those days, selling fixtures with lenses called 6250. Instead of using a four-light fixture, and all the energy that a four-light consumed, you could be more efficient using a three-light with the 6250; but they were very expensive, the Rolls-Royce of lighting fixtures.

Faced with their prices, I decided it would be smart to be my own source. I bought the lenses from Holophane; then bought the metal cheaply from someone else, put them together and competed directly with Holophane. I was the first person in America to buy their lenses and put them in somebody else's fixture.

I've always tried to surround myself with talent wherever I found it, and Bill Warren and Bill Langone were former Holophane vice presidents whom I convinced to come in with me to form a new company that made injection-molded lenses for fluorescent lighting fixtures. This company became US Lighting.

Bill Warren was brilliant – he should have been a professor at MIT instead of in the lighting business. Bill Langone (pronounced Lang-GOH-nee) was from Boston. His family was in the funeral home business. We ended up competing directly with Holophane and making a lot of money.

We partnered with MSL Industries, a California company with a 180,000-square-foot factory on Mannheim Road in Chicago which had previously fabricated injection-molded fronts for Motorola TVs. MSL was owned by Joe Zoline, who also owned Osh Kosh Luggage. MSL had lost the Motorola contract to Japan – their molds were out of use, they didn't know what to do with all that factory space and they were looking for production. That's where we ended up making the lenses to compete with Holophane. These were the lenses we used for the Hancock Building.

US Lighting was a great company. The molds we used to make our lenses were huge, the size of a trailer, and cost up to $800,000 each. They produced a clear acrylic plastic lens that provided comfortable light, really a wonderful product.

✧   ✧   ✧   ✧

In addition to CSL and US Lighting, I helped create another successful company in the '60s – although my relationship with it ended in a way that ultimately upset me a good deal.

With the explosion in construction of larger supermarkets and shopping malls in the mid-1960s, the need for more and better outdoor lighting increased exponentially. Our objective with the exterior of shopping malls, supermarkets and shopping centers – illuminating parking lots and storefronts – was to make them warm, inviting and visible to the public passing by on the roads. A giant fixture called the GBB (or "Great Big Bastard") was just the ticket – we were Sylvania's biggest customer for those fixtures, and together, we were literally lighting America. But Sylvania was based way off in Massachusetts, and the thought occurred, why remain dependent on Sylvania when I could do it myself?

So, as a first step toward developing my own line of outdoor lighting, I hooked up with a Moline sand caster named Don Robbins. (The difference between sand casting and die casting is the initial cost of molds.)

We created a flat outdoor lighting fixture that was like a square box, and we put them on poles and lit the shopping center parking lots. It turned night into day. That's how EMCO was started – Electrical Manufacturing Company. I went to the bank, and we set up the company and the plant.

My partners In EMCO were Bennett Levin, a consulting engineer from Philadelphia – an excellent specifier who was also a railroad buff with a real train engine in his back yard – and of course, the brilliant Bill Warren.

The three of us put up the money to start the company, and then brought in Ed Manning from Curtis Electro in New York to run it. Ed Manning was a very talented guy, a micromanager who had helped me with the luminous ceiling job for John Deere.

I gave Ed a piece of the company with no cash investment, and he moved to Moline and became the president of EMCO. Roz and I arranged a nice house next door to ours for Ed, his wife Barbara and their son and daughter.

Ed was secretive, a difficult man to understand, but he was very efficient. The company hummed. Bill Warren designed, Don Robbins produced, I marketed, and EMCO, with Ed Manning running the day-to-day business, became a full-fledged company selling outdoor lighting. Initially I was my own biggest customer, but soon I was selling to companies across the country, and EMCO flourished.

We eventually built a new factory in Milan, which is outside Moline, near the airport. (Always build your factory near the airport for optimum shipping efficiency and minimum costs.) I left Ed in charge of the plant in Milan in 1976 when we moved to California. Once in Los Angeles, I really didn't have much to do with EMCO other than being the majority owner.

In 1978-79, Ed called me one day and said, "Jack, you're in California, I'm here, I'm doing all the work – would you sell me back your initial investment at twice what you paid for it?"

At that time, I didn't care, I had other things cooking, so I let him have it. Not long after that, they squeezed Bill Warren out. It wasn't long before I learned what Ed Manning had pulled; I'd been conned and Bill had been forced out, leaving just Ed and Bennett Levin.

Six months later, the lawyer who was handling everything in Chicago called. He was a cousin of mine, the brilliant David Parson, a partner in a major firm called Kirkland, Fleming, Martin, Green and Ellis, today called Kirkland and Ellis. Dave told me that Ed had just sold the company to Thomas Industries for multiple millions of dollars. Both Bill Warren and I had been blindsided – Ed hadn't told us he intended to sell it and he'd certainly understated its value to us.

Efficiency and class don't always go together. Ed Manning was a good manager and ran a profitable business, but as a human being he was unreliable. Ed was interested in Ed. With him, the dollar always trumped loyalty; feelings, relationships, people all came in second to the buck. I saw him once more a few years later but didn't have anything to do with him, didn't speak to him. He passed away eight or ten years later. EMCO is still making outdoor lighting, going strong.

✿   ✿   ✿   ✿

Now in case I'm giving the impression that I myself have been the One Good Man in the business world throughout my career, I'll tell of the time my salesmanship ran a little bit ahead of my production department.

One day Bill Warren and I went to a lighting show in Miami where all the manufacturers displayed their wares and I fell in love with a product for supermarkets. It was similar to a Holophane lighting fixture, made out of acrylic, and it fit into a two-by-two metal pan. After the show, I talked the people into letting me buy this item.

Then I contacted Publix Supermarkets. Bill and I went to Lakeland, Florida, where Publix is based, and met with the president of the company, George Jenkins. Jenkins, affectionately called "Mr. George" by his employees, had started his supermarket empire during the Depression and was a great innovator. In 1940, he mortgaged an orange grove and built Florida's first supermarket. His "food palace" had piped-in music, air-conditioning, cold cases, in-store donut and flower shops, and electric-eye automatic doors! Today Publix is a Fortune 500 company and the fourth-largest privately owned company in the country.

George Jenkins and his staff loved the fixture. We told them we manufactured it. They wanted to use it, but required that their head of construction approve it. Jenkins said, "We'll send him to your factory in Moline to see how you make them."

We'd never made them before.

So they sent their man to see our factory on a quick turnaround visit. I picked him up at the airport.

"We've got plenty of time," I told the man from Publix. "Let me show you the sights."

I drove him to Peoria, 80 miles away, "to show him the town" – really to kill time. We ate a nice leisurely lunch. I was in no hurry to take him back to the factory in Moline, which was not at all impressive and had none of the fixtures I'd claimed we manufactured. The Publix man had a 3:00 p.m. flight back to Florida.

"That's Browning Field," I said, back in Moline, slowing the car down. "I played ball there when I was a kid. Let me tell you about the time I was batboy for the Moline Plows."

"But Jack, shouldn't we go to the factory?" the Publix man asked.

"There's just enough time," I said, speeding up. "We'll go there now, take a quick look and make the plane. We have a half-hour window."

That's when a police siren started blaring behind us.

A cop pulled me over. He ran my license.

"We'll be done with this in two shakes," I told the man from Publix.

But the cop took his sweet time. Minutes passed while he studied my license and talked on his radio. Finally he came back.

"Well, Mr. Zukerman," he said, "it appears that—"

I cut him off.

"Do you know who this man is?" I demanded. "He's the head of construction for Publix Supermarkets, the biggest chain of markets in the whole USA. He's here to see our factory and you've just caused a major delay!"

"But sir –"

"No buts!"

I proceeded to rake the cop over the coals with vehement indignation. I said it was outrageous. I said it was one thing to pull us over, but then to keep us there indefinitely while he went back and played with his radio, causing a delay that could ruin my guest's ability to do his job – that, mister, was unlawful detainment, and if I had any influence in town he was going to hear plenty about it. I mean, I gave him both barrels.

The cop apologized profusely.

"I'm so sorry, Mr. Zukerman, it'll never happen again. I promise you. I apologize on behalf of the police department and ..."

By the time he finished this amazing aw-shucks apology, we had to break the speed limit just to make the flight.

"It looks like we don't have time to stop," I said to the man from Publix.

I pointed out a large factory and said, "That's our factory."

He said, "Oh, okay, good!" And we put him on his flight home.

Back in Florida, he reported that he'd seen all the fixtures and we were a great company, that I was a respected man in the community with an impressive factory. We got the contract and ended up lighting all the Publix stores.

Later, I sent a dozen roses to the cop's wife. It had been a set-up. The officer was an old pal, Tom Ott, who moonlighted in the construction business. I'd called him and planned the gambit.

I'd feel guilty about it, but the Publix guy turned out to be right – we really did make a fine fixture.

CHAPTER 6

LIFESTYLES OF THE RICH & FAMOUS

I moved west in the '70s, but before doing so I ran into another example of the way business was done back east – at least if your business brought you into contact with the "wise guys."

Food Fair Properties had become about the biggest food chain in America in the mid-1960s, with stores in Florida and Pennsylvania, and had plans to expand nationwide. Food Fair contracted me to light two new buildings in Newark, New Jersey, called Gateway One and Two in the Gateway Urban Renewal Project.

The Gateway project was intended to bring life back to Newark's fiscally blighted inner city, which was rife with corruption and violence – a hard, tough, depressed place.

Mayor Hugh Addonizio was, it seemed, doing everything he could to get Newark out of its rut. The Gateway was an attempt to reinvigorate New Jersey's largest city and attract business investment after the racial rioting of mid-July 1967, one of the decade's worst civil disorders, with grim numbers – four days, 26 dead, more than 1,000 injured and more than 1,000 under arrest. It was a nightmare.

This was the landscape I entered when I took on the Gateway job. The electrical contractor I had to deal with was Valentine Electric. A friend of mine from Lightolier warned me that they were Mafia.

I went to meet the head man, Andy Valentine, who sat at his desk in his office while another man stood behind him in a threatening hoodlum stance ... a scene right out of *The Godfather*.

I said, "I've got the contract to furnish the lighting fixtures for the

Food Fair Properties job, and you've got the electrical contract. What's it gonna take for you not to break up my lighting fixtures and cause all the havoc you can?"

Just like that.

Valentine looked at me and said, "Sit down, kid. You've got a lot of guts, walking in here and talking like this."

"So?" I asked.

He looked me over and then smiled.

"Okay, I won't break up your lighting fixtures, but it'll cost you two dollars apiece."

I was shipping 20,000 lighting fixtures, so I paid him $40,000; and every time I shipped another thousand fixtures, I brought him two grand more in cash – my "insurance policy."

It's hard to figure, given our arrangement, but I came to like the guy. Andy Valentine ended up becoming a customer in his own right and bought all his lighting from me.

Andy was connected but he wasn't Italian. He'd been in the Navy in the submarine corps and they made him into an electrician. He probably was one of the ten smartest guys I ever met in that business, sharp as a razor. He didn't own his own company – he had a piece. The mob had put up most of the money and called it Valentine Electric. Everyone in the lighting and electrical business was scared of him, but he was a friend to me.

Roz met him, not knowing of his connections. She liked him. We would have business parties in our NY apartment building across the street from Lincoln Center. We threw Christmas parties in the penthouse, by the swimming pool, and Andy would always come – a regular guy.

I later found out that Andy, along with Hugh Addonizio, the mayor, was indicted for billing the city of Newark for work that was never completed.

Addonizio, who had won the Silver Star in the Army during WW II, had served Newark in Congress from 1948 to 1962, when he quit and successfully ran for mayor. He ruled the roost until 1970 when his re-election bid got knocked dead by Kenneth Gibson, an African-American.

Addonizio was convicted after he was out of office; according to former U.S. District Judge Herbert J. Stern, Addonizio and others indicted with him were guilty of "literally delivering the city into the hands of organized crime." The court went on to state, "It is impossible to estimate the impact upon and the cost of these criminal acts to the decent citizens of Newark, in terms of their frustration, despair and disillusionment.... Their crimes, in the judgment of this Court, tear at the very heart of our civilized form of government and of our society. The people will not tolerate such conduct at any level of government."

As related by one of the witnesses against him, when asked why he left his nice cushy job in Congress to "come up here in this mess," the bald, paunchy former war hero Addonizio stated, "Simple – there's no money in Washington, but you can make a million bucks as mayor of Newark." You can also get ten years hard time in the federal pen.

Addonizio's two immediate successors were also convicted of corruption-related crimes. The city of Newark was steeped in crime and slime. And my pal Andy, who was also convicted of bribing the mayor of Ft. Lee, New Jersey, was in it up to his neck.

Addonizio, who had been touted as a contender for the New Jersey governor's mansion, served five years and two months in prison and came out broken in many ways. Fourteen others were indicted, including Anthony Boiardo, son of legendary Newark godfather Richard "The Boot" Boiardo who always fancied that the Godfather character Don Corleone was based on him. Anthony, a.k.a. "Tony Boy," had taken over the rackets for his father, but during the criminal proceedings, Tony Boy had a heart attack and never stood trial.

✿   ✿   ✿   ✿

In the fall of 1971, Marti, our oldest, went off to Northwestern University in Evanston, Ill. It was very hard for me to let her go. She was the buddy I had always wanted, and we enjoyed all our sports together. It took many months to accept her departure from the nest. We consoled ourselves with the knowledge that Evanston wasn't that far away, a couple hundred miles, and Marti had chosen a good school.

Marti was an outstanding student at Northwestern and also organized a women's powder puff football league, starring as quarterback on one of the teams. She would graduate Summa Cum Laude and Phi Beta Kappa, the highest honor any senior can achieve.

She would also start a Zukerman offspring troop movement, because Steve would follow Marti to Northwestern, and Jeff would follow Steve. So we were a little surprised in 1976, when Mike was a senior in high school and told us he wanted to go to the University of California, Berkeley.

Roz and I thought, California. Hmmm …

We were really sick of the cold, and I figured that by then I could run CSL from the West Coast, so we moved to Los Angeles.

I came out first and bought a house in Beverly Hills, at 1168 Hillcrest Drive in the Trousdale section. Next door, at 1174 Hillcrest, was Elvis Presley's former home! Elvis had bought the house in 1967.

The Presley house was now occupied by Paula Kent Meehan. Paula started as a young actress and model and in 1960 founded a small company, Redken Laboratories, with an initial investment of $300,000. She ended up making a fortune from shampoo bubbles and beauty products, and in 1993 sold Redken to L'Oreal.

But tourists looking for Elvis still arrived by the busload to see where the King had kept his blue suede shoes. Some believed he still lived there.

One day Roz and I were out of the house, but my mother, who was visiting, answered the door and was confronted by a busload of Elvis fans who insisted that our house was Elvis' house.

Mom proceeded to give them a tour. She said: "Elvis watches TV here, he takes a shower here, and he sleeps here." And they believed her. My mother was really funny.

When I came home and she told me this, I said, "Are you crazy?"

"Well, they were nice people!"

Across the street from us lived Irv Levin, a businessman who owned the Boston Celtics. Irv became a good friend. He owned the Celtics in 1974-75 with Bob Schmertz, a developer of retirement communities who was indicted in 1975 for bribery but died soon thereafter. Irv owned the Celtics by himself in 1978-79. Irv was not a popular custodian of the fabled Celtics franchise. The rabid Boston fans gave him hell, the team was in such terrible decline at the time – so he ended up trading the Celtics for the Buffalo Braves. He moved the Braves to San Diego, where they became the Clippers. How do you ditch the Celtics for the Clippers?

To add insult to injury, in the deal, the Celtics ended up with the draft rights to the great Larry Bird the next year. It was the mistake of the century, at least in basketball terms.

Two doors away lived the great comedian Danny Thomas, star of TV's *Make Room for Daddy,* and his wife Rosemary, the parents of Marlo Thomas. I saw Danny and Rosemary often, they were lovely people. Most people don't know Danny Thomas was actually born Amos Alphonsus Muzard Yaqoob in Deerfield, Michigan.

Down the street from me on Hillcrest lived the singer, film star and Rat Pack regular, Dean Martin. Hillcrest Drive was full of movie people coming and going, show-biz folk wandering around in their bathrobes, with coffee cups and the morning paper. Having come from Moline, Illinois, I have to admit to being a bit star-struck.

When I bought the house, I was fortunate enough to retain the services of James E. Lewis III, a houseman who was a can-do fellow. The house had belonged to a man in New York. It was beautiful, I thought, but Roz didn't care for it; she thought it looked like a motel.

Nine months after moving in, I was in Chicago at a meeting and Roz called me up and said, "I just sold the house!" I said, "Are you nuts?" She said, "No, somebody knocked on the door of the house and they liked it and so I sold it." I said, "That's great," and she said, "And we made a 35 percent profit!"

By selling that house, we ended up neighbors to Hollywood's Master of Suspense. We found a house on a four-and-a-half-acre estate in Bel Air and Jimmy moved with us. The address was 880 Strada Vecchia. Three doors away lived the great movie director Alfred Hitchcock.

I used to see Alfred all the time. He was very funny and likable. We used to sit in the gardens or on the patio and talk – he was very interested in where I was from. He was English and eccentric and I was a small-town Midwesterner, but we had great rapport; we found each other exotic.

Our new house had belonged to a man named Ben Smith, a member with me at Hillcrest Country Club, but it had earlier been the property of Alfonso Bell, of Bell Petroleum Co. Bell used his profits to develop upscale real estate communities in West Los Angeles, including parts of Westwood, Pacific Palisades, and Beverly Hills, luring the Hollywood elite and other well-heeled residents. In 1922, Bell founded Bel Air Estates on 600 prime acres, sprucing up the area with lush vegetation, new roads, utilities, and a world-class country club. Bell's son, Alfonso E. Bell, Jr., later became one of California's most popular congressmen.

For his own home, Alfonso Bell picked the choicest piece of property in all of Bel Air. It boasted a 360-degree view as far as the eye could see, which meant that on clear days you could see from the ocean to the valleys, snow on the San Bernardino Mountains or all the way to Catalina – but when the pollution was severe, you couldn't see in front of your nose. LA in those days had terrible pollution problems, a plague of brown skies and bad air, but our property was wonderful, with a fabulous pool and pool-house and amazing rose gardens that bloomed lushly, magically, all landscaped with exquisitely fitted stone walls, a garden fit for royalty – really a magnificent, enchanting piece of property.

Hitchcock lived a few doors away on one side, and on the other side was Jim Kilroy, a real estate magnate, major California developer and legendary sailboat racer. Jim was on my board of directors; I was on his. We became great friends, as did his wife Kathy and Roz.

Jim showed a flair for enterprise at an early age. When he was ten, during the Depression, he was co-partner in a bicycle repair shop and earned money in a number of ways: he sold magazine subscriptions, mowed lawns, hauled trash, sold scrap paper, made up newspapers and sold and delivered them, navigating his crowded city routes on a skate-wheeled scooter and the residential areas on his bicycle. He also worked as a lifeguard, grocery-store checker, inventory stocker and haberdashery clerk. He was occasionally a butcher and a baker. He ended up attending one year of college at Santa Barbara State.

"What a beautiful thing it was to grow up scrounging," Jim once said. "It gave me a lot of smarts."

Jim was a very competitive man. He built a series of legendary maxi-yachts and raced the seas around the world, braving sleepless nights and violent storms in his quest for victory. His boats, the Kialoa series 1 through 5, were luxurious and fast and won a lot of races. His vast real estate empire spread across Southern California, and he was one of the savviest and most visionary developers of the LAX area.

We played a lot of tennis over at the Kilroys', and through Jim, I met such men as Chrysler CEO Lee Iacocca, as well as the president of Hughes Aircraft, the president of Rockwell – interesting, high-flying guys.

It was an idyllic time. My business was thriving; Roz had completed her legal training and started her own practice in family law. And we had our beautiful home, until we suddenly didn't.

It was a Thursday. I was at my office, Roz in court, when we each got a call that the house was on fire.

We rushed home to find the house burning like crazy, flames everywhere – a goner. The police determined that a burglar had broken in and set it on fire – arson. We were instantly homeless. Upscale, but homeless.

We moved into the Westwood Marquis Hotel. We were starting over as far as possessions went, and since the fire had wiped out our clothes, Kathy Kilroy took Roz to Paris to buy a new wardrobe. Kathy showed Roz where to buy everything, took her shopping. Everything was cheap in Paris at that time; the exchange rate favored the dollar. Besides wonderful new clothes, Roz bought all sorts of fantastic things for our home on that trip.

I had mixed feelings about the fire. The truth was I hadn't really liked the house itself; I didn't like anything old in a house. But the grounds were truly magnificent. I wanted to rebuild, but Roz didn't want any part of it.

Jim Kilroy bought the land from me. I'd given him an option to buy the house once – he wanted the land to expand his property. He took the land, added three of the four acres to his home and later sold the other acre for big money.

Jim had five 100-foot racing sailboats stashed all around the world – some of the sleekest, swiftest, priciest and most comfortable on the seas. After the fire he asked us, "Please, since you guys had such a trauma, take a boat for a week or two, any boat – how about the one in St. Thomas?"

Roz and I flew to St. Thomas. Our son, Jeff, had graduated Northwestern and had married by then, becoming an attorney himself, and he and his wife joined us. We spent a week on Jim's 100-foot sloop, sailing the warm, beautiful blue seas with a crew of five, including a fantastic cook. It was a fun week and we sailed all over the Caribbean, stopping in Little Dix Bay and other interesting ports.

When Jim was racing, his sailboat crew included the president of Hughes Aircraft, who was his navigator and brought the latest top-secret navigational equipment from Hughes on board – high-tech stuff they'd developed for the military which gave Jim an edge on the competition in races. Before Ted Turner or any of the software boys got into boats, there was Jim Kilroy.

Big boats – that's how some corporate big shots express their egos. My boat's bigger than your boat, my boat's faster than yours. Big boats, big egos and big, big business. I wasn't used to an environment where guys were tooting their own horn all the time – but if you didn't take it too seriously, it could be big fun.

On the other hand, there was a dark side to the good life – and the boat world too, for that matter. A friend of mine, an ex-employee, got himself inextricably entangled in that other side – so tangled that it destroyed him.

✧   ✧   ✧   ✧

On March 2, 1990, I read the following in the *New York Times*: "Jack Kramer and Ben Kramer were found guilty of federal money laundering."

Previously, Ben, Jack's son, had been sentenced to life imprisonment without parole for having imported 500,000 pounds of marijuana into the U.S. He'd already done time on drug charges from the mid-'70s to the early '80s.

I met Jack Kramer in the late 1960s when I was in Philadelphia visiting an old friend, Barry Lieb, who owned Quaker City Electric, a lighting fixture manufacturing company he'd taken over after his father died. Quaker City had been one of my first suppliers as a national distributor. Kramer was one of their salesmen. His duties included calling on architects and specifiers to sell lighting.

Jack was planning a move to Hollywood, Florida, to find a new job and get away from the long bitter winters in Philly – just an ordinary guy looking to provide a better life in a sunnier climate for his wife, Maxine, and his two sons, Ben and Mark. I liked Jack immediately. He was quiet, well-spoken, charming, bright, and most importantly for doing business, he had that fire in the gut a salesman needs in order to succeed.

Building nationwide sales teams requires meeting and hiring many potential reps and assessing their character and skills, so when I spot talent, I zero in on what makes the man tick – his passions, his weaknesses – and then find ways to make that talent work for me.

Jack was an easy read. He just wanted to get out of Philly, live in warm weather and provide well for his family. After some negotiations, I hired him as CSL's man in Florida. We'd opened an office in Hollywood – a good excuse to visit my mother, who had relocated to Hallendale, Florida.

Jack worked for me for many years selling lighting in South Florida, and he was very good at it, as I'd figured he would be.

I got to know his family quite well, too. When Roz and I took the kids to Florida and stayed at the Deauville Hotel, near his house, we would often have dinner together. Jack's son Ben was a bright young man who helped teach my daughter Marti how to scuba dive.

I helped Jack buy a beautiful house on the lake in Hollywood. He paid $96,000 for a four-bedroom house right on the Intercoastal Waterway! One of Jack's neighbors was Meyer Lansky, who lived in a small, unobtrusive bungalow which hardly seemed appropriate for one of America's most notorious crime bosses.

When in town, we often ended up at the Forge, one of South Florida's top dining destinations, the Miami hangout for Frank Sinatra, Dean Martin, Sammy Davis, Jr. and the rest of the Rat Pack. Judy Garland and Richard Nixon were other guests. The Forge was owned by Al Malnik, a young lawyer with purported links to underworld doings.

Al Malnik has been called the heir to Meyer Lansky's throne and over the years has palled around with celebrities while earning a fortune as a high-interest money lender. Once, even, his Rolls-Royce was blown up. In later years, he was a great friend of the singer, Michael Jackson, hosting the eccentric entertainer in his South Florida mega-mansion for many months and reportedly helping the King of Pop with his many debts and legal problems.

Roz and I dined at the Forge on numerous occasions and Mr. Malnik was very gracious to us. Years later, Roz represented a developer from Florida who was a business partner of Al Malnik.

During Jack Kramer's working years with me, he often came to Los Angeles for meetings. On one occasion I introduced him to Sam Gilbert, a millionaire general contractor who was remodeling the home we'd purchased in Bel Air. The introduction I made that day between Sam and Jack had fateful consequences for both men. What followed became national news.

Sam Gilbert was the No. 1 booster for UCLA basketball – he donated millions to John Wooden's incredibly successful program and was known to the players as "Papa Sam." Sam always got me center court seats for UCLA games. Of course, I had to pay a large premium for those seats.

UCLA, coached by Wooden, known as "the Wizard Westwood," dominated men's college basketball from the early '60s through the mid-'70s, winning seven straight NCAA championships from 1967 to 1973, and 10 in a 12-year span. During this amazing run, they went undefeated a record four times. Some of the great UCLA players of the era included Lew Alcindor (Kareem Abdul-Jabbar), Bill Walton, Sidney Wicks, Curtis Rowe, Walt Hazzard, Henry Bibby, and Larry Farmer. I was courtside for many magic moments.

When a player needed a "boost" – friendship or counsel or a favor – he turned to "Papa Sam." And what a friend he was. Sam pushed the NCAA rules to the limit. Whatever an athlete needed – books, an apartment, car, clothes, pin money, help for a sick aunt – Sam arranged it. He arranged it so often that in 1981 the UCLA basketball program was placed on probation and UCLA ordered to disassociate from Papa Sam.

Jack Kramer had left my employ a few years earlier and had not stayed in close touch. One sunny California day in 1978, a black stretch limo pulled up to my Los Angeles office. Out stepped Jack, trim and dapper in a Brioni suit, looking tanned, healthy and very prosperous. Quite a change from his days selling lighting fixtures.

Jack was in town, he told me, because he was involved in a construction project with Sam Gilbert. Together they were building a massive gambling enterprise called the Bicycle Club. The Bicycle Club was to be located in Bell Gardens, in a 100,000-square-foot building, and would be the largest card club in the world, operating 24/7/365. The club, predictably, became a huge success.

Between the years 1982 and 1987, Jack's son Ben Kramer imported an estimated half-million pounds of marijuana into the U.S., the newspapers reported, at a profit of $60 million. The Bicycle Club served as the perfect money-laundering operation for Ben's marijuana millions, according to the government's case.

Ben and Jack Kramer were tried, prosecuted and convicted. Sam Gilbert and his son Michael were served a subpoena and indicted two days after Sam died. Michael was convicted, but later had his conviction overturned.

As Papa Sam moved on, Uncle Sam moved in. The Bicycle Club became government property.

In 1990, the year Ben was convicted of racketeering, conspiracy to possess marijuana, and conducting a continuing criminal enterprise, the Bicycle Club generated an after-tax profit of $23 million and was estimated to be worth $150 million. The government now was in control of the Gilbert/Kramer operation, a huge cash cow.

How the Kramers and their business ventures connected to President George Herbert Walker Bush becomes even more interesting, according to *George Bush, the Unauthorized Biography*, by Webster G. Tarpley and Anton Chaitken, and a report by journalist Matt Meltzer of the website MiamiBeach411.com.

We have all seen President George Bush 41 on TV in his speedboat

Fidelity, on the waters of his family's getaway in Kennebunkport, Maine. Fidelity is a powerboat capable of operating on the high seas at fantastic speeds – a thrilling experience for anyone. This boat belongs to the category called "Cigarette" – the Aston Martin of power boats.

The boat was purchased by Bush 41 from South Florida celebrity Don Aronow, preeminent powerboat racer of the '60s and designer and builder of the top powerboats in the world.

Aronow had made his money in the construction business in New Jersey in the late 1950s, then moved to Miami in 1961 where he began racing boats for a hobby – living, by most accounts, a flamboyant playboy lifestyle. He'd had several boat companies, and in 1966 he formed Magnum Marine and the Cigarette boat was born. This sleek, sexy monster of a muscle boat was capable of speeds up to 80 mph on flat seas. Aronow won the world offshore powerboat racing championship with the Cigarette, named for a prototype used in Prohibition times to smuggle cigarettes.

It was no great surprise, then, that the Cigarette became the boat of choice for South Florida drug smugglers. It was perfect for the job: difficult to detect by radar and so fast that it easily outran the Coast Guard and other law enforcement agencies. Cocaine was sweeping across America like wildfire and Miami was the gateway from South America for much of the drugs coming into the country.

The amount of drug money in Miami was incredible. It rebuilt the city, literally – drug money was funneled into construction projects all over town, altering the skyline, waking up and beautifying South Beach. It is not a stretch to conclude that the Cigarette boats played a major role in the renaissance of Miami.

There were many rumors that Aronow was connected to drug smugglers, according to Tarpley and Chaitken's book.

President Bush 41 met Don Aronow in 1974 and bought his Cigarette boat the same year. Other notable Aronow clients included the Shah of Iran, King Hussein of Jordan, King Juan Carlos of Spain, the Prince of Kuwait, Charles Keating, Robert Vesco, Malcolm Forbes, "Baby Doc" Duvalier, President Lyndon Johnson, Prince Rainier and Princess Grace of Monaco, Eastern Airlines CEO and ex-astronaut Frank Borman, Kimberly-Clark heir Jim Kimberly, and Ben Kramer.

Ben Kramer idolized Don Aronow. And Don loved Ben. They had something in common in the '80s: they were both living their wildest dreams, two insanely glamorous lives of money and speed and pleasure.

Bush, ex-head of the CIA, served as Ronald Reagan's vice president from 1981 through 1989. On March 23, 1983, Reagan put him in charge of the National Narcotics Border Interdiction System, which was supposed to help curb the flow of drugs into the U.S. He also ran Operation Alliance, which involved 20 federal agencies, 500 additional officers and a budget of $266 million. Bush's famous "War on Drugs" proved a dismal failure.

Vice President Bush and Don Aronow were, against all acceptable logic considering the speedboat king's alleged connections to organized crime, good friends. They went on several fishing trips together, and Bush consulted Aronow many times about the upkeep of his boat. They were pen pals, too – a mutual admiration society.

Aronow piqued Bush's interest in a new boat he had designed and built: a high-performance catamaran. On January 4th, 1984, the vice president gave a rousing "War on Drugs" speech at the Omni International Hotel in Miami. Later that day, he hooked up with Aronow at Islamadora in the Florida Keys and, accompanied by Secret Service and customs agents in Cigarette boats which had been confiscated from drug dealers, they took a ride in the new "Blue Thunder" catamaran. Bush, wearing futuristic eye goggles, even took the wheel. It was a wonderful photo-op. Ten days later Bush wrote Aronow a personal letter thanking him for the experience and indicating how much he admired the new boat, apologizing for his bad typing.

On February 4, 1985, it was announced that Aronow's company had received a contract from the U.S. government for the Blue Thunder catamarans at a cost of $150,000 apiece. The government ordered two boats, to be followed by an additional 12. The contract culminated with a public ceremony with Florida's senior senator, Paula Hawkins, and U.S. Customs Commissioner William Von Raab.

It was later determined that this powerful catamaran was a dud; it couldn't hack it on the high seas, not against the drug runners. It was an embarrassment, puttering along at just above 50 mph – no match for the hotshot smugglers zipping across the waters in the faster Cigarette boat. George Bush had gotten ripped off. He couldn't have been happy.

To further compound matters, when the government did place the order for the catamarans, the company was no longer owned by Aronow – it was owned instead by none other than Mr. Jack Kramer, of the Super Chief South Corporation. (Jack and Ben Kramer also operated Fort Apache Marine, located on Thunderboat Row on 188th street in Miami.) By then, Ben had done time for drug-related offenses and the Kramers were persons of interest to prosecutors in the Bicycle Club case. It looked like the foxes owned the henhouse.

The government, fearing a public relations disaster if it were discovered that drug traffickers had sold them the ineffectual boats, canceled the order for the remaining twelve. Kramer's company was left with no business, so Aronow bought the company back.

The entire situation stuck in Ben Kramer's craw, and he found it even harder to get down when the government reinstated the order for the 12 boats from Aronow.

On Feb. 3, 1987, Don Aronow was shot and killed, execution style.

He'd been in his office, it is reported, and had had a visit from a stranger calling himself Jerry Jacoby, who claimed to work for a rich man wanting to purchase a 60-foot boat. "Jacoby" left the office, followed soon after by Aronow.

Aronow drove his white Mercedes a few blocks to see an old friend at Apache Boats. After a short time there, he got back in his car and drove off, but was approached by a Lincoln Continental with tinted windows. The driver of the Lincoln exchanged a few words with Aronow, window to window, and then pumped him full of lead. The king of the powerboats was dead.

When the distraught widow Aronow started hearing clicks on her phone she called George Bush, who promised to look into it. The clicks stopped, and Bush later called her back, according to Tarpley & Chaitken, to reassure her that she and her children were in no danger.

The Miami police searched for the assassin but drew a blank. There were many theories floated – pointed fingers that didn't pan out in arrests. Some claimed it was the government, embarrassed by the drug-and-weapons shenanigans in Central America, eliminating a rogue asset whom they had promoted and then wanted to hush up. Some said it was retribution from Aronow's old enemies in the Jersey construction trade.

The government seized Ben Kramer's marina and assets in 1987 and the conviction for Jack and Ben followed in 1990.

Jack Kramer got out of prison early in 1994 and I met with him in Fort Lauderdale. He was living in a small apartment, a far cry from the plush home on the Intercoastal, but still near the water. I asked how he'd gotten out, but his lips were zipped about how he'd swung it.

"It got done," was all he'd say.

Jack was starting over and he needed a car, so I leased a new car for him. He said he'd pay me back but he never did. Jack did come to California a couple times – he wanted to get back into the lighting game. Hard as it was, I had to say no. He was just too hot to handle. We stayed in touch, but eventually he stopped calling and his phone no longer answered.

In April 1989, while Ben Kramer was being held in the Dade County jail, a spectacular attempt to break him out of the jail yard by helicopter failed when too many other inmates grabbed onto the copter, causing it to crash. In 1996, Ben, according to the Tarpley book, told authorities that he had hired the Aronow hit man, a pimp named Bobby Young from the Dixie Mafia. Young took credit for the hit while already in the can for other crimes.

Ben never fully admitted guilt, though. He claimed he was confessing so he could be relocated from the Dade County jail, that he was physically sick after years of being housed in degrading conditions and just wanted to be transferred to a federal penitentiary where he could get some health care and relief from the horror.

Time passed, and he continued to appeal his conviction, pointing out that the cases against him were constructed on the evidence of convicted felons and snitches.

To this day, the case is shrouded in controversy, innuendo, misinformation and unproven allegations, with tentacles stretching deep into the fabric of American political and financial life. These high-octane-lifestyle gents were part of a bloody, ugly, sometimes glamorous and fascinating chapter in American criminal history – drugs, guns, political skullduggery, fast women and faster boats on the high seas, against the exotic backdrop of Miami vice and murder.

Tarpley and Chaitken's book states that George Bush used to covet a guest-starring stint playing himself on the iconic TV show *Miami Vice*. He wanted to ride the waves of Miami with Detectives Crockett and Tubbs, the sun in his face, the wind in his hair, busting the bad guys, and it is said that he was disappointed not to get his wish. Perhaps, though, with Don Aronow and Ben Kramer, he got a taste of it in real life.

I was sorry about what happened to Jack Kramer. I always liked him. I think he started a ball rolling that he couldn't control; after a certain point, things happened to him more than he initiated them, and by the time Jack saw where the high life was taking him, it was too late to go back.

CHAPTER 7

THE THREE WISE ~~GUYS~~ MEN

We tend to think of the people we know as either good or bad; we're a little surprised when we hear of behavior that doesn't fit our picture. But we're all a mixture of noble and shabby, generous and ruthless, and our opinion of others is based on the side of them we see. When a guy's good-bad mix has a strong tilt – say, 6 to 1 one way or the other – we can gauge him pretty easily. But some of us aren't so easy to figure.

Among my friends in California, as the years went by, were a few men whose influence stretched across the country from Chicago to Las Vegas, from Hollywood to the White House. They were good friends, sophisticated businessmen and stalwart Southern California community leaders – and, if the reporting in some recent journalistic books can be trusted, they were mobbed up.

They didn't do business in the same way as Andy Valentine and Sam S. back east. Their essence may have been similar, but the style was different and the stakes they played for were higher. You couldn't tell them from the upright citizens with whom they socialized. You really couldn't tell the good guys from the bad guys.

♢   ♢   ♢   ♢

When we first moved to Los Angeles, the only people I really knew in town were the Ziffren brothers – Lester, Leo and Paul Ziffren, all attorneys from Chicago, but originally from Davenport, Iowa. My grandmother had taken care of Lester

Note from the Author
This Chapter on the three wise men ties into my business venture because, if I wanted a certain project, it was handled by one or two of these men…I didn't ask how, I just knew it was done "the old fashioned way"…

Ziffren when he was a small boy. Naturally, I looked them up, and I became very friendly with Lester and Paul.

Paul was actually my sponsor when I joined Hillcrest Country Club. Hillcrest was located on the south side of Beverly Hills, on Pico Boulevard, across from the Fox Studios. It was the country club for the LA Jewish community when other clubs were restricted; hence all the biggest Jewish stars, producers and moguls in Hollywood made it their home away from home. The movie moguls would gather there in the 1930s to outdo each other in generosity to the United Jewish Fund and other Jewish causes. George Burns played bridge there daily for most of his life and stars such as the Marx Brothers, George Jessel, Eddie Cantor, Al Jolson, Jack Benny and Danny Kaye were all regulars.

There were no big flashy signs announcing the club: just a long wall on Pico, with a stone gateway bearing the number 10000, behind which lay a green paradise with an 18-hole golf course, tennis and all the fascinating socializing you ever could want in this new exciting city we'd moved to. (Our neighbor Danny Thomas, a Lebanese Catholic, was one of the first non-Jewish person to belong.)

They'd even discovered oil on the property in the 1950s; Hillcrest allowed drilling and members who held shares received tax-sheltered dividends on their original initiation fee. These "B.O." – Before Oil – memberships became so valuable that they are now passed, in wills, from father to son.

Through the Ziffrens and Hillcrest, I made many excellent friends and solid acquaintances, including Paul's lifelong friends from Chicago, the famed lawyer Sidney Korshak, and Lew Wasserman, the most powerful man in the entertainment business, head of MCA (Music Corporation of America), which eventually gobbled up Universal Studios.

Paul, Lew and Sidney participated in a fascinating scenario of which I was aware at the time, but which now reads like a blockbuster:

A group of bright young Jewish lawyers, trained at top universities and in the butcher shop of Chicago's cutthroat world of Democratic politics, move to California and front for the Chicago crime syndicate in the worlds of entertainment, real estate, Las Vegas, and politics, with repercussions all the way up to the presidential level.

What I've learned of this history only came to light in recent years. It has been documented in many books, such as *Dark Victory*, by Dan Moldea, *Supermob* by Gus Russo, and *The Last Mogul* by Dennis McDougal, that these sons of the Midwest were bound together by their Lawndale, Chicago roots and connections to the Democratic political machine of Jake Arvey.

According to the books, the Chicago syndicate – what remained of the Al Capone gang – moved to California in the mid-'40s and invested millions of mob dollars in the state, and of course, Las Vegas, buying up much of the valuable real estate and turning the West into their private kingdom – a total bonanza for mob interests. These men became wildly successful, rich and powerful on a global level. In plain words, they took over.

Paul moved to Los Angeles in 1943 after graduating from Northwestern Law and working at the law firm of Jake Arvey. Paul was a tax lawyer, and by the mid-1950s had become quite prominent in national Democratic politics. He started with campaign fund-raising – money would appear from mysterious sources – and then, in 1950, he helped stage Helen Gahagan Douglas' losing effort against Richard Nixon for the U.S. Senate.

Paul was named Democratic national committeeman in 1953, and was instrumental in modernizing the Democratic party and pushing its liberal agenda, as well as promoting the use of the new medium of TV in political campaigns. Democratic Senator Estes Kefauver warned in 1956 that if Adlai Stevenson were elected president in the contest against President Dwight D. Eisenhower, Paul Ziffren would become the czar of California. Stevenson lost, but Paul Ziffren never stopped winning.

A bump in the road: In 1958, Paul's brother, Herman, was arrested in Illinois on three counts of violating the Mann Act. He was charged with transporting three women across state lines, across the Mississippi from Davenport to Rock Island. This was really a set-up to get at Paul. Paul dismissed the charges against Herman as "scurrilous nonsense," implying that the government, in the person of Nixon crony and fellow Communist-hunter Sen. William Knowland, was anti-Semitic. Fifteen months later, Herman was slapped with a $4,000 fine and the case was dismissed. It was back to smooth sailing for Paul.

Paul was also the prime lobbyist in bringing the 1960 Democratic convention to Los Angeles. *Harper's* magazine called him "California's cure for tired Democratic blood." John Kennedy and Hubert Humphrey both sought his powerful endorsement. Paul's friend Sidney Korshak was an old friend of Joseph Kennedy, according to the Russo book. John Kennedy took the nomination, of course, and the White House.

In 1979, Paul became chairman of the Los Angeles Olympic Organizing Committee, sponsor of the controversial but incredibly successful 1984 Olympics which the Soviet Union boycotted. A *Los Angeles Times* editorial said: "Although the hands-on operator who put the games together was Peter Ueberroth, it was Ziffren, as Chairman of the LAOOC, who coalesced corporate support behind the games and gave Ueberroth the necessary freedom to make things work. It is fitting that the soft-spoken civic leader wielded his influence so quietly that most residents probably don't know who he was. Yet many people were affected at least indirectly by the public activities he worked at so effectively, usually behind the scenes."

Paul was quiet and serene, comfortable working behind the scenes. He loved his solitude. A quirky thing that few knew about him, but I did: Paul used to golf Hillcrest all by himself. He'd just go out on his lonesome and shoot 18 holes, with only his caddy for company. Hillcrest was his retreat from the moving and the shaking.

But Sidney Korshak, another Jake Arvey golden boy, was anything but quiet. He was closer to the street, in a sense – a hotshot Chicago tax lawyer who, according to Gus Russo, was actually the front for the Chicago mob's interests in California – even rumored to be the head of what was later called the "Kosher Nostra." He was known in Hollywood as "The Fixer."

In 1978, after a lifetime of brokering huge deals and fixing labor contracts between his clients the unions and his clients the corporations, Sidney was named in a report released by California Attorney General Evelle Younger as a major mob figure.

After years of keeping his name out of the newspapers, except on the social pages, Sidney roundly denied the allegations, saying: "I've never been cited, let alone indicted, for anything."

Sidney operated from a corner table at the Bistro restaurant in Beverly Hills. According to Robert Evans, onetime Hollywood studio chief and close Korshak crony, Sidney told him he had been the "consigliere" to Al Capone at the age of 21. Evans said Korshak and his Chicago associates all ended up in Beverly Hills at the same time because, as bank robber Willie Sutton once explained, that's where the money was.

Using money from organized crime, according to Russo, the "Supermob" bought up land throughout Southern California, tipped to the best deals by Chicago tax attorney David Bazelon, Paul Ziffren's roommate at Northwestern Law School, who was serving as director of the Office of Alien Property in the Truman administration. Bazelon handled the disbursement of land seized from Japanese-Americans rounded up and sent to internment camps during World War II. The Japanese were herded like cattle, stripped of dignity and possessions, and lost everything. The Chicago mob cashed in, snapping up the properties – much of California's best farmland – for a song. The Truman administration rewarded this travesty by giving Bazelon a federal judgeship.

According to the 1978 report, Sidney was a "senior advisor" to organized crime groups in California, Chicago, Las Vegas and New York, and over the years was linked with such figures as Bugsy Siegel, Tony Accardo, Lucky Luciano, Meyer Lansky, Sam Giancana, Moe Dalitz, and controversial Teamster chief Jimmy Hoffa, whose pension-fund loans to the "Supermob" interests ensured a steady cash flow for new projects. An FBI report states that when Korshak came to Las Vegas one night in 1961, Hoffa agreed to let Sidney have his luxurious suite at the Riviera Hotel. The report says Hoffa "was moved across the hall to a smaller apartment when Korshak checked into the hotel." Sidney was at the top of the pecking order.

By 1984, while Paul Ziffren was enjoying his success with the Olympics, Sidney's power was in decline. In 1985, New Jersey turned down Korshak's client, the Hilton Hotels, in its application to operate a $300 million hotel and casino it had built in Atlantic City. In rejecting Hilton's request for a gaming license, the commission found that Sidney Korshak, who had been Hilton's labor consultant for 13 years, was "a key actor in organized crime's unholy alliances with corrupt union officers." Hilton chief Barron Hilton, in an attempt to distance himself from his old pal Sidney, told the commission: "I wish to hell we would have never hired him."

The past caught up with Sidney Korshak, but it never overtook Lew Wasserman, who ran MCA all the way into the early 1990s. Lew, another Chicago product, was the most powerful and feared man in show business. MCA, Music Corporation of America, was founded in the 1920s by Jules Stein – Dr. Julius Caesar Stein – a Chicago eye doctor and musician with a good head for numbers and a love of music who was a natural at booking and managing other people's talent. At first, Dr. Stein would fit patients for eyeglasses while booking bands on the phone. One of his early acts was Louis Armstrong.

The company flourished across the mid-century, going from the most powerful talent booking agent in the country to ownership of the multi-media conglomerate, Universal Studios.

Lew Wasserman ran the show with an iron fist. His career spanned the history of the movies, from silent pictures on, and he was guru to my neighbor Alfred Hitchcock as well as Marilyn Monroe, Marlon Brando, Jimmy Stewart and on and on to Steven Spielberg and George Lucas – and his good friend Ronald Reagan.

Lew, Paul and Sidney were great friends. They socialized together; they hung out at the Mocambo nightclub, with its live aviary full of squawking birds; their wives were also friends, and of course they all backed each other's charities, showing solidarity at various functions. Their success and influence only grew with the years – they were the recognized social and civic leaders of the entertainment industry, the people who supported the arts, at the top of the community A-list – but according to the above-cited authors and other sources, the crooked interests they still represented back in the Windy City flourished as well. Mob money had been legitimized and multiplied.

Paul Ziffren and Lew Wasserman were Teflon figures, up front for the civic works and relatively free of scandal. Sidney was more daringly prominent. He wasn't in the Yellow Pages under "shady," but he could be reached if you had a deal in mind.

If you wanted to settle a labor beef that was costing you too many millions, you'd go see Sidney at the Bistro. If you wanted a good deal on a way to beat Uncle Sam on taxes, it was Sidney you called. If you were soliciting a donation for charity, you'd go to Sidney. Movie and union people bowed to him. He was smooth as silk, charming as a Swiss diplomat, and, according to all who dealt with him in business, tough as nails. Sidney always got his fee.

Iconic network TV reporter Brian Ross summed up Sidney's position in a rare on-air expose, stating, "Sidney functioned as a gangster. He was their straight man. He would go to the corporations and those places that the gangsters couldn't get into simply because they were such slobs. A guy like Korshak is essential for that bridge between polite society and criminal society."

It didn't hurt that Sidney's brother, Marshall, was straight as an arrow, a state senator in Illinois. Sidney loved his brother, was very proud of him, and a day after Marshall died, a grief-stricken Sidney also passed on, in January 1996. He was 88.

Sidney also helped make the Chicago-based Pritzker family billionaires. These tough magnates built a vast commercial and real-estate empire which included the Hyatt hotel chain, among others. But they started as loan sharks in Chicago, lending immigrants five dollars for seven dollars back – they called it "five for seven." No wonder they later banked offshore in the Cayman Islands and skipped paying taxes – they were accustomed to getting great deals. Like many "Supermob" beneficiaries, they received huge loans from the Teamsters pension fund, and by the 1980s, their business dealings were under investigation by the government, according to Russo.

Russo quotes journalist Sy Hersh on Sidney: "He was the Godfather. There's no question he ordered people hit." Los Angeles FBI man Mike Wacks waxed nostalgic and admiring in the same book, *Supermob*: "He had clout all the way until his death. He was active until the day he died. He's an amazing character."

Perhaps Lew, Paul and Sidney's most remarkable achievement was the transformation of their old buddy from Chicago, Ronald Reagan, known as "Dutch," from B-movie actor to president of the United States. Reagan was represented by Wasserman and MCA and his road to the White House ran straight through Lew's office. It was a half-century marketing job of "the Gipper" that ended in the Oval Office, Reaganomics and the end of the Cold War, as well as Iran-Contra and other less celebrated moments.

In 1950, Reagan was elected head of the Screen Actors Guild. One of his first services to the Chicago faithful was skillfully shifting the government's investigative focus from the mob's muscling into the movie business and California real estate – and mob influence in politics – to the congressional witch hunt for Communists in Hollywood. Reagan was a star player during the investigation and hearings by the U.S. House Un-

American Activities Committee (HUAC), serving as both an informant for the FBI and a friendly witness for the committee. Reagan was rewarded for his Red-baiting performance before Congress by being elected president of the Screen Actors Guild, serving five consecutive one-year terms.

In 1952, Reagan engineered a "blanket waiver," exempting MCA from stringent SAG rules which prohibited a talent agency from also engaging in film production. MCA was the only firm granted this favored status which placed the company in a position to directly hire the actors it represented. Other talent agencies complained that this gave MCA an unfair advantage. But MCA retained its privilege and as a reward Reagan was given a network show, *General Electric Theater*, which helped showcase his friendly style for the nation.

Jules Stein helped Reagan invest his money and the future leader of the free world quickly became a multi-millionaire. Reaganomics was born.

When Reagan became governor of California and later president of the United States, Paul Ziffren, Lew Wasserman and Sidney Korshak's friendships were rewarded with unprecedented access to the upper echelons of government. When MCA became the object of a government probe and the efforts of investigative reporters to "out" the "Supermob," the investigations eventually dried up and blew away, squelched in consideration of Lew Wasserman's longstanding friendship with President Reagan and the Chandler family who owned the *Los Angeles Times*.

Just as these men had friends in high places, they also consorted with the most notorious, including a man I also knew, Johnny Roselli, a famed Capone associate who as a young man in 1925 was sent to California on account of his asthma. I met Johnny Roselli at the Los Angeles Friars Club, a private show business club started in 1947 by comedian/actor Milton Berle as an offshoot of the New York Friars Club. The original members of the LA Friars Club were Jimmy Durante, George Jessel, Robert Taylor and Bing Crosby, among other celebrities who had moved from New York. Later members included Al Jolson, Frank Sinatra, Jack Benny,

Dean Martin, Jerry Lewis, the Marx Brothers, Sammy Davis, Jr., Billy Crystal and Johnny Carson. Like the New York club, for many years the West Coast Friars Club was known for its celebrity members and "roasts." The NY and the LA clubs later broke up after a lawsuit, and the Los Angeles club has been disbanded.

Roselli, known as "Handsome Johnny," sported a full head of slicked-back, bone-white hair and was rumored to have pulled the stunt made famous in *The Godfather* – cutting off a horse's head and putting it in the bed of a Hollywood producer in order to get a career-changing part for Frank Sinatra in *From Here to Eternity*.

In the early 1950s, Roselli shifted his attention from labor and other activities toward the highly profitable gambling paradise of Las Vegas. Roselli was the Chicago and Los Angeles mob's chief representative in Vegas. His job was to ensure that the mob bosses each received their fair share of the burgeoning casino revenues through "skimming" money off the top of the daily gambling take. He was also directly involved in the Bay of Pigs fiasco when the U.S. invaded Castro's Cuba, hosting a training camp for the invading forces; the mob had always resented the loss of their Havana casino interests.

In 1976 he was found in a steel drum floating in the water near Miami, strangled, shot and dismembered. Not a happy ending for "Handsome Johnny."

The figures of national prominence who played a part in the life and times of Sidney Korshak included the Kennedy family, Marilyn Monroe, Frank Sinatra, Hugh Hefner, Henry Kissinger, Howard Hughes (to whom the mob basically sold Las Vegas in the 1960s, although they continued to milk it by skimming the count of gambling dollars), Estes Kefauver, the crusading Republican pit bull who was muzzled with blackmail pictures, and many other potentates, gangsters, politicians and show-biz folk, according to Gus Russo's meticulous reporting.

When weighing the ultimate worth of men like Paul Ziffren, Lew

Wasserman and Sidney Korshak – complex and dynamic men whose influence spread in every direction – there is much to set on both sides of the scales. Despite what people have come to say about their activities, I found them to be positive contributors to the community, sponsoring many good works. Sidney was actually instrumental in forging an agreement with Cesar Chavez and the farm workers' union to end a bitter strike. Where others had failed, Sidney, as usual, succeeded. And you can bet he got his fee – this time from the Schenley Distillers liquor company, whose growing interests were at stake. He was a force of nature.

So what's the final score on these men? Of the three, I knew Paul the best, but I never heard him speak on the subject of where any bodies were buried, figuratively or literally, so I'm in no position to deny what Russo and others wrote about him and Sidney and Lew Wasserman. I can only say from my own experience that they were remarkably enjoyable company and they did a lot of positive things.

All three are gone now. Were they good guys or bad? In their prime, I'd say it probably depended on whether or not you were in their way.

CHAPTER 8

FORM OVER SUBSTANCE —
FORTUNE 500 CULTURE
(OR THE LACK THEREOF)

How does an entrepreneur fit into a Fortune 500 culture? He doesn't, I don't, and no one with any backbone ever does.

In the decades following our move to California, my business had ups and downs and then ups again, the culmination of which was RSA Lighting in Chatsworth, my architectural lighting company, specializing in high-end residential and boutique retail lighting systems.

We were a lean, mean company; my years in the business had given me strong relationships with reps all over the U.S., and I built one of the best R & D teams anywhere.

I've always been an exponent of the better-mousetrap theory – that if you keep ahead of the competition creatively, you will stay ahead of them in every other way as well. In my years at RSA I kept that framed Rudyard Kipling verse I mentioned before on my office wall:

They copied and they copied and they copied
But they couldn't copy my mind
So I left 'em sweating and stealing
A year and a half behind

It might seem a little self-satisfied, but I didn't think of it that way. To me it was a constant demand and inspiration; it meant I couldn't get smug, soft and comfy. It meant I had to keep thinking, coming up with new designs, new ways to produce them and new ways to market them. It was the only way to keep that year-and-a-half lead. The day you say "I've made it" and put your feet up on the desk is the day you start to decay.

In Southern California, I had a great example in front of me in the movie industry. The studios that kept ahead were the ones who thrived – and survived. When the Warner Brothers studio got rolling in the first days of talkies, back in the 1930s, they stayed in the forefront with fast-paced, tough, topical gangster pictures starring young James Cagney and Humphrey Bogart. Sixty years later, the company, now known as Warner Bros. Pictures, saw the quality and potential in the *Harry Potter* books and acquired the rights to the most successful film series of all time. They've been leaving other studios choking on their dust for generations by thinking fast and acting accordingly.

I didn't have Warners-level resources, but I did my best to keep RSA in the forefront of its lighting-industry niche by hiring, and keeping, the best talent available.

It was 2004 and RSA was thriving – our products were excellent and top-to-bottom the company was running like a well-oiled machine. At the heart of this success was my firm belief that a company is only as good as its next product – not its last product, its next product. In other words, technological creativity. So my R & D team was continually pushing the envelope, developing, designing and producing new products every day, rolling out something fresh every month or two. We would bring five or six brand new, cutting-edge products to the marketplace each year.

Nonetheless, in the back of my mind lurked the nagging question: What would happen if I fell ill or became incapacitated? Who would take my place? My three sons were not interested in the business. My daughter Marti actually could have taken over, but her husband was working in the company, and I didn't think that would work. That left no one; RSA would fall apart. I had been pondering this for some time, so when I was approached by some financial gurus advising me that the time was right to sell the company, I was in a quandary. To sell, or not to sell, that was the question. (Not quite *Hamlet*, I know, but the situation had me talking to myself almost as much as he did.)

We interviewed many companies and were interviewed by others, and in the end it came down to an American company, Cooper Lighting, a division of Cooper Industries, and the dynamic Italian company, I Guzzini. We were captivated by the Italians – so smooth, so far ahead of the rest of the world in their approach to tooling and automation in manufacturing. Their sophistication (and their pure charm) was captivating. The only problem with them was that they didn't understand the American marketplace. I wanted so much to make a deal with them, but believed, perhaps incorrectly, that we'd never make them understand the unique complexities of selling in America. Perhaps I underestimated the value of their entrepreneurial spirit and design brilliance in making my decision to go with the U.S. company, Cooper Lighting, the second-largest lighting company in the world.

I entered into negotiations with Cooper Lighting's president at the time, David Feldman. I liked him. He was charming, cosmopolitan, a real salesman. He convinced me that a big company – his big company – really cared for its employees. I believed all the sugar he fed me, but it proved not to be altogether true. Big companies, as I soon found out, care about one thing and one thing alone: the bottom line.

On March 25, 2004, Cooper gave me a lot of money and my employees and I became part of the Fortune 500 culture, which fosters form over substance – a culture that is showing signs of decay.

Back in the '80s, Tom Peters and Robert H. Waterman, Jr., wrote a great book called *In Search of Excellence* which was read by CEOs everywhere. In it, Peters praised some great companies, and much of corporate America adopted his book as its business bible.

In a few years some of these great companies, including Xerox, Sears, IBM, Polaroid and K-Mart, were in serious trouble and everyone was asking what happened.

Why do good companies fail?

It used to be my belief that although humans were mortal, institutions lived forever. I have since read that a corporation's life expectancy is 15 years and declining, either through mergers and acquisitions or chapter 11 protection.

Several elements stand out as likely to factor into the failure of a company, the primary ones being regulation, competition, and of course, technology.

The business environment never stays the same, which means companies can't either. The lighting industry, for example, faces strict new regulations regarding the use of certain lamp sources which will soon be abolished by law. If companies don't react soon enough to make the transition to correct technology, they will be left behind.

Many companies fail to adjust to new conditions. We saw this in the recent meltdown of the airline industry. The 20th century telecommunications industry fell apart when faced with competition and new technology. We went from simple dependence on Bell systems for our home phones and AT&T for long distance to an environment in which the home-phone ground line has been conquered by cell phones and the old established companies are reeling.

Most companies come into existence through what we might call entrepreneurial opportunity. Company success is much like human behavior, a result of nature and nurture. The entrepreneur needs to have a vision, but also needs an environment conducive to success. Most managers take all the credit themselves, but in actuality many business people succeed by accident and not by plan.

When you succeed by accident, you often cling to your belief system even more tightly afterward than you did before. You become superstitious.

Next to baseball players, entrepreneurs may be the most superstitious people on the planet. This brings resistance to change – and the problem is that what worked before will not always be successful over time.

In 2001 alone, 257 public companies with $258 billion in assets declared bankruptcy. Each month seemed to bring another giant to its knees – Enron, Worldcom, Global Crossing, K-Mart, Polaroid, Arthur Anderson, Xerox, Qwest ....

You ask the CEOs why and they will tell you bad economy, market turbulence, competitive prices and so on, and will add that these things are all out of their control. But the truth is that many of these companies – Polaroid and Xerox, for example – were slow to react to a changing business environment. Both companies blamed other circumstances, but the real problem was a bad business model in a changing world.

What undoes formerly successful companies is a failure to execute a flexible business plan, and the components of this failure are ego, denial, wishful thinking and poor communication – both with customers and employees.

Corporations spend an enormous amount of money and energy marketing themselves to the world, attempting to give the appearance of caring about the welfare of its employees. This is often far from the case. One method of promoting this fiction is the use of the term "human resources," a phrase meant to be warmer than the term it replaced, "personnel." But at least with the word "personnel" you never forgot you were dealing with people, whereas the ambiguous term "human resources," meant to show that the corporation values its employees as resources, also implies that they are something to be used, and then, sadly, used up. Once these employees are no longer of value to the corporation they are discarded like so much trash and left to fend for themselves. Sometimes they're discarded *before* they've lost their value.

The welfare of a small company is directly connected to the welfare of its members. But in a big company, the small mind sometimes flourishes.

Much like the military, corporations are buttoned up tight against criticism coming from below. In this hierarchical structure, it's up to the employees and the managers to implement the policies that are set down. While these policies are designed to make the company profit, they often reveal that the corporation is completely disconnected from the customer, with no comprehension of customer needs or desires.

For the most part, Fortune 500 companies end up swiftly and systematically gutting the small company they bought of the qualities and innovations which attracted them to buy it in the first place.

Individuality is not encouraged. The only way to get ahead in the corporation is to think like everyone else. Even when criticism is offered constructively, it is not encouraged. If you rock the boat, expect to be thrown overboard. So much time is spent on conforming to the form, to the norm, that the substance and reason you are there often gets lost in the translation.

And that's the irony – a company which thinks only of keeping itself secure undermines itself. Unless people have the courage to risk their jobs, speak out against the trend and correct it where wrong, the company becomes part of the Fortune 500 culture (or lack thereof) and becomes stagnant and outdated.

RSA was a progressive company specializing in new products long before we sold it. Why, as a small company, could we run rings around the big ones? Because big companies can't act as quickly. They take many meetings to accomplish the obvious, while a small-company manager can act on his own initiative. At RSA, we didn't rely on ivory-tower corporate "product people" who make their decisions while watching the stock market report on cable TV. We listened to the customers. We found out what they wanted and worked closely with the lighting designer to make sure we gave it to them.

Somehow in the corporate culture the customer becomes the enemy. It sounds insane, but that seems to be the attitude that pervades the corporate world. Sure, we like to think we are enlightened business people, but without realizing it we are telling the customers they must do business our way or no way. A big New York general contractor I met for the first time, who was involved in a huge retail store rollout, told me he didn't trust anyone in our business; he had been lied to so many times regarding delivery, he couldn't take anyone's word at face value.

So how do we, in this wonderful world of lighting, build loyalty with our customers, our reps, and the lighting specifiers? Is customer loyalty extinct? Many of my business associates think it has forever vanished, that the only thing that keeps the customers returning is the lowest price. But I tell you customer loyalty is alive and well and still translating to profits. Look around at today's list of best companies: Home Depot, Google, Apple and many more. These companies still earn customer loyalty while their competitors stumble and fall by the wayside.

It is true that in today's marketplace, maintaining customer loyalty is complex and difficult – but losing it is quite simple. Why do customers lose faith in companies? They are underwhelmed, overpromised and under-delivered. We in the lighting industry are totally guilty of these three deadly sins.

How does a Lightolier, a Cooper or a Lithonia transform a good company which they have absorbed into a great company? By and large, they don't. (Sadly, you have never seen these three companies listed in *Forbes* among the most admired companies.)

The secret of good-to-great company transformation is a complex one. There is no foolproof formula or miracle moment. Those companies which succeed at it, however, share a pragmatic dedication and commitment to excellence, a program that keeps its leaders *and* its employees on track for the long haul. This is very hard to do when the CEO is focused on nothing but the next quarter's earnings because his personal rewards are tied to profits. The obsession with the bottom line is ultimately the anchor that sinks the corporate ship.

It is entrepreneurs who build companies, but when Fortune 500 giants buy those smaller companies and administer them, they do not support the entrepreneurial spirit that made them successful and attractive in the first place; they do not encourage original thinking. Corporate thinking is regimented and unoriginal, forged in the image of the bean counters at the top. It discourages innovation in the acquired companies, hence they do not flourish.

In the case of RSA, the Cooper corporate system does not retard new product development; in fact, it is encouraged. But RSA's previous success was based on creativity, and the present situation does not lend itself to creating new products. It is extremely difficult to create new products without the proper motivation and people. It takes many years to build up an engineering group that understands what is needed, and when that group is eliminated in one fell swoop due to financial constraints and a decimated economy, your capacity for innovation is crippled.

Another problem is that for the people at the top, the sole criterion for product approval is how much it will cost and how much revenue it can make. But you cannot know how much revenue a product can generate until you actually bring it to market.

When Cooper took over RSA, and I ran it for two years, we developed two or three new products each year. With the economy in its current troubled state, we have no R & D department. Most of what we do is take orders based on our previous reputation.

This company cannot grow without new products and a dedicated sales force. How can we develop a rapport with customers if we don't have our own specialists calling on architects and specifiers? How can you do business in this country if you don't have a dedicated sales force in the marketplace?

Loren Kessel, a fine young man and brilliant creative and marketing mind whom I brought into the game early on, has moved up the corporate ladder at Cooper and is doing something else. So, sadly, we're left without a Loren Kessel. It is most difficult to create and sell without a star. Without exciting new technology, it's virtually impossible. It boggles the mind and leaves me scratching my head and thinking wistfully about the Italians I left at the altar.

The Cooper executives aren't bad people; nor are they fools. It's just that they are committed to a culture in which bigger is worse and innovation is stymied by bureaucracy and short-sightedness.

In these troubled times, it's particularly difficult to get approval to get things done. Whatever metaphor you choose to use – penny-wise and dollar-foolish, tripping over dollars to save pennies – it's madness and business suicide.

The bottom line is that if you don't produce, you wither, and you have to sit with your hands tied and watch helplessly while the little companies run rings around you.

I've found that in corporate America, if you want to get something done, you don't ask for permission – you do it and then ask for forgiveness.

The ideal Fortune 500 culture, I believe, would allow the individual companies under the corporate umbrella to retain their unique entrepreneurial style and do their own thing while answering to the big corporate brother as far as costs and profits. But the corporation must allow each company the freedom to act independently, and it must stay far enough away from the day-to-day so as not to fool with the originality and energy and enthusiasm of its small companies.

In other words, let them create, let them get excited and develop new products, and then let them justify them in the marketplace. *Trust the company you trusted enough to buy*.

Corporations shy away from the potential cost of doing this. But how can you be an industry leader unless you continue to improve your technology? This is why America is lagging in development and implementation of new products – the Europeans have not lost the entrepreneurial spirit. They are not afraid to spend money and take time to develop a product. And because they are not owned by conglomerates and are for the most part free of corporate interference, the Italian and German companies come up with some of the most wonderful, fascinating innovations you have ever seen – which is why they clean up at the IALD and other industry awards. When all is said and done, they've spent a fortune to create a product – but their products sell. And that's an honest kind of bottom line.

You have to have leadership when you are developing new products. You have to have somebody who has the ideas, and trusts those ideas. At present, in our company, it isn't my function to come up with ideas – and after a lifetime of coming up with them, and adapting the great ideas of others, I feel like a caged lion eating tofu.

But I won't be in that cage for long. Someday soon you'll see me roaming the wilds of the business world again, looking for fresh meat on the horizon, and pouncing.

BOOK TWO:

THE

DESIGNERS

PUSHING BACK THE DARKNESS

In the second part of this book, a section which might also be called "Geniuses I Have Known," I'm going to step aside while the top artists in my profession tell of their greatest individual lighting challenges.

Before they each take the floor to tell their stories, I'll set the stage by introducing some of them, along with the Hall of Famers who preceded them – pioneers in a field which took its first great strides in the America of the 20th century. These brilliant lighting design innovators may not be as well known as some of the architects with whom they collaborated, but they deserve to be; their work has had an influence and impact not only on those who followed them in their profession, but on all of us.

The practice of lighting design has advanced "light years" from the 1940s, when my brother Bill was first putting together simple fluorescent fixtures in the basement of the Blue Ribbon Market in Moline, to become an integral component of architectural and interior design. Until the '60s, much of the lighting design in the country was done by electrical engineers like Syska and Hennessy, but as the industry evolved, the advent of more sophisticated architectural imperatives and new technologies demanded a specialist with a profound vision of what light can do.

Enter the lighting designer, whose career is dedicated exclusively to the art and science of lighting. The lighting designer examines each project, whether interior or exterior – residential, commercial, industrial, theatrical, sporting, artistic, even automotive or aeronautic – and provides cost-efficient, aesthetically pleasing solutions for all site-specific challenges.

In a world in which technology advances at "light speed," with hundreds of new products hitting the marketplace each year, lighting designers keep abreast of industry innovations by continually updating product information from manufacturers, as well as attending national and international trade shows, in order to provide cost-effective solutions to even the thorniest of design challenges.

The lighting designer paints with light, creating ambience, mood and comfort. He or she can be said to be a poet, a musician, a sculptor, a magician. Let there be light, indeed.

Lighting design is, in my opinion, the ultimate marriage of art and science, and stands on its own as one of the highest and most powerful of all the arts.

One day in 1979 I met the man who is universally acknowledged as the first true professional lighting designer, the legendary Abe Feder. Abe's brash, burly exterior hid a brilliant mind and sensitive spirit – he was a true genius of light, full of amazing ideas.

Born in Milwaukee in 1909, Abe was fond of telling how he fell in love with the magic of stage lighting when he watched a magician named the Great Thurston perform in a local theater and was fascinated by the dazzling lights onstage. The theater had always been the traditional "staging" point for innovation in lighting in America.

"I went home in a dream," he said, adding that after that, every time he closed his eyes, he saw the lights. "I have been obsessed with light ever since. Other boys played with footballs and postage stamps. I played with light."

Abe went on to study engineering and theater at the Carnegie Institute of Technology (now Carnegie-Mellon University) in Pittsburgh. He got bored after two years and moved to Chicago where he became the lighting director of the Goodman Theatre.

His next stop, logically, was the center of both the lighting and the theater worlds, New York City, where he prospered and invented and innovated for over 50 years. Abe's favorite saying was "Push back the darkness!"

Although he actually invented the position of lighting designer and was called "a genius in light" by legendary drama critic George Jean Nathan – a label he wore to the end of his days – Abe humbly referred to himself as "a worker in light." Works which carry the "Lighting by Feder" credit include 300 Broadway shows, among them his first show in 1932, *Trick for Trick*, Nazimova's productions of *Ghosts* (1935) and *Hedda Gabler* (1936), *I'd Rather be Right* (1937), *Inherit the Wind* (1955), *My Fair Lady* (1956), and *Camelot* (1960). Between 1935 and 1939 he lit more than 200 projects for the WPA Federal Theatre.

He also created the basic lighting arrangements for many new theatres, including Washington's Kennedy Center, and taught workshops in several universities. In 1975, he won a Tony for the best lighting design for his work on the show *Goodtime Charley*.

After establishing his theatrical brilliance, he formed an architectural lighting design company which, unsurprisingly, he called Lighting by Feder.

Although he kept up with his theater work, he was increasingly drawn to what he referred to as "the larger stage of life." His various projects took him all over the country and included the El Paso Museum of Art, the Tulsa Civic Center and the Beverly Wilshire Hotel in California. Major department stores boasting "Lighting by Feder" included Bergdorf-Goodman, Saks Fifth Avenue and Neiman Marcus. In 1964 he did the lighting design for the New York World's Fair, highlighting Buckminster Fuller's famous geodesic dome.

Other major structures he was responsible for lighting include the Empire State Building and United Nations Building, banks, concert halls, many universities, and the main altar of St. Patrick's Cathedral. In addition, he lighted the lion cages and the penguin house at the Bronx Zoo, a terminal at Kennedy Airport and Roosevelt Raceway, as well as many buildings in other countries, including the Montreal Cultural Center and the Israel National Museum in Jerusalem.

Although known for lighting the exteriors of buildings, he was equally adept at interiors, from supermarkets to restaurants to ocean liners. His range was incredible. I worked with him on Rockefeller Plaza and on the RCA/GE Building in Rockefeller Center and had nothing but wonderful experiences with him.

At the end of his career, when asked which he preferred, theatrical or architectural lighting design, he replied, "How can you get excited about a 50-foot stage after you've lit a 50-story building?"

In a 1960 profile of Abe in *The New Yorker*, Joseph Wechsberg wrote: "Feder has used light as if it were a building material – plaster, concrete or wood. He picks up a light and places it elsewhere, or piles light beams on top of one another, as if they were bricks. Feder plays with light as a composer plays with sound."

In that profile, Abe was quoted as saying that light was a material that "can fill space without actually filling it" and that it had phantasmagorical possibilities: "Lighting – especially lighting at night – can make you see things you've never seen before."

Abe was pursuing his great dream to light the Sistine Chapel and the Wailing Wall in Jerusalem when he died in 1997 at the age of 87, after a lifetime devoted to the art of illumination. In his honor, the lights at Rockefeller Center and the Empire State Building were turned off for one hour. He was truly a magician, an inspiring man to know.

Early in 1969 a small group of lighting designers met at the home of pioneer lighting consultant Richard Kelly to brainstorm about their industry. Later, they regularly gathered informally in a local Manhattan restaurant, squeezing into one booth. You could count those who called themselves lighting designers on two hands. Most of these people were IES (Illuminating Engineering Society) members, and their sole means of support came from design fees. They believed they could create an understanding of the importance and benefit of their craft among potential clients – and incidentally obtain group insurance benefits.

One of the prime movers in that group was my friend Lesley Wheel, a proud graduate of Bryn Mawr. Like many others, Lesley began her career in theatrical lighting design early in the 1950s, lighting nightclub acts, fashion shows and industrial shows, but, like Abe Feder before her, she made the natural transition into architecture.

"It took me eight years in theater to find out where I belonged," she said in a March 2001 interview with Architectural Lighting magazine, "but once I got started in architecture, I knew I was in the right place."

In 1957 she became Hilton Hotels' in-house lighting consultant and a year later opened her own lighting design practice, becoming the first woman to practice full-time in architectural lighting design. In 1961 she co-founded the firm Wheel-Garon. It is said that without her, there would never have been an IALD – the International Association of Lighting Designers, the great organization that is the heartbeat of the industry.

Lesley recalled that Charles A. Bell, the executive vice president of Hilton International, once told her, "Hotels are theater. Don't you ever forget it." And Lesley never did.

"The hotel lobby," she said, "is a theater set in which the people coming and going are the performers." But the cast of characters is always changing, and to create lighting that is warm and inviting, even exciting, so that the customer returns, is always a challenge. "Six years from now, a hotel should look just as good as it does today."

Also of utmost importance in lighting for hospitality: establishing mood and atmosphere; providing the right quantity and quality of light for guest and worker tasks; reducing glare; creating a safe, secure environment with adequate lighting in parking lots, garages, corridors and other public spaces, and keeping cost and energy efficiency in mind.

I met Lesley early in her career in New York on a job Tishman had contracted her to design. She was a woman in a man's game and to keep from being overwhelmed or dismissed, she had developed some hard bark. When I went to see her, she was brisk and somewhat standoffish.

"Why are you bothering me?" she asked.

"I furnish all the lighting for Tishman's projects," I informed her.

She was bewildered by that at first and took a while to understand my role in furnishing her lighting. She let me know early in the game that what she put down on the drawings was what she wanted. No more, no less – and no ifs, ands or buts.

"I want what I want and I expect to get it," she said, tough as nails.

I was still pretty new to the game in New York and too young and scared to do or say anything that would offend her.

"You'll get it," I said.

It was a chilly start, but Lesley and I eventually became great pals and over the years she encouraged me to manufacture products she thought the industry needed. She was the first person who demanded I make a low-voltage shower light. Funny, it doesn't seem like a big deal, but to get that MR 16 low-voltage fixture with a UL wet label wasn't easy. UL had to establish a criterion for this product. I think we were the first to accomplish this feat.

Lesley and Don Gersztoff formed a partnership in 1977. Their strength was in the hotel and hospitality industry. Some of Lesley's most notable projects include the Willard Hotel in Washington, D.C., the Monte Carlo Hotel and Casino in Las Vegas, and Union Station in Los Angeles. Among her countless accomplishments and contributions to the industry: she was a founding member, fellow and past president of the IALD; she was also recipient of the Designers Lighting Forum Honor Award in 1979, the Reader's Choice award from Architectural Lighting magazine in 1990, and the IALD Lifetime Achievement Award in 1999; she was a former director of the Lighting Research Institute; and she was a founder and board member of the Nuckolls Fund for Lighting Education.

Her generosity in mentoring and passing on her knowledge to the next generation of lighting designers was legendary.

"Goodness," she said. "After you realize something remarkable, you want to pass it on." And "pass it on" she did, to all, even to competitors. It is said that almost everyone in the industry either worked for Lesley or worked for someone who worked for Lesley.

One of Lesley's most prominent students was Babu Shankar, a pillar of the architectural lighting community. His company, Integrated Lighting Design, is recognized all over the world in hotel lighting design. On the evening of April 1, 2004, industry members were all in Las Vegas at Lightfair, watching as Babu Shankar accepted an award of appreciation from IALD President Charles G. Stone for his outstanding volunteer achievements as IALD Awards Co-Chair for several years, when we learned that Lesley had passed away in her home in Los Angeles. She is missed. Lesley was a great inspiration and a true friend to me and many others in the lighting industry.

Between 1978 and 1995, Lesley's protégé Babu Shankar cut his teeth on such celebrated Wheel-Gersztoff projects as the Willard Intercontinental in Washington, D.C., the Waldorf Astoria in New York City, the Peninsula and the Beverly Hills Hotel in Beverly Hills, and the famous Regent Halekulani Hotel in Oahu, Hawaii.

Since branching out on his own, Babu has gone on to light over 200 top hotels and restaurants around the world. Some of his clients include Nikko, Loews, Hyatt, Westin, Ritz Carlton, Starwood Group and the Okura Group, as well as the Taj hotels in his native India.

Since his early years working with Lesley, Babu Shankar has found that hotel lighting has changed. The hotels, he told Architectural Lighting magazine, "are more concerned with their profit margins, which are much tighter now than in the 1970s when they were just beginning to experience the oil-price crunch. Now, consideration of energy consumption is of paramount importance. Also now, due to economizing, there is much less hotel staff for maintenance."

Like Abe and Lesley before him, Babu understands the intrinsic connection between theater and hospitality lighting design, and how improvements in dimming technology have allowed designers to manipulate lighting much more than in the early years.

"A hotel is a stage in a lot of ways," Babu said in his AL interview. "Like a theatrical lighting director, the hotel lighting designer uses the dimming technology to pre-set different lighting levels to set scenes at different times of the day and different seasons as well."

Modern dimming systems can be monitored and controlled from one central location, making maintenance that much easier, but as Babu observes, the human factor still exists:

"Less maintenance staff in hotels underscores something I tell my designers: our lighting is only as good as it is maintained. We can do a great job, go back to visit in six months, and it's not the same. Some operators are very conscientious – Japanese hotels, for example. I visited a project we designed, and after two years, it was maintained the same way we designed it. Unfortunately, this is not always the case in other parts of the world."

Through his travels and work in over 40 countries, Babu has noted the differences in lighting tastes between East and West:

"Here, we like warmer, incandescent light, perhaps because most Americans come from colder, Northern European countries. In Japan and other parts of Asia, they feel the more light the better. I was always fighting with Asian clients about this when I first started working there. For instance, I designed lighting for a restaurant that would have been lauded in the States but was told it was too dark. Look at the typical Japanese home – mostly they are lit by cool fluorescent lamps. We like contrast in America, and do not light every square foot of the space evenly. For example, the Chinese consider dark spots as places where evil spirits lurk, so it is important that we understand cultural norms and design accordingly."

Babu is also an expert in the shifting requirements in lighting restaurants:

"For example, for a three-meal restaurant in a hotel, you want to make sure there's enough light during breakfast for a patron to read the newspaper without trouble. The same restaurant has to be made interesting enough, with softer, candle-like setting, to attract a dinner clientele."

Restaurant lighting, like hotel lighting, is changing with the times.

"There was a time we pin-spotted the tables in fine dining restaurants and kept the ambient lighting low, but the trend is changing with a younger crowd. They don't want the dark, ambient, atmospheric lighting, but something lively. We need to highlight what is architecturally interesting. Restaurant lighting has to come from all different directions – not just the ceiling, but from candles, wall sconces, concealed lighting from banquettes – in other words, a combination of different components to make it more interesting."

Edison Price is one of the most interesting and brilliant men I have had the pleasure to know, a pioneer in the building of lighting fixtures. Edison went to work for his family's stage lighting company in 1935 when he was 17. He is credited with inventing everything from glare-free recessed filters to track lighting systems, and he became the confidant of great architects Ludwig Mies van der Rohe and Philip Johnson, for whom he provided the recessed fixtures that bathe the Four Seasons restaurant in light. Edison is also credited with lighting over 200 museums around the world.

He formed his own company, Edison Price, in 1952. Edison was a Renaissance man in the field – inventor, engineer, designer and craftsman – and is recognized as the innovator responsible for recessed and track lighting.

Edison was ahead of his time with low-brightness, glare-free fixtures and established industry conventions, setting the bar for future product development. "Edison Price" – the company and the man – is synonymous with lighting design.

In addition to van der Rohe and Johnson, Edison has worked with some of the most notable architects of the 20th century – Louis Kahn, Marcel Breuer, Buckminster Fuller, and I.M. Pei. Equal parts inventor, engineer, designer and craftsman, Edison Price has long been recognized as a fantastic innovator.

I first met Edison when I was working on the 100-story John Hancock Building in Chicago. He asked me to introduce a fluorescent fixture he had designed, with a parabolic louver, something I had never seen until he showed it to me. This fixture became an industry standard after Columbia Lighting saw and copied it – it was my old pal Walter Tolle, the same person who hung up on me back when I called about the John Deere Building, who latched onto it.

Edison was a pure genius, always tinkering – the ultimate professor. I found him inspiring.

He didn't hesitate to express his opinion, either. I remember when the city of Chicago wrote in its electrical code that all recessed lighting fixtures had to meet the "Chicago Plenum Requirements." Edison sent a blistering letter to the chief electrical inspector of Chicago calling this code ridiculous. The chief inspector posted this letter on his wall. For many years after, Edison had problems shipping to Chicago, but he'd said his say.

Edison's great company is run today by his bright beautiful daughter, Emma Price, and Joel Segal.

Another great early innovator was Sylvan "Sy" Shemitz. Sy was born in Long Island in 1925 and served in the navy during WW II, going on to complete his education at the University of Pennsylvania and the Wharton School. Throughout his life this brilliant man kept in touch with higher education and gave back to the community, mentoring the young – this is one of the noble traits I have found in all truly great lighting designers, this nurturing of young talent. He was a fellow at the Illuminating Engineering Society of North America and a visiting lecturer at a number of prestigious schools, including Yale, RISD and Princeton. It's safe to say he was loved by students lucky enough to hear him expound on the art and science of lighting. Sy was also an avid boat and yacht racer, competing in and completing the race from Newport, R.I., to Bermuda a dozen times.

Sy invented a type of "ambient office lighting" called Tambient and also held patents for a number of innovations regarding asymmetrical lighting, which he marketed under the Elliptar brand. Asymmetrical lighting is used in many famous public buildings, including the New York Public Library and the Nelson-Atkins Museum of Art in Kansas City, Missouri, O'Hare Airport in Chicago, and the Thomas Jefferson Memorial in Washington, D.C. He is probably best known for his famous lighting of Grand Central Terminal in New York City, about which Sy told the *New York Times* in 1991, "I think the most important issue is to make New York a lively, friendly and joyful place." He used blue filtered tints and magenta-colored lighting to accent the exterior façade and help the terminal exhibit a magical, majestic aura, an otherworldly glow that makes it one of the most aesthetically pleasing and harmoniously designed public spaces in the world, matching any train station in Europe.

Sy died in 2007 while sailing on his beloved, poetically named boat "The Light Fantastic."

In a May 2006 interview for Architectural Lighting magazine, Richard Kelly recalled opening his first lighting consultancy in 1935 in New York City: "There weren't lighting consultants then. Nobody would pay for my ideas, but they would buy fixtures."

Richard was so frustrated that he began to write and lecture on the integral relationship between lighting and architecture, giving voice and name to, and helping to shape, the emerging practice of lighting design. Kelly furthered the relationship between the lighting and architecture communities, and cemented his role as the prime liaison between the two, by graduating from the Yale School of Architecture in 1944. He was equally at home in the architectural and illumination engineering communities;

you might say he brought them both under one roof.

By the early 1950s, Richard Kelly had coined much of the vocabulary for modern architectural lighting design, the bedrock of which included the three "light energy impacts" – focal glow (highlight), ambient luminescence (graded washes), and play of brilliants (sharp detail).

He also lectured at such top institutions as Harvard, Yale and Princeton, where he happily shared his philosophy of light and his wisdom with the next generation of lighting designers.

Over the years, his training and unwavering belief in lighting design garnered him the respect of some of the most dynamic architects and designers of the era. He worked with Mies van der Rohe, Philip Johnson, Eero Saarinen and Louis Kahn, and helped realize a number of the 20th century's most memorable and iconic buildings, including Saarinen's General Motors Technical Center (1946-55), Johnson's Glass House (1949), Mies's Seagram Building (1954-58), and Kahn's Kimball Art Museum (1967-72).

Richard Kelly refused to be confined by available lighting solutions and was always pushing the envelope to develop new products and lighting technologies to meet the challenges of a constantly evolving industry landscape and marketplace.

One of Kelly's early devotees was Harry Gerstel of Gotham Lighting, located in the Long Island City section of Queens, N.Y., who was driven by the convergence of two significant trends of the day – the advancement in the technology of electric lamps, which were quickly replacing gas lamps, and the growing international influence of modernist architects, whose preference for minimalist interiors called for unobtrusive, even hidden, light sources.

In 1958, Harry Gerstel designed and patented the "recessed accent light," which was easily adjusted, providing vertical aiming up to 45° and a full 360° rotation. Other Gotham Lighting innovations included small-aperture recessed downlights with ellipsoidal optics, precision-machined die-cast baffles, and velvet black finishes which maximized optical control.

The company became widely known for setting trends. Gotham was also the first to use deep-finned heat-radiating socket assemblies to extend lamp life.

All these important innovations were born of Gotham's unique problem-solving mentality and its close, collaborative relationship with top architects, engineers and lighting consultants of the day. Gotham installations include such architectural classics as the Seagram's Building, Lever House, McGraw Hill, and the CBS building in NYC.

Ray Grenald is a practicing architect who has won international recognition and almost five decades of raves for his lighting designs. He was one of the founding members of the IALD who squeezed into that Manhattan restaurant booth back in 1969. His philosophy of design evolved from a sensitivity to, and awareness of, human perception and how behavior responds to the physical environment, especially the visual. His extensive studies and his observation of behavior modification have resulted in an entirely unique approach to lighting design.

He is a member of the American Institute of Architects (FAIA), a past president and a fellow of the International Association of Lighting Designers (FIALD) and a fellow of the Illuminating Engineering Society (FIES). He currently serves on the board of directors for the National Lighting Research Organization.

If you want to see things in a dynamic new light, talk to Ray Grenald. His projects are often ambitious and sometimes controversial, such as the gingerbread lighting of the outline of 12 Victorian boathouses on the Schuylkill River in Philadelphia, and the World Trade Center in Baltimore, where light beams shining up the corners of the Trade Center's five sides bounce off two mirrors attached at the roofline, so that you can see ten white lines radiating from the heart of downtown Baltimore, a breathtaking, immensely satisfying effect – magic, theater, man playing God.

Ray's company Grenald Waldron also lit one of America's famous early feats of suspension engineering, the 1926-vintage Benjamin Franklin

Bridge (a precursor to the Golden Gate Bridge), which spans the Delaware River from Philadelphia to Camden, New Jersey. Boston-based Color Kinetics outdoor fixtures were used to meet the design goals of changeable color, long life, low maintenance, and a kinetic quality to make a bigger show.

The bright color-changing LEDs are invisible to those in cars driving across the bridge but can be seen from numerous vantage points for several miles along both the Philly and Camden sides of the river. This is truly light as entertainment. There are two main shows: a five-minute show at the top of the hour and a two-minute show at the half-hour. The top-of-the-hour show focuses more on color, while the other show is more about movement and the dynamics of the bridge.

The LED colors and movements are programmed in patterns, such as the "Chime," which starts at the center of the span and moves toward the banks of the river. There is also the "Big Bang," whose light sequence runs from the shores to the center of the span and back to the shores, and the "Train Chase," which is as exciting to the senses as it sounds. The bridge also turns on and off based on an astronomical clock, adjusting itself to the time of year – a show for all seasons.

Paul Gregory of Focus Lighting, Inc., of New York City is often said to paint pictures with light. His excellence is reflected in his numerous awards, including multiple Lumen and IALD Awards, Waterbury, ASID Awards, and the *Lighting Dimensions* "Lighting Designer of the Year" Award. He was also inducted into *Architectural Lighting* magazine's Hall of Fame.

Paul trained in theatrical lighting at Abe Feder's old stomping grounds, the Goodman Theatre School of the Art Institute of Chicago, and in architectural lighting design at the Parsons School of Design in New York City. Like so many before him he was a theater man through and through, until in 1975 he founded Litelab Corporation and branched into major design projects in museums, restaurants and entertainment facilities.

For Paul, lighting is Show Biz – beautiful, bright and engaging – of the moment. One of his primary goals is to ensure that a patron's initial impression of a space or facade is as stunning and memorable as that moment when the curtain rises on a Broadway stage. His focus with Focus since 1987 has included hotels, resorts, retail (toy stores galore), restaurants, museums, nightclubs, offices and private residences around the world.

Paul feels that great lighting has a profoundly positive effect, not only on the look of a space's architecture, but also on the people within that space – their state of mind, sense of well-being, productivity, happiness – and ultimately their quality of life, health and life-span. Paul is an industry jack-of-all-disciplines, fusing, in his theory and practice, theatrical lighting design with architectural design, interior design, graphic design, all the fine arts, computer technologies, psychology, medicine and construction.

The bright lights you see today on Broadway were a result of special legislation, written by lighting designer Paul Marantz, which has resulted in a gluttonous orgy of glorious lighting in New York's Times Square. Let's face it, Times Square is Broadway's greatest show, the greatest canvas for lighting design in America – an amazing planned and random amalgamation of lights which creates a mind-blowing tapestry for the brain. Paul Gregory's Toys R Us is an amazing example of what is possible given a relaxation of lighting laws which many in the industry think are unfair energy-conscious government restrictions. Lighting designers want the lights to stay on.

Paul Marantz got bitten by the lighting bug when he was a ten-year-old puppeteer, but came into the business from the architectural end after studying architectural history at Oberlin and graduating in 1960. He went on to study theater at Case/Western Reserve University and Brooklyn College. At the start of his lighting career, Paul specialized in theatrical projects, working as chief engineer for distributor Lighting Services.

"Jules Fisher was the wizard of off-Broadway in those days," Paul told Architectural Lighting in 2002. "Jules would come into Lighting Services to look for ways to solve lighting problems on the cheap, and we got to be friends. Since he preferred theatrical projects, Jules would send any architectural lighting jobs that came his way to me under the table."

The architect in him loves to light theaters. He says, "Both museums and theaters are places for the enjoyment of visual things."

Paul was working for Century Lighting in 1971 when the company decided to relocate to the West Coast. Paul opted to stay in New York and partner with Fisher to form Fisher Marantz.

"On the day we opened our office," Paul recalled, "I went to a stationery store and bought a small file box. I wrote down the names and addresses of all the architects I would like to work with on index cards and put them in the box. I forgot about the file box until ten years later, when I opened it and riffled through it. It turned out that I had worked for most of the firms I had listed on the cards."

Although his firm has illuminated a wide variety of buildings, Paul's knowledge of and interest in art history has led him to a special expertise in lighting museums.

"As a class of building, the museum is the most interesting to me because the purpose of the lighting has only to do with enabling people to see – and you get to work with both electric and daylight."

He is not much of a fan of the trend in contemporary lighting design toward theatrical glitz:

"The kinetic visuals of television and the increase in consumers' leisure time and wealth have led to a tendency to incorporate entertainment components into architectural venues, typified by sprawling, glitzy Las Vegas hotels and restaurants. Some of it is fascinating, but some of it is too much. I prefer that the lighting technology be simple and that ideas rule over technology."

His best advice to new colleagues fresh to the industry was always "to learn about light. It's an invisible material and you have to work with it. The benefit of working in theater is that you go quickly from one show to another, work fast and get a lot under your belt in a little amount of time. Material moves and interacts with light - focus on learning about that. Use your eyes and look at great art and architecture."

Marantz' philosophies and transformation of space with light have earned him all the highest industry awards, including Lumen Citations from the Illuminating Engineering Society of North America (IESNA) for the Audrey Jones Beck Building, the Museum of Fine Arts in Houston; Radio City Music Hall renovation, New York; Times Square New Year's Eve ball, New York; J. Paul Getty Museum, Los Angeles; Byzantine Fresco Chapel, Houston; Procter & Gamble corporate headquarters, Cincinnati; Gas Company Tower, Los Angeles; Minnesota Orchestra Hall; Denver Symphony Hall; Palladium Discotheque, New York; Boston Museum of Fine Arts; St. Louis Union Station rehabilitation; and the Royalton Hotel, New York. He received an IALD Citation for the Rainbow Room in New York's GE Building and an IALD Award of Excellence for both the Islamic Cultural Center in New York and the San Francisco Museum of Modern Art.

Howard Brandston set up shop in 1966 with BPI – Brandston Partnership Inc. – and ever since has been one of the most ingenious and fantastic lighting designers in the industry. BPI's philosophy is to make the work beautiful. His Expo '67 in Montreal and his Expo '70 In Osaka were industry high-water marks. He did the Pan-Am Building at New York's JFK, as well as NY's Carlyle Hotel and the Cathedral of St. John the Divine, which is ongoing. Howard has also lit Battery Park City, The Oklahoma City National Memorial, the Petronas Towers in Kuala Lumpur, and the Cheung Kong Center in Hong Kong. The recipient of countless awards, he's lit everything from the fossils at the American Museum of Natural History to the Toronto International Airport, among a staggering 3,000-plus completed projects.

Another industry giant is Honolulu-born William Lam, who served three years with distinction in the U.S. Army Air Force as a B-25 pilot before earning a degree in architecture from MIT in 1949.

Bill's entry into lighting design was accidental – it stemmed from his interest in the work of Finnish architect/designer Alvar Aalto, who has been considered a master of functionalism.

"I designed a lamp for myself," said Bill. "People were admiring it and seeking to obtain one, and the rest is lighting history."

It was a floor lamp with a wood base, brass stem, goose neck and a fabric shade that featured a clip-in diffuser to minimize glare from the lamp. This was a revolutionary feature at the time – the best-known contemporary model had a metal shade with a bare bulb sticking out at the bottom.

Encouraged when some friends wanted to know where they could buy the lamp, Bill told AL magazine in 2001, he "made three sales calls in Boston and got three orders. I made five sales calls in New York and got five orders. I went out the next day, rented some space, hired one employee and started making these lamps. That lamp and a coffee table were selected for a 'Good Design' award by the Museum of Modern Art and exhibited in museums across the U.S. That really got things off to a great start."

It was 1951 when Bill founded Lam Inc. - now Lam Lighting. However, after eight years as president of the company, Bill resigned to return to his original love and calling, architecture, founding the firm of William Lam Associates, Consultants-Coordination of Lighting with Architecture and Urban Design in 1959. For the next 40 years he won acclaim for notable projects including the Tennessee Valley Authority headquarters complex, government centers in Quebec and Vancouver, Union Station restoration in Washington, D.C., and the San Diego Convention Center.

For years Lam has waged an often-solo battle with the light and power industry against its promotion of ever-increasing light levels and energy use. His long public battle with the Illuminating Engineering Society (IES) began in the early 1960s and ran through the energy crisis of the '70s. "Quality not quantity" was Bill Lam's battle cry. He related that at the time, the IES arbitrarily set high lighting levels at the expense of good design.

"I wanted the emphasis on quality, judgment and common sense rather than numbers," he said. "More footcandles usually led to more glare and worse environments. Lighting is about design and not engineering; engineering is the last thing you do. If you know what a good environment is, you can create it. Lighting is applied perception psychology. You have to know what makes a good environment."

As a result of his efforts, the light levels once recommended by the standards committee have been reconsidered and lighting design is not compelled to adhere to what Lam would term "ridiculously high requirements." It has evolved into contemporary design – a combination of ambient lighting with task lighting. Bill Lam's advocacy was critical to changing the way we perceive our environment.

Lam's work has always integrated lighting with architecture and urban design, based on the conviction that lighting is an integral part of the architecture. This is the philosophy he has taught in his lectures at universities including Harvard and MIT, and in his writings.

"What motivates me is designing buildings from the inside out. It's creating a space that people want to live and work in."

One of the best examples of his collaborative approach is the Washington Metro System. For this project Bill worked with Harry Weese Architects and De-Leuw, Cather Engineers. In Harry Weese's letter of recommendation to the American Institute of Architects (which bestowed honors on Lam in 2000), he wrote, "In a field which is peopled with all manner of … mountebanks and stage lighting experts, Lam is one of the few who combines a respect for the scientific method, aesthetic judgment and a penchant for elimination of cant. He does not go by the book; he sets standards rather than follows them."

All great lighting designers, from the first caveman who put on a show by firelight, to the Elizabethans who positioned candelabra to illuminate Shakespeare's plays at the Blackfriars theater, to the Kliegl and Century Lighting companies that dominated American theater lighting of the 19th and early 20th century, to today's and tomorrow's artistic adventurers in the wondrous and ever-evolving world of light, where technology is invented and applications and fixtures follow suit, where magic is the norm and dreams of men and women are brought to light – all these designers shared and share a common goal: the illumination of life, and the improvement of the human condition.

IN THEIR OWN WORDS:
THE GREAT LIGHTING DESIGNERS AND THEIR GREATEST CHALLENGES

During the 2009 Lightfair, held in New York, I had the pleasure of attending a session at which six of the founding members of the International Association of Lighting Designers [IALD] discussed how it all began. As I listened to their amazing lighting design stories, I thought that someday the new young members of this talented group would wonder how it all began and what the early years were like. They would also want to know how these icons thought about the creative process that propelled them to accomplish their greatest lighting challenges. Since time passes so quickly, I wanted to include some of these great minds in my book.

I have asked a few of those with whom I have had the pleasure of working to write a piece for the book. True to form, they all graciously accepted the opportunity. Some told of their early years and what happened thereafter. Some wrote brief articles on their greatest lighting challenge. I am indebted to all these talented people, for much more than just writing these stories.

There are so many more great lighting designers in this industry to whom I am indebted as well, that it would be impossible to acknowledge them all. But here, I think, we have a strong sampling of the best minds in the field.

We have had the pleasure of working with lighting designers from other countries and I would like to acknowledge two who have made major contributions to this industry.

Metis Lighting Srl, Milan, Italy – Paolo Giovane has been a friend for many years and has done most outstanding work all over the world.

Speirs and Major, London, England – Jonathon Speirs with his innovative designs, has been a pleasure to work with.

The Jefferson National Expansion Memorial Gateway Arch (Randy Burkett)

Image by Debbie Franke Photography, Inc.

RANDY BURKETT LIGHTING DESIGN
ST. LOUIS. MO.

Beginning his lighting practice in 1978, Randy is a Penn State graduate and an architect. His lighting credits are so diverse that you marvel at the level of inspiration, from corporate offices to underwater sea museums to the largest retail mall portfolio in the country. I'm continually amazed at this man's productivity – and at his product. He has also found time to serve as president of IALD (1996-97) and teach lighting at the University of Colorado and Maryville U. in St. Louis. His right-hand man, Ron Kurtz (another Penn State alum and architect), is one of the most creative men I have had the pleasure to work with.

Randy writes one of the most interesting lighting-challenge stories in this book: the story of the fabulous St. Louis Arch.

THE JEFFERSON NATIONAL EXPANSION MEMORIAL GATEWAY ARCH

RANDY BURKETT, FIALD, IESNA, LC

INTRODUCTION

I often get asked by clients how and why I got into lighting design. My answer, a story I have also recounted to students and other would-be lighting professionals for many years, is one with which many of my colleagues can identify.

As I was considering my options for college, I could not decide whether I wanted to be an architect or an engineer. In high school, I frequently found myself sketching ideas one moment, and cranking out math problem solutions the next. I enjoyed doing both, and I did not want to choose between them as I pursued a higher education.

I was fortunate to grow up in Central Pennsylvania, and on

a high school career day trip to Penn State, I discovered Architectural Engineering. It was the ultimate fence-straddling degree. I could spend five years exploring whether I wanted to be an artist or a nerd; architect or engineer. However, it was within this AE program that I found my true calling – a discipline that drew equally on both the right and left side of the brain. I found lighting design.

The 30 years since graduating have brought a lot of lighting design challenges, many of which taxed both my aesthetic and technical acumen. None, more than the lighting of the Jefferson National Expansion Memorial – the Gateway Arch.

THE CHALLENGE

In late 1999, I was approached by a private foundation about illuminating the Jefferson National Expansion Memorial. They had gotten our firm's name from a respected local client, with whom we had worked on several major commissions. The Gateway Foundation, a privately funded organization that had been involved in the financial support of civic enhancement projects in the St. Louis area throughout the years, was inspired to attempt the Arch lighting when they saw it temporarily illuminated as a backdrop for a series of national television news shows during a visit of Pope John Paul II to St. Louis in 1999.

The 630'-high structure was one of the crowning achievements of Finnish architect Eero Saarinen. He had won the commission in an international competition for design of the Memorial in 1947. The park and Arch is a memorial to Thomas Jefferson's role in opening the West and to the pioneers who helped shape its history,

Nearly 35 years had passed since the Arch's dedication in 1966, and not a single successful permanent lighting design strategy had been put forth.

Hurdles for the project abounded, not the least of which was a history of failed proposals to light the Arch proffered by a collection of both the well-intended – but ill-fated – and the self-serving, seeking to sell equipment or gain political favor. The lack of success with these attempts had soured the local National Park Service (NPS) authorities on the very idea of illuminating the monument, and convinced them it just could not be permanently done. Additionally, it had been just a few years prior that a decree had come down from Washington, that taxpayer money could not be used to fund aesthetic lighting projects. The government would not pay for any of the design, construction, or maintenance and operation over the life of the installation. This meant that should the project proceed, the Foundation would not only have to fund the design and construction, but commit to maintaining and operating the system throughout its life.

As the project was finally granted permission to commence a preliminary design phase, the headwinds seemed to increase yet again. The NPS insisted that any lighting scheme would have to be virtually invisible during the daylight hours. It could not cause a hazard to the users of the Park, nor could it in any way distract from nighttime security requirements. Additionally, it would have to be shut down during a number of the Park's yearly festivals, and protected from potential damage during special events.

When the Arch was first constructed, historic artifacts were discovered on the site, including remnants of the original St. Louis settlement, as well as even older pieces from Native American villages. Any excavations in support of a new lighting system would be under the watchful eye of the Park Services' archeologist.

Beneath the Arch lies the nationally recognized 25,000-square-foot Museum of Westward Expansion. The museum's footprint overlays a large portion of the area directly beneath the monument, and with only 18 inches of cover above the underground roof, it virtually eliminated 2/3 of the best locations for lighting equipment.

There were many who did not want to see the Arch lighted at all. They felt that its nighttime presence, seen only through silhouette, and its reflections of the city's lights, were enough to recognize its importance.

Those opposing the project would say, "If Saarinen had wanted it lighted, it would have been part of his original design." In an ironic twist, during the early research for the project, we uncovered an old television news clip showing GE engineers working with members of Saarinen's team on a lighting mockup at the soon-to-be-opened memorial. The footage clearly demonstrated a desire to illuminate the structure, although the results were apparently less than satisfactory. Nonetheless, the mere presence of this recording helped rally support of our client's intention to make this a reality.

THE DESIGN

Exhaustive study of the Arch, its magnificent site (designed by noted landscape architect Dan Kiley), and the surrounding cityscape, informed the design team as to the strengths and weaknesses of various lighting concept approaches. Its perch on the banks of the Mississippi allowed glorious views to the Arch when traveling into the city from the east. The view from the city to the west was varied, yet remarkably stately. It was important to celebrate the Arch as an architectural icon, while being mindful that the 60-story stainless steel catenary form was, indeed, a memorial. The lighting had to reveal it as grand structure, yet its acknowledgment had to be both reverent and respectful.

Since attaching any lighting source or equipment to the Arch directly was ruled out at the beginning, lighting concepts would have to concentrate on locating luminaires on the Arch grounds. The sheer projection distances involved made light intensity and beam control of the utmost importance.

As simple and elegant as the Arch appears during the day, its geometry and stainless steel skin posed onerous technical problems for the lighting at night. Almost any conceivable lighting position presented problems of reflections or compromised views. While one scheme might hold promise when seen from downtown, vantage points to the highways and approaching boulevards did not seem to receive the same beneficial returns. When light positions were optimized to provide impressive renditions from a distance, the more intimate, close-in results appeared, at least from the mathematical models, to be excessively compromised.

About six months was spent in design and formulation of lighting concepts, with periodic presentations to the Park Service for the required progress approvals and blessings. When the project first began, Park officials were quite skeptical, but by the time the design neared completion two years later, they were among the staunchest supporters of the effort.

MOCKUPS

Despite countless hours of computer-aided calculations and technical review, it became increasingly apparent that the only way to effectively assess the myriad of reflections and sight-line combinations for the project was to conduct full scale mockups.

Due to the number of lighting fixtures that were believed needed to provide the necessary results, it was not practical to procure enough samples to fully illuminate even one leg of the Arch. Instead, it was decided to obtain eight fully operational 3000-watt xenon luminaires, and use them in studying segments of the structure's surface.

Once the equipment arrived in the City, we had just four nights to complete the segment studies. It is more accurate to say four *mornings*, since we were forced to work from midnight to 6 a.m. so that the local and regional press corps would not discover that plans to illuminate the Arch were well underway.

The goals for these mockups were as follows:

- Idealization of the lighting equipment locations
- Determination of final luminaire wattages and light distributions
- Detailed examination of key views to the Arch
- Assessment of the visual impact of light source reflections on key views and on nearby highways

The process involved set-up of the six to eight luminaires in pre-calculated positions beneath and around the Arch. Once each luminaire positioning scenario was prepared, the units were illuminated and focused onto different Arch leg segments for study. As the aiming adjustments were fine-tuned, vehicles were sent to various parts of the city, county and across the river to examine the results, recording the effects of the specific tests on video for later use. The assessment teams would then drive back into the city, toward the Arch, with each traveling a different route. Video was taken during the return trip to provide a record of what would be viewed from each approach. Time coding permitted later synchronization of the clips for analysis.

This painstaking process yielded a great deal of valuable information, permitting critical technical and aesthetic decisions to be made with a high degree of confidence.

THE SOLUTION

As a result of the mockups, final selections of lighting equipment and preferred positions were made.

A total of 44 3000-watt xenon source floodlights were determined to be needed. The luminaires would be deployed to four 8' x 10' x 55' subterranean concrete vaults, located on the east and west sides of the Arch, just over 100' from the stainless steel legs. The open air vaults are covered with a lightweight, high strength metallic grating, which protects the public above and the lighting equipment below. Positioned over each luminaire is an independently adjustable circular grating section which allows for the rotation necessary to maximize optical transmission of the grating material by aligning its cross members parallel with the light beam's dominant axis of distribution.

Each xenon luminaire has an adjustable, motorized reflector system, permitting precise beam shaping. A mechanical dowser allows for incremental light intensity control without impacting source color or beam distribution. Four different lens types provide further light beam modeling, tailoring each fixture to its optical assignment. This combination of reflective and refractive manipulation also maximizes control over direct spill light to the sky.

A centralized computer control continually monitors xenon lamp and luminaire system health through an on-board processing chip within each lighting fixture.

THE BIRDS

Since the Arch had never been permanently illuminated before, attempts to do so now drew the attention of several interested wildlife groups. Both the United States Fish and Wildlife Service and the National Audubon Society expressed apprehension over the potential impact of lighting the Arch on birds, both indigenous waterfowl and migrating bird species.

After sunset the surface of the earth cools, and columns of warm, rising air dissipate. As a result, turbulence aloft decreases and the atmosphere becomes increasingly more stable. In terms of energy expenditure, birds can maximize their efficiency by flying in a less turbulent atmosphere. Many species of birds migrate at night to reap these energy-saving benefits.

The principal concerns centered on two issues. First, on foggy nights or evenings with heavy particulates in the atmosphere (such as hot August days along the Mississippi), there was a strong possibility that light scattering into the sky around the Arch would disorient or confuse birds, heightening the likelihood of strikes of the structure. Secondly, there were several migration periods during the year when bird flight traffic would be so intense that the volume would ensure a significant number of Arch "encounters." After close consultation with both of the concerned organizations, as well as with the NPS, it was decided that several design-related actions would be necessary in order to satisfy all involved.

The first, and most straightforward, measure was to extinguish the lighting system during the prime migratory periods (two to three weeks during early March and September) when the bird traffic was at its peak along the Mississippi flyway. The Arch would be made to go dark an additional couple of weeks in July due to the presence of naïve young birds during their dispersal from breeding areas.

The unpredictability of weather made safeguarding the birds during foggy and low cloud conditions a more difficult challenge. Since the Park could not provide nightly human monitoring of the sky conditions, it was determined that any solution for this problem had to be automated. We turned to a technology frequently used at airports – the Laser Detecting Ceilometer. This is a device that uses a laser to determine the height of a cloud base or to measure the aerosol concentration within the atmosphere. It consists of a vertically pointing laser and a receiver in the same location. A laser pulse with a millisecond duration is projected through the atmosphere. As the beam travels upward, tiny fractions of the light are scattered by atmospheric particulates (aerosols), which produces some degree of light scattering. A small component of this scattered light is directed back to the receiver. In this way, each pulse of laser light results in a vertical profile of aerosol concentration within the atmosphere. The presence of clouds or water droplets can produce strong return signals compared to background levels, which allows for cloud height determination, and an estimate of overall atmospheric particulate concentration.

Once low clouds, fog or dense particulates are reported by the ceilometer, a signal is sent to the lighting system ordering it to extinguish itself using the on-board mechanical dowsers. The mechanical occlusion minimizes lamp degradation and permits a quick return to an illuminated state once weather conditions improve.

REFLECTIONS

Nearly nine years have passed since the Arch lighting was installed and illuminated for the first time. It has helped to bring people back into the City at night, and its now preeminent appearance on the evening skyline is a source of pride for the community and all who visit. Most importantly, it remains, day and night, a moving and memorable acknowledgment to Thomas Jefferson, and to the pioneers, whose exploration of the Louisiana Territory commenced the greatest expansion in the history of America. Playing a small role in helping to honor this history remains one of my most satisfying experiences.

The World War II Memorial (Barbara Horton)

Image by Corbis

BARBARA HORTON
HORTON LEES BROGDEN LIGHTING DESIGN
NEW YORK, LOS ANGELES, SAN FRANCISCO

Barbara is such an icon in this industry that her name evokes the upmost respect. She came to Horton Lees in 1981 after working as an interior designer. She has taught lighting design at the Fashion Institute of Technology and the Parsons School of Design. Her company has tackled such varied and exciting projects across the U.S. as the Cedars Sinai Comprehensive Cancer Center in Los Angeles, San Francisco's Federal Building and the LA Museum of Art, and others across the world from Taipei to Stuttgart and Bavaria. I have had the pleasure of working with Barbara for many years.

She writes below of her greatest lighting challenge: the World War II monument in Washington, D.C. – a project of which we should all be proud.

THE WORLD WAR II MEMORIAL

BARBARA HORTON
WASHINGTON, D.C.

Architects: Friedrich St. Florian and Leo A. Daly
Lighting Designer: Horton Lees Brogden Lighting Design Inc.
Designer team: Barbara Horton, Stephen Lees, Chad Grosshart, Nam Choi
IES Lumen Award of Merit – 2006

There are very few opportunities in my career, thus far, that I can say were an honor to be part of the design team; the World War II Memorial in Washington, D.C., is one of them. We were on the winning team with Friedrich St. Florian and Leo A. Daly, one of 400 competitors for this prestigious project.

The World War II Memorial is located on the National Mall's central axis between the Lincoln Memorial and the Washington Monument on a

7.4 acre controversial lot. The client was officially the American Battle Memorial Commission, comprised of many survivors, including military men and women who served in this war, as well as historians and an Auschwitz survivor. As part of the team, we engaged with these people to understand the nature of this monument, the war and the era. It was a history lesson like none other. I found myself reading every book I could get on FDR to understand the era, books about the war, and sought out family members who served in the military or were victims at labor or death camps to find a significant metaphor or symbolic element of light that would transcend time.

What I learned from the history lessons and reading was aptly put in Tom Brokaw's book *The Greatest Generation* – "this was a war of honor and all Americans were united as one." The lighting elements that would support the sentiment of this war in this era were embodied in the phrase "the darkness of global conflict and a light of freedom." Light and darkness, chiaroscuro, all concepts a lighting designer could use to transform the monument from the day to the night experience, were powerful imagery.

The project is classical in design, in three parts: formal colonnades represent the 50 states; two baldachins with enormous eagles represent both the Atlantic and the Pacific Theater, and the Rainbow Pool, centrally located, represents the light coming out of the darkness. The Freedom Wall sits in a reflecting pool with 4,048 gold stars, each representing 100 American lives lost. The gold star was proudly displayed in windows during and after WWII as a symbol of family sacrifice and it continued during the Iraq and Gulf War.

It was opposed by critics who believed that the location of the memorial would interrupt what had been an unobstructed view between the Washington Monument and the Lincoln Memorial. The most important criterion we established for lighting this project was to always be discreet. The architectural elements, the stories, the symbols were always the most prominent element. Our lighting would never interfere with the images of the Lincoln and Washington monuments' reflections in the Mall Reflecting Pool. This rule, along with the myriad others from the various parties that had a voice in this project, was the most sacred in our minds.

Our lighting approach was to discreetly light the colonnade from across the rampart wall, highlighting each state represented and the bronze wreath. The columns were cascading from 30'-0" high to 8'-0" which meant a unique aiming position for each of the columns. A custom fixture was designed using low voltage Par 36 and AR111 lamps to obtain the desired effect, control of light and brightness. The fixtures have custom vertical louvers, each louver precisely angled to shield direct view of the lamp. Visitors pay homage by walking along the rampart wall passing through the light. The effect not only softly illuminates each column but animates the monument at night, casting long shadows on the columns. The concealed fixtures and low light levels supported our criteria to minimize intrusion on adjacent monuments.

The main plaza, which was about a football field in size, was illuminated strictly from light sources located in the fountains, the wash of light on the baldachins reflected from the fountain beneath them and the concealed bench lights which further emphasized and revealed the curvilinear form of the rampart walls.

The Rainbow Fountain was illuminated with Par 56 – 500 watt lamps to light the 90'-0" high water elements in the center as well as the classical arching water jets surrounding the oval pool. The fixtures were fitted with color changing filters and controlled on dimmers as part of a requirement from the ABMC Owner. It was their desire to have the monument have multi-scene controls for various events. Dimming and color change was an important part of their vision for future events at the memorial. Regrettably, LED technology was not advanced enough in 2000 when we began this project to be able to consider what would now potentially be a more appropriate source. Low wattage metal halide lamps were very desirable from our point of view and recommended but of course do not offer the ability for dimming.

Using the dimmer system we reduced light output minimally to extend lamp life. The parks commission was very concerned about all incandescent but as we researched some of the existing monuments, we discovered that fiber optics and LED were equally problematic for maintenance.

The Freedom Wall sits in a reflecting pool independently of the Rainbow Fountain with 4,000 gold stars in three dimensions. Water is a beautiful means to magnify light. Opposite the wall of stars, in a low knee wall to contain the water, we located the Par 38 underwater lights to highlight the stars. As the light passes through the water it reflects off of the stars creating a million tiny reflections.

During the photography session for the project, our photographer made a wonderful observation about how he watched the visitors moving through the memorial from dusk into night. The play of shadows, from those visitors walking the rampart walls casting shadows, to children jumping from one uplight to another, totally animated the memorial with shadow play. A video would have been a better choice to demonstrate the lighting effects at night.

The lighting effect we created was simple, discreet and reverent out of respect for the lives lost while keeping their memory alive.

Crystals at City Center (Paul Gregory)
Photography by Jaun Pablo Lira (Focus Lighting)

Museum of Science and Industry (Paul Gregory)

Photography Courtesy of Evidence Design (Museum Designer)

PAUL GREGORY
FOCUS LIGHTING
NEW YORK, NY

Paul formed his lighting design firm in 1987, but long before that was a theatrical designer; he also started a very important lighting manufacturing company. He truly paints with light and is one of the lighting geniuses in this country. I am always amazed at his creativity and philosophy of design. I remember the Toys R Us store in New York, which featured a real Ferris wheel, a dollhouse you could walk into, and lighting so unique I shall never forget it.

Paul is a perfectionist and a micro-manager, something needed in this industry. He writes a great story about the philosophical and practical approach to lighting design.

BUILDING A PHILOSOPHY OF LIGHTING DESIGN
PAUL GREGORY

It is 1969 and I am a young man of about seventeen on a trip to New York City to see my first Broadway show. It is a Saturday matinee of Dale Wasserman's *Man of La Mancha* starring Richard Kiley. As my friends and I climb the stairs I am impressed by the incredibly rich details of the painted plaster ceiling and intricate balcony in the Martin Beck Theatre. I notice the velour drapes in the boxes and the gold sparkle on the proscenium as we settle into our seats in the nosebleed section next to the follow-spot booth. The atmosphere is electric!

The house lights go to half; then the house goes out. All detail disappears, but not the memory of what was just there. There is darkness, not normal, but darkness filled with drama and excitement.

The orchestra begins playing the overture and themes of "Dream the Impossible Dream" come through the music. Light from the follow spot, just a foot in diameter, pierces the darkness like a knife and illuminates only the head of the conductor. The follow spot cuts out. It is as dark as I can remember. Slowly the lights come up to reveal a stage and a large creaking stairway descending from the back wall towards the orchestra pit. The judges of the Spanish Inquisition come down the stairway and the show begins.

I remember that moment like it was yesterday and still get excited by it. THAT is the emotional drama we try to bring to our work as architectural lighting designers. If we do a good job it gives us an emotional link to the experience and strengthens our memory of the visual.

After 35 years of being inspired by Mitch Leigh's musical score for *Man of La Mancha* I had a chance to show my gratitude in 2004. I was able to work with architect Emanuela Frattini Magnusson to design the lighting for Mitch and Abby Leigh's New York residence. It was an honor to have the chance to impact someone so influential in my choice of career path. I channeled the same drama and emotion he helped to inspire in me into the lighting design of his home. I can only hope I was able to evoke the same reaction he helped to produce in me!

THEATRE

My instant enthusiasm for what I saw on the stage led me to theatrical lighting. Lighting for me has always been the synthesis of art and physics, which combined my interests. The theatre was a place filled with creative people and it was a great fit for me.

I began in summer stock during my senior year in high school. I was allowed to design one of two shows that first summer. During the next five years I designed theatrical lighting for over 100 productions, including *Company* (when it was first released from Broadway), *1776*, and *Promises! Promises!* Often designing lighting in "one show a week" summer stock meant honing your skills to develop a concept, create a light plot to support it, and hang, focus and cue a show very quickly. Sort of like MASH surgery during the Vietnam War, you got good quickly because you had no other choice – the audience showed up Friday at eight o'clock.

The experience I gained on those 100 shows – the testing of color and angle on the drops, scenery, actors and dancers – was some of the best training I received. During previews I often got to sit next to the director and watch the audience response to different effects: a blackout, or a three-second fade to black at the end of a scene; a cyclorama during the opening scene lit in steel blue, or the amber of a sunrise. We discussed which color supported the moment and why. These lessons helped me form the techniques I used in writing the color-changing programs for the Entel Tower in Chile in 1994 and the Marcus Center for the Performing Arts in Milwaukee in 2008.

If I could give only one piece of advice to a young designer I would say: "Get the most experience you can." Each director (or architect) has something important to teach you. Accumulate as many points of view as you can. It is your ability to see the world through someone else's eyes that makes you valuable. To be able to confidently answer the question "How will they feel when they see this?" is critical.

NIGHT CLUBS

In 1973, I graduated from The Goodman Theater School, a conservatory school in Chicago. I moved to Houston for my first real job: two seasons as the lighting designer at The Alley Theater. Though I enjoyed my time there and continued to enrich my experience and views, I began to be a bit disheartened by regional theatre. We put all that hard work into making a good production only to see it wiped out when the show closed after a five-week run. I decided to leave the Alley and shift from theatre to architectural lighting, where my mark would be more permanent.

In 1975 I started my first company, Litelab, with my friend and business partner Rick Spaulding. We found our niche in designing and providing lighting systems and control equipment for clubs. Club owners were getting sick of hiring bands each week that showed up late, played too loud, and trashed their clubs. They wanted to control their business, which meant controlling the sound and lighting. We started with smaller clubs in Chicago and over the period of five years grew to 150 people with offices in Chicago, New York City, Boston, Buffalo and Los Angeles. We worked on nearly every major nightclub or disco in the world and it was one of the most thrilling experiences in my life.

Our only rule was "Make it fabulous," which often meant trying to create architecture with light. For example, in the Paradise Garage in New York City we made eight small dance floors by projecting shapes on the ground with 512 pin beams arranged in 8 rings of 64 fixtures. People could dance in a small square of white light and watch their friends dancing in a heart of red light a few feet away. The more spaces we designed, the more we saw that what made a great club was a strong relationship between sound and light. Control equipment was the critical key to that relationship. We started designing controllers to allow patrons to feel the music through the intensity and color of the light. Our controllers were an instant hit and became the most widely used entertainment lighting controllers worldwide.

For twenty years my Litelab business card was a ticket into any club in the world. I saw my equipment controlling dance floors in Paris, Rio, Basra, Baghdad, Tel Aviv, Taipei, Hanover, Moscow, Buenos Aires, Rome, Reykjavik, and of course New York City. We created electric drama for New York clubs like The Saint, Paradise Garage, The Electric Circus, Xenon, and some of the effects for Studio 54.

One day in 1977 I got a call from Robert Stigwood. I had no idea who he was. He got my attention when he mentioned that the letters RSO written on the little pink pig on the BeeGees record label stood for Robert Stigwood Organization. We designed the club lighting, the dance floor and control system for a movie project starring John Travolta that was being filmed at 2001 Odyssey, a dance club in Bay Ridge, Brooklyn. No one anticipated the hysteria that would result when *Saturday Night*

Fever opened in December 1977. The Disco business became enormous worldwide and Litelab was leading the way.

The club business was a wonderful training ground. It gave me a chance to continue developing my creative process and emotional connections that I had learned in theatre. It also helped me develop my own formula for success. Each person needs to find a special corner of the market, and then make it work for him or her. By capitalizing on frustrated club owners and terribly behaved bands, I was able to gain entrance to a blossoming industry. The key from there was hard work on strong ideas and the intelligence and ingenuity to make them work. As simple as it sounds, I still apply this formula to the operations of my design firm today.

FOCUS LIGHTING

Looking for something that was more about lighting design and less about manufacturing, I left Litelab in 1984. I wanted to apply all the experience I had gathered through the years to architectural lighting with the objective to create beautiful, evocative spaces. I started my current company, Focus Lighting, in 1986. At first it was just me and I worked in an office in my home. When the workload became too much for one person to handle I hired Chris Harms and then Carlos Inclan to help me. We continued to grow person by person and today Focus is an Architectural Lighting Design firm of thirty talented designers doing projects all over the world. Our approach, built on dedication and experience, has opened up opportunities to explore some really worthwhile projects such as children's hospitals, retail boutiques, schools, design offices, residences, restaurants, hotels, and other specialty projects like the lighting and programming for the 100th Anniversary of the Times Square Ball.

Though it may have seemed like starting over again, getting into architectural lighting design was really the culmination of all my years in theater. I was able to pull together all of my knowledge and experience and apply it to the architectural field. The process of all those years of observation and evaluation led me to develop my own philosophy of design.

EVOKING ONE EMOTION

The best way I have found to create meaningful design is to create spaces and effects that evoke specific emotion. Feeling the drama created during the opening of *Man of La Mancha* burned the experience into my memory, where it remains to this day. In the same way, when two young lovers go to the beach and watch the sunset together, they remember the image for the rest of their lives. One reason their memory of the sunset is so strong is because it is tied to the emotion of the moment. The memory of the image is strengthened by the emotion. If you can create that response in a viewer they will always remember a space as important to them.

A project is successful when a person walks in and instantly feels affected by the space. For this to occur, the architect, interior designer, owner and lighting designer must articulate and agree on what emotions the space will evoke and which moods will be created. Specifically, the lighting design must serve and enhance this vision by controlling the light that is reflected off the surfaces and forms created by the architectural designer. We paint the image that the viewer sees. This way, we can transform a space into an atmosphere that embraces all the deliberate, well-thought-out expressions of the design team. We strive to construct an image or a feeling so great that the patron will want to keep that lasting impression.

The Marcus Center for the Performing Arts in Milwaukee, Wisconsin, is a wonderful example of a project that evokes emotion. Home to the local symphony orchestra, opera, ballet and theater companies, the building was designed by architect Harry Weese. With so much art and culture on the inside of the building, we wanted the creativity exhibited on the stage to bleed through the building and express itself on the façade. Using individually addressed color-changing LED fixtures, we treated the concrete facade as a blank canvas and painted the building with subtly blended color-changing compositions. Color palettes were inspired by natural scenes such as the Northern Lights and the paintings of Wisconsin native

Paul Gregory   177

artist Georgia O'Keefe and have universal appeal. Locals feel a connection and sense of pride in seeing their cultural center adorned with the art of a Wisconsin native. Since the new lighting was first unveiled, Marcus Center employees have reported getting visits from Chicago residents who drove two hours just to see the new look. A visiting couple saw the Northern Lights "painted" on the façade of the building and said it reminded them of a trip they took to Reykjavik years ago. This is the evocative design we strive for in every project. It was a pleasure to create a lighting scheme that not only expresses and adds to the art and culture of Milwaukee, but inspires an emotional connection in locals and visitors alike.

Striving to evoke emotion is not always easy. Through the years I have developed a few strategies that help me and my designers at Focus Lighting to achieve this goal. A great team must think about the artistic composition while they analyze a project, push the envelope, and go the extra mile to turn out a great design.

BUILDING A TEAM

As Focus Lighting grew, I took a great deal of time picking each designer. They are all incredibly talented, but also kind, considerate, wonderful people, and I am proud to work with them every day. I try to pass along everything I have learned from the theatre and club designs, which starts with "how to see." Ultimately, you don't see the paint on the wall, the wood beams in the ceiling, or the texture of the stone tabletop. You only see the light reflected off those surfaces into your eyes. *All you see is reflected light.* This is not an opinion; this is the physics of the situation.

As lighting designers, we are only one part of the greater design team that makes a project work. I believe it is our role to understand which emotion the project will evoke, and affirm it in the minds of architects, interior designers, engineers and contractors on the team. We try to anticipate problems that will arise, and come up with solutions proactively. We research and mock up tricky lighting conditions so that we can say without a doubt whether a treatment will work or not. If there is considerable risk, we make the client part of the decision of how to proceed. By transmitting this sense of passion and importance, lighting designers can gain the respect of the design team.

We had a great team experience when we designed the Tourneau Store of the Forum Shops in the MGM in Las Vegas. The design featured a domed ceiling which we were grazing with the light from half a million dollars of LEDs. In every conversation we had with the contractors we mentioned the importance of a perfect, flawless finish on the dome since the light would be coming from such a steep angle. When they turned the lights on, it was a disaster. Every crack and irregularity of the poorly plastered ceiling was highlighted. Because we had brought it up so many times, the contractor brought in thirty men and refinished the ceiling at his own expense without holding up the project. The project later received the IALD Award of Excellence. This story shows how important it is for the team to understand the lighting design and for us to stick to our convictions.

PAINTING WITH LIGHT

I see the world as a series of compositions. For example, let's say you are entering a hotel. As you approach the building, through your car window you see a rhythm of columns and windows with a central porte cochère, set off against the blue sky. You enter the lobby and a hotel employee stands behind a mahogany desk and in front of a framed red mural. As you walk to your room, you pass a corridor with a repetition of chandeliers and elevator doors that terminates in a leather wall with a credenza and a brass lamp. I see each of these views as a composition. They have a central focus, foreground, background and a frame. I believe that the first step in any design is to discover these critical views, and to prioritize where you want to focus your attention. Only then can you create a "light painting," by highlighting the focus, creating contrast in the background, balancing the foreground and transition spaces and emphasizing the frame to stop your eye. By focusing on particular views, you can create stunning compositions with visual relief in between. As patrons move through the space and come upon these compositions, they experience a sense of discovery and excitement.

The important views were very clear when we were asked to do the lighting design and programming of the New Year's Eve Times Square Ball for the 100th and 101st anniversaries. It was our challenge to reinvent a classic icon viewed by people all over the world and make the custom cut Waterford crystal sparkle from every angle. We decided that there were three critical viewpoints in this design. First there was the view from 5 feet, experienced by the press who were standing next to the ball. Next there was the view from 50 feet, which was what the ball looked like on TV. Finally, there was the view from 500 feet that the crowd saw from the street below. Our design would not only stand out in the nocturnal Manhattan skyline, but also be compared to other illuminated symbols across the globe. With "a glistening gem in the sky" as our design concept we took steps to address each of the three critical views.

To enhance the 5' view, we analyzed the materials, light source, and detailing of the ball, doing several rounds of mockup with patterns of Waterford crystal during the process. We finally requested that they cut facets into each crystal triangle on both sides, something they had never done for the ball before. The additional sparkle created by the double layer of facets made the close-up view brilliant.

To address the 50' view, we created an extruded triangular mirror form that held the LEDs away from the crystal. This allowed the chamber behind each triangle to be a different color without affecting the triangle next to it and virtually tripled the perceived light sources behind the crystal. The addition of this form prevented any "off axis" viewing problems that could produce light leaks or dark spots in the television view.

To maximize the 500' view we thought very carefully about the source. The previous balls had incandescent lighting which was perceived by the crowds in Times Square as a tiny dot very far away. The choice to switch to LEDs allowed crisper, more vibrant colors and patterns unlike anything possible with incandescent sources. In addition it was four times brighter than the previous ball, which made it much more prominent in the long view.

We made sure to take all three views into account when we programmed a series of themed shows that would start at the top of each hour. Some of these themes were "The Changing Seasons," "Flags of all Nations," and "Diamonds in the Sky." Some shows had bolder patterning that would be read well from the 500' view, others had more intricacy and sparkle that could only be seen in the 50' and 5' views.

By attacking the project with the three views in mind, we were able to foresee problems that might arise in the actual installation. We made sure viewers could see something different and interesting depending on their vantage point and we came away with a comprehensive design whose beauty not only had sparkle, but depth.

PUSHING THE ENVELOPE

We had an amazing chance to use our creativity when the New York office of the architecture firm Gensler asked us to design the lighting for Toys R Us in Times Square. When we tackled the lighting of the glass façade wall, our first question was: "With all the visual stimulus, what would attract attention in Times Square?" I developed the concept of covering the building with a white sheet to contrast the busy blinking lights on the surrounding buildings. On a bright day, it would appear to be brilliant just by reflecting the natural 10,000 footcandles of sunlight. Periodically, in an eye-catching moment, you could pull the cloth away to reveal the exciting interior complete with a Ferris Wheel, two story animatronic T-Rex, and more toys than any child could imagine. To achieve our desired effect, we covered the glass with façade panels that would roll away quickly for the reveal moment.

Through extensive research we found Diazit, a blueprint machine company that made a 3' x 3' scroller and had years of experience moving large format paper. We studied the thickness of the rolls, the number of images that could be stored, the size of the motor, and the type of non-stretching plastic that would accept ink from printers. We finally laid out

165 scrollers each with six images and a clear panel so that the entire wall could become transparent. To address the night view, we added 66 arm-mounted 1,000-watt metal halide sport lights that would floodlight the facade. We built plywood mockups to ensure that the fixtures did not block the view of the billboards from the street. We even tested the luminance of surrounding signs in Times Square to prove that our lighting was bright enough to compete. Our creative, comprehensive approach turned out a great project that won the Clio Awards Gold Statue for Environmental Design, the GE Award of **Excellent** in 2001 and the NY Construction News Retail Project of the Year in 2002.

GOING THE EXTRA MILE

Clients want a "proactive lighting consultant." That is one that designs the lighting, and if necessary pours the concrete, installs the conduit, hangs the steel and mounts the light on it. Of course that is a joke, but on opening day of Town Restaurant at the Chambers Hotel in NYC it was clear that the electricians would not be able to install the lighting in the back-lit wood veneer banquettes in time for the press party. We sent half of the office to the site and wired the 120 electrical boxes and sockets, installed the PAR38 lamps and connected the load to the dimming system. The point source quality of the lamp enhanced the wood grain while the full spectrum of the light brought out the complex tones of the wood and complemented the flesh tones of the diners. It was a great opening and one of our most beautiful projects; people just looked great sitting in those banquettes. Getting the design done with a great attitude and a confidence in your design is the key.

- Take the initiative.
- Make the extra phone call.
- Overcome the obstacles.
- Never let anything get in the way of creating a wonderful project for the owner.

GREAT DESIGN SELLS

The lighting profession is not about tallying up meaningless experiences just to build a resume and pay the bills. Slowly building up a mental database of quality experiences, studying and reevaluating is what great design is all about. For example, Cirque du Soleil is one of the most successful enterprises I can name. They have fifteen shows in four freestanding theaters across the country, and there is talk of opening a village in Hong Kong with hotels, restaurants and even training schools. It takes the Cirque du Soleil team eighteen months to develop a new show. During the first six months, the design team sits in a room and works only on concept. In months seven to twelve they design and assemble the actual show, and in months thirteen to eighteen they are in technical rehearsals. Six months of concept development is the key to success. When you encounter difficult design problems, a strong concept will guide you to the solution that will not only answer your questions, but reinforce your original ideas. By continually falling back on a strong concept, each detail works together to produce a thorough and powerfully evocative design.

People want good design. They don't want just any mp3 player. They want Apple's iPod because it is sleek, sexy and small. They want to come to New York, see a Broadway show, eat at a world-class restaurant and have a quality experience. They don't want glitz and glamour and superficiality. They want good design, period. If you can put that quality within their reach, success is yours.

CONCLUSION: A LIGHTING DESIGNER'S DREAM

Imagine if when they first unearthed the Great Pyramids at Giza, there were copper terminals at the base of the structure. By clipping on power leads you could light up the pyramid and it would look just as great as it did 4,500 years ago when the Pharaohs and their subjects basked in its grandeur.

As far-fetched as it is, we as lighting designers can all take something away from this anecdote. We strive to create memorable, powerful projects that will outlast us as an expression of our art and culture. We can only dream that our successful projects will last centuries unharmed. But in every design we strive to find simple, maintainable strategies to ensure that the emotion we convey in our work will remain strong for years to come.

Lighting design is not easy, but the satisfaction I get from my work makes it all worthwhile. There is nothing better than using my experience, developed by years of testing and reevaluating spaces, to turn out great, evocative designs. This is what happens when a great team works together to analyze the artistic composition, push the envelope, and go the extra mile. I love knowing that I helped create a space that makes people look great, feel great and allows them to enjoy themselves. To have such a direct effect on the lives of the people who experience our spaces is a powerful thing.

Bellagio Hotel (Mike Gehring)
Image Courtesy of Getty Images

MIKE GEHRING
KAPLAN GEHRING MCCARROLL
ARCHITECTURAL LIGHTING
LOS ANGELES

When this firm was established in 1985 Mike Gehring was an architect, and to this day, in order to be a member in KGM you have to be a licensed architect, making it the only firm I know of with such requirements. It has paid off because KGM has visions that other firms don't. I have worked with Mike for a long time, and I particularly remember the Bellagio Hotel in Las Vegas. At the time, Mike wanted to use my lighting but wasn't sure how good it was, so he tried me out on a small project. I didn't know what he was auditioning me for until after the fixtures passed his criteria, when he gave me that enormous job called the Bellagio. His firm had to focus over 20,000 fixtures – no easy task.

If you take a walk down the Strip in Las Vegas, many of the hotels were done by KGM. The KGM portfolio also includes everything from Royce Hall at UCLA to office buildings to large retail complexes and hospitals.

Mike writes about the early days of his career and his most challenging project: lighting the massive Bellagio Hotel in Las Vegas.

THE BELLAGIO HOTEL
MIKE GEHRING

I'm an architect. I specialize in lighting design.

That's how I answer people when they ask what I do for a living. I decided to focus my career on lighting design 15 years ago, and believe me, it was not a smooth process.

ARCHITECTURE SCHOOL

When I graduated from the USC School of Architecture in 1981, lighting design was not really a profession, at least out here in L.A. The only lighting consultant I knew of was Ray Grenald (who is also an architect, by the way). Though I did not see it then, there were a few events in school that portended aspects of my future.

Ten semesters of Design Studio were required for our degree in architecture. All of our final drawings were hand-drafted ink on mylar or vellum. We made countless three-dimensional models out of Strathmore, chipboard, foamcore, or wood. The whole experience was almost monastic in its rigor, dedication, and discipline. However, while we were drawing our 500 circulation diagrams, we missed out on the university experience during some of the best years of our life. Architecture school was an island on campus, full of people who felt superior to those we didn't have time to get to know.

In our third-year structural engineering class, we did the classic "egg drop" exercise. The object was to drop a raw egg from the roof of the three-story building onto the concrete patio below, without it cracking or breaking. Since I was preoccupied with design studio, I rushed through my egg drop exercise with some half-assed paper bag full of balloons. My egg didn't break, but I was not proud of my solution. I will never forget the winning design; it continues to serve as an inspiration to me. I wish I saw whose it was, but there was a cardboard cone about one foot tall (like the spool in a roll of paper towels) with little wings at the top. The egg was simply set on top of this cone, naked for everyone to see. The designer hung it off the roof, and spun it. It slowly twirled down to the ground and fell onto its side, with the egg gently rolling out onto the ground, unscathed. So beautiful! So elegant! Damn! Why didn't I think of that?

Our electrical engineering professor at USC was Saul Goldin…it was over 15 years later that I learned that he was one of the pioneers in lighting design. He rarely taught us anything about electricity. He only talked about lighting, with statements such as "get the lights off of the ceiling!" Our final project each semester was to photograph a project we thought had good lighting, create a slide show (this was WAY before Powerpoint), set it to music, and show it to the rest of the class. It was nothing but fun … and a nice break from the REAL work of design studio. We would laugh at how easy Saul's pointless class was…I guess he knew better than we did at the time.

The young people in my office would not believe this today, but I loved computers back in architecture school. I excelled in Fortran programming and land planning on the computer. This was back when USC's computer (that's right … singular) was an IBM 360 that filled a whole building. We had to enter data on separate computer cards. In my land planning class, the largest project to date was a few acres. I decided I wanted to do Santa Catalina Island, which was many, many times larger. There were 20,160 individual computer cards in the data base. This was my first hint at working on huge projects. I remembered what our high school chemistry teacher taught us about doing long chemistry problems, "It's just like eating a steak … one bite at a time."

Our thesis advisor told us a story about a world-famous German structural engineer who defected to the Allies during World War II. There was a heavily-damaged bridge that we needed for moving our troops the following week. The engineer walked along the top, looking at all the holes in the roadway. He then crawled underneath, and studied the missing, broken, and shattered structural members. As he returned to the group of Seabees with their clipboards, they were ready to order tons of steel and concrete to hastily rebuild the bridge. The engineer said, "All I need is a can of red paint and a three-inch brush." He then painted a serpentine line on the roadway, and told the team, "Just make sure your troops walk along that line, and the bridge will hold." To me, that is the best example of an elegant solution. They didn't need to rebuild the bridge; they just needed to move the troops.

WORKING AS AN ARCHITECT

I was one of the few people in my class who did exactly what we were prepared to do in school…I went to work as a designer in an architectural firm. At Welton Becket Associates, my first project was to help one of the senior designers do schematic design for Fluor Corporation's Houston headquarters. As I would develop his sketches, I would do alternate schemes on the side. Eventually, he told me that the owner wanted to see two alternate schemes at every meeting, so the senior designer would design Scheme A and I would work on Scheme B. Week after week, the owners would choose Scheme B. My bosses thought I looked too young to attend the conferences, so the clients would always come out to the studio and say hello to me after each meeting. I never got to go see the building in Houston (since I was too young), but I did design that 1.3 millionSF building complex for $8.50 per hour. Once again, doing big projects was natural for me. After the groundbreaking, which was attended by all of my superiors, I received a package in the mail from our clients. It was a cattle brand in the shape of Texas with Fluor's name on it. They knew who designed that baby. I still have that 25-year old brand on my desk.

After three years at Welton Becket, I moved on to Dworsky Associates. The projects were not as large, so I was able to learn more about how buildings go together. The Westwood Community Center was only 50,000 square feet, with a wide variety of program elements. We were able to really think about daylighting, glare, contrast and views, though not much of our original design was actually built. We thought about electric lighting, too … indirect, color-mixing, protecting fixtures, etc. I am proud to say I have learned much about lighting since then, however.

The Landau Partnership was my next stop, back to huge projects. However, the economy in the late '80s was beginning to slow down in some sectors, and I was only able to work on two built projects in six years. I learned a lot about the business of running an architecture firm while I was at Landau. We had many tough developer clients who looked upon the architect's professional liability insurance policy as a profit center for themselves. Every day was a study in contracts, liability, value-engineering, contractor budget manipulations, getting paid…oh yes, sometimes we got to design buildings, too.

I worked on one office building in Glendale for four years. That was really boring for me, but I accepted it. I didn't know any better.

TRANSITION TO LIGHTING DESIGN

The big recession of the '90s finally hit, and Landau laid off 80 percent of our staff. There were only seven of us remaining, out of 35. There was no work, and we were down to four-day work weeks on top of a 10-percent pay cut. Since my wife was seven months pregnant with our first daughter, there was only one obvious choice for me, so I did it. I resigned … then I called my wife and gave her the news.

I started my own sole practitioner architecture firm, and luckily I never had the proverbial two waiting rooms (the one I waited in, and the one nobody waited in). I did small residential remodels and consulted to architectural firms as an independent contractor. I was rakin' in the cash, and working my butt off! However, I didn't feel like I had a business or a career … everything was piecemeal.

I used to hire Joe Kaplan as our lighting consultant while I was at Landau. When I was consulting to WWCOT for a religious project in Los Angeles, Joe was our lighting designer. We had a great meeting where we were able to untangle some nagging architectural problems by introducing lighting into the mix. Joe then asked me if I had some time to help him for a couple of weeks, since he was just starting to get a little too busy. Two weeks has become 15 years and counting.

Joe saw the potential for our successful working relationship before I did. He often asked me to commit to working together for the long term, and I resisted. After all, I was a licensed architect, a former Director of Design. I wasn't a lighting guy. Why would I want to move down the food chain? Why would I leave architecture?

By the way, I had spent four years at night earning an MBA at the

UCLA Anderson School of Management, with the intent of becoming a developer. Why? Because I wanted to make more money than an architect. There, I said it. I don't recommend attending four years of night school on top of a career as an architect. I entered UCLA with one wife and came out with another.

As I agonized about my decision whether to become partners with Joe Kaplan, Andrea (my current and favorite wife) asked me why I went to business school. When I told her I did it to become a developer, she pointed out that I had intended to get out of architecture anyway. Mmmm, good point.

Joe then told me a joke about the circus parade. The last guy in the parade followed the elephant, to pick up the poop. One of the spectators asked why he didn't quit that job. He responded, "What? And leave show business?" Oh, I get it.

Five months later, I committed my career to lighting design. Joe and I were having fun. We would say we were like chocolate peanut butter cups. His lighting knowledge was the peanut butter, and my architectural experience was the chocolate.

The economy was picking up, we were working on a variety of homes, condominium units, offices, etc. We had just completed the home of a major casino owner in Las Vegas, and he decided to try us out on a few small remodels in some of his properties. Things were not perfect, however, since we were working many hours on probably too many projects. Our process was a little rough, and some of our clients and contractors shared their frustration with us. One of our home projects in Las Vegas had the fluorescent lamp color reversed between the master closet (supposed to be 3000K) and the garage (4100K). Shortly, it became clear that the contractor was not going to fix this, and the owner was irate. Joe and I flew to Las Vegas, got on a ladder in the garage, and began to open the lenses. It was 114 degrees outside, and probably 130 inside the garage. When I looked up to open the first lens, a dead bug fell into my mouth. I spat it out in disgust, remembered that I used to be a Director of Design for high rise buildings, looked down at Joe, and asked, "What the hell are we doing?" Then his cell phone rang. They wanted us at Atlandia's office right away to propose on a new project. Some big hotel in Las Vegas called Beau Rivage or Bellagio or something like that.

It's always darkest before the dawn…

THE BELLAGIO HOTEL

Be careful what you wish for…

The Bellagio project overwhelmed us. Besides the fact that it was our first CAD project, we immediately had to hire a number of people, buy computers, lease more space, and work at a much faster pace. We were working 80-hour weeks in an attempt to simply keep up. The clients and contractors in Las Vegas were the toughest I have ever worked with in my 30-year career. Besides their unreasonable demands and intimidation, they never stopped changing their design. These guys did not distinguish between consultants and employees…they thought they owned everybody.

The Bellagio was huge, fast, mean, and was ever-changing! As much as I wanted to run away, I kept plugging away, day after day. It was a matter of sheer guts and will that we finished the project successfully. In the final weeks, I was directing aiming teams for six spaces at the same time…as soon as they were ready for us. There were 20,000 fixtures to aim, since the owner forced us to use only recessed MR16 adjustable downlights with slot apertures. This is the only project that required aiming while we wore hard hats. We had to guess where the art and furniture were going to go…if we waited until they were installed, we would never open the building on time.

How did we do it? One bite at a time. That massive project is a collection of simple lighting moves. I kept thinking of that egg drop and the curving red paint line on the bridge in Europe…elegant. We had to run our part of the project like architects…that is the only experience I could call upon. Our office today looks, sounds, and acts like an architect's studio…these are our roots.

I finished my part of the Bellagio at 7 p.m. on opening night. My last task was to work with the lighting control system to set the scenes at the Villas (6,000SF each). I walked through the Casino during the VIP party with three of my toes wrapped in bandages from blisters, on the way to my rental car in the remote construction laborer parking lot. When I got to the car, half a mile away, I turned around and looked at the building. WOW!

I have never felt that way since.

Our participation on the Bellagio brought us many other casino resorts in Las Vegas and elsewhere. Since casino owners tend to be volatile, we knew we had to protect ourselves by diversifying our project types and locations. For every casino resort we got, it was our goal to bring in the equivalent fee amount of other types of projects. This also gave us a chance to rotate designers in and out of the gaming projects, to minimize burn-out.

CHALLENGES FOR ALL LIGHTING DESIGNERS

The Bellagio was my biggest one-time career challenge, but there are a number of challenges I continue to face. I suspect that many lighting designers would agree with me.

There is a huge disparity between the lighting designer's AUTHORITY and our RESPONSIBILITY. On many projects, we will participate in design meetings with architects and interior designers who dictate what they think the lighting should be, and how it should be implemented. After deeper discussions and gentle coaxing, most people come around to agree with our way of designing the lighting for a project. However, some designers are stubborn and inflexible. When they "tie our hands" and force us to design lighting a certain way, they are usually disappointed in the results…then they blame us, saying, "Well, YOU were the lighting designer!"

The smoothest projects we do are for repeat clients who tell us WHAT they want to achieve with lighting, then we tell them HOW we will achieve that.

Since our fee is so small compared to other members of the design team, there is a tendency to downplay the importance of lighting in a project.

Many owners and architects can get free design work from a lighting manufacturer's representative, so they don't see the point in paying a fee to a lighting designer.

Lighting distributors won't disclose unit pricing of various light fixture types on a project, so it is impossible to know how much the owner is paying for specific fixtures. The world of packaging, distribution, mark-ups is a black art.

Back when I designed buildings, the architect was responsible for coordinating the structural members, HVAC ducts, piping, and light fixtures, to avoid conflicts. We don't see that much, anymore. Many architects try to leave coordination up to the various consultants. There are many situations in the field during construction where our light fixtures don't fit because there is a duct in the way. This could have easily been solved on paper by the architect during the design phases.

OUR ARCHITECTURAL APPROACH

My path to lighting design certainly was not traditional.

During 18 years of education and practice as an architect, I strove to create places. Not just spaces, but places. A place is distinguished from any other place. It has its own culture, history, feeling. It takes years to learn how to create a place, and light is one of its most important aspects. We determine how a place is formed, and how we want it to feel…only then do we begin to design lighting. The feeling, the effects, the lamps, and then the fixtures…in that order.

That's why I often tell clients, "There is a big difference between 'lighting' and 'lights.'"

Chek Lap Kok Airport, Hong Kong (Charles Stone)

Photograph Courtesy of FMS

Chek Lap Kok Airport - Station, Hong Kong (Charles Stone)
Photograph Courtesy of Michel Porro

Chek Lap Kok Airport - Station, Hong Kong (Charles Stone)
Photograph Courtesy of FMS

Chek Lap Kok Airport - Station, Hong Kong (Charles Stone)
Photograph Courtesy of FMS

CHARLES STONE
FISHER MARANTZ STONE
NEW YORK, NY

Charles joined Jules Fisher and Paul Marantz in 1983 and has been one of the most important innovators in the lighting industry. Fisher Marantz Stone has done some of the most important lighting designs the world has seen, from New York to Shanghai to the Middle East and Europe. I had the pleasure of working with Charles's firm on many important projects with Enterprise Lighting. The FMS portfolio includes such diverse challenges as the Four Seasons hotels in New York and Boston, the Washington Monument, the Grand Hyatt in Tokyo and the outstanding office building at 2000 Avenue of the Stars in Los Angeles. Were I to list all their most important projects it would take 25 pages. Charles has also found time to serve as president of IALD.

Here he writes about lighting the Hong Kong Airport, which required him to make over 60 trips to Hong Kong from New York. The tale of his experience makes for one of the best contributions to this book – a story well worth reading.

HONG KONG AIRPORT
CHARLES STONE

I moved to New York to join Jules Fisher & Paul Marantz in 1983. I soon figured out that I would have to get out from "under the wing" of these lighting giants in order to make something of a name for myself. It was the '80s and opportunities would quite literally stop by the office from time to time. And so I remember the late great engineer Gordon Rigg from Melbourne sitting in our conference room and asking if we might be interested in working in Australia.

Gordon's firm, Rankine & Hill, was at the time the leading building services engineering firm in all of Australia, New Zealand, and much of the Pacific Rim. I leaned forward as I noticed that my partners had all leaned back.

My parents are avid lifelong travelers – and I think it must be genetic. I went down to Melbourne and before long we were working from Melbourne and Sydney to Singapore and Hong Kong with an interesting mix of American architects and various expatriate consultants and a few local clients.

In 1991 I received another call from Gordon asking if we would be interested in working on the new Hong Kong Airport and did I ever come to London. I was there the next week and had an interview at Sir Norman Foster's office. A few months later I was in Hong Kong and we were on the project.

Looking around that first day in the project office I saw many Australian friends I had made in Melbourne years earlier. Thus with terrific Australian engineers and terrific English architects I embarked on the greatest challenge in my lighting career (so far).

In advance of the 1997 "handover" of Hong Kong back to China, the Hong Kong government was determined to spend some 61 billion U.S. dollars on new infrastructure – including, perhaps most prominently, a couple of billion for the largest airport in the world – plus bridges, tunnels, rail lines, port facilities, roadways. The furious schedule and massive scope of this once-in-a-lifetime boom was exhilarating. The facilities and infrastructure they were planning to build was like no other. And they would need lighting, lots of it.

The airport design team assembled in Hong Kong. And there I met and worked with some of the brightest young architects in the world – really well-educated, hard-driving and exceptionally creative people. They drove their consultants hard. I learned that every meeting is a presentation, that no option is a good option until all other options have been studied and eliminated. The rigor of process I learned in those years can be found today in our New York studio. The days were long and emotionally draining. I remember that once my wife came along for a three-week trip, but we only got out a couple of evenings because the 12-hour office days and daily presentations just wouldn't quit.

At the height of the design work we had a staff of four in Hong Kong working on the airport and several other transit projects. Our hotel rooms looked like drafting rooms. We worked on paper – this was the old days. And although the project drawings were done in CAD, all the supporting documents were on paper. In the end everything was scanned as .tiff files and delivered on disc. I wonder if any machines exist that can read the discs today. This was cutting-edge stuff. Email was just beginning. The fax machines sat there grinding away all night. We started to say, "The sun never sets on FMS." We would send questions and sketches to New York before a late dinner, sleep for a few hours, then get up and retrieve the morning faxes.

As the design developed, I made several trips around the world to visit potential fitting manufacturers. My first trip was mostly a goodwill mission to gauge interest in the project, and my strategy was to dispel any ideas the manufacturers might have about using standard product. At each manufacturer I visited, there came a point in our discussions where I actually told them they should not pursue the project because they couldn't make a profit on all these custom things. I guess everyone likes a challenge. The friends in manufacturing I made during that experience are on four continents … and they still welcome my calls warning them not to go after a particular job, advice they still ignore.

It was the uplighter that was the greatest challenge of all. The airport design is fundamentally made up of 121 roof sections, each 36 meters square (imagine more than 40 American football fields under roof). The basic general lighting idea was that the roof would be uplighted and thereby indirectly provide all of the general lighting for the entire airport. We wanted to use one really robust and efficient fitting (4,000 of them) using just one lamp type for both interior and exterior application of this idea. We began by looking at an Australian manufacturer of mine lighting – that's how serious we were about the need for robustity. In the end we found a U.S.-based manufacturer who worked with us to design an easily maintained "clamshell" design with a vertically oriented lens – so the dirt falls off. After drawings and prototypes, we did a successful full-size mockup in a mosquito-infested warehouse at a place called Lok Um Pi, accessible only by boat. There were long days and nights swatting mosquitoes while we struggled to get meaningful illuminance measurements from the mockup. Now I can laugh about the screaming matches I had with the suppliers about the quality of the reflector, the importance of the constant wattage ballast, the consistency of manufacturing tolerances, and on and on.

In the end, we had made over 60 trips from New York to Hong Kong in the service of the project. The uplighter was surely the most important but by no means the only custom fixture. In all, we designed over 100 bespoke, yes, truly custom, light fittings that populate the new Hong Kong Airport, over 100,000 fittings in all. Point source downlights, linear downlights, surface mounted projectors, special wall washers, furniture integrated fixtures for customs and immigration, all in addition to the main event – the roof uplighter.

It was a challenging time with a rewarding result and 10 years later, the airport still looks good. I joke that I had hair before that project. Funny thing is that it's true, but I'd like to do it all again starting tomorrow.

Grand Hyatt Melbourne, Australia - Lobby (David Singer)

Image Courtesy of Grand Hyatt Melbourne, Australia

Grand Hyatt Melbourne, Australia - Lounge (David Singer)

Image Courtesy of Grand Hyatt Melbourne, Australia

DAVID SINGER
ARC LIGHT DESIGN
NEW YORK CITY

D avid formed his company in 1992 and is one of the accomplished mentors in this industry. He has worked on six continents. He not only knows lighting design but also fixture design and helped me design an AR70 product which is unique. I have cherished his friendship from day one. If there is one man more than any other who has helped educate this writer about lighting equipment, David is that man.

His greatest lighting challenge was in Australia: the day before he was to make a presentation to the Grand Hyatt, he learned the government had outlawed incandescent light sources. What did he do? Great story ….

THE GRAND HYATT MELBOURNE
DAVID SINGER

22 February 2006 is one of the most notable days as a professional lighting designer I can remember. This was the day after the Honorable Malcolm Turnbull, Member of the Australian Parliament, announced that Australia should be the first country to ban the sales of incandescent lamps and promote the use of high efficacy lamps. He announced the ban the day before our final Lighting Design Presentation of Grand Hyatt Melbourne Public Area Renovation to the new owners of the property. You can only imagine my concern, as our entire design was based on incandescent tungsten filament lamps!

Though we use the higher efficacy incandescent lamps, this announcement came to me as a complete surprise. During my presentation, I brought up this new event and stated that I could only assume the lamp companies would provide suitable replacements as in previous lamp bannings. At the end of my presentation, I humorously suggested the concept of warehousing ten years of lamps – it was not taken as the joke that I had intended!

On the plane back to New York, all I could think about was whether or not I would be able to continue our business of lighting 4- & 5-star hotels, which we believe requires the use of incandescent technology to be able to achieve the atmosphere expected by owner, designer and guest alike. Critical to achieving this 5-star atmosphere is the ability to have a clean bright white light during the day and seamlessly be able to shift to a dimmer candle-colored light for the evening. The need for both dimming light levels and color shifting is unique to hotels and restaurants. These lighting adjustments need to be made in a subtle unobserved manner so as not to be disruptive to the atmosphere of high income generating periods which often occur during sunset. There is only one technology currently available that is able to achieve both dimming and color shifting and that is incandescent.

Without the use of incandescent lamps, I had no idea how to be able to achieve the design for hospitality. I even considered closing the business altogether to go into A/V design where there are no codes yet! It was a long trip.

The first task when I returned was to make good on a promise to my client to call the three major lamp company representatives to find out what this was about. The family of incandescent lamp technology is often broken into four categories: line voltage "general service"; line voltage/low voltage "halogen"; "decorative," and "specialty" lamps. It was clear that the lamp companies were targeting the "general service" lamps starting at 40 watts and going higher.

These lamps are being targeted because they make up the majority of lamps used in residences, which is a huge potential retrofit market. The lamp technology the lamp companies were promoting was the compact fluorescent lamp with the screw-in E27 base. Per their specification this lamp has a 50 to 60 lumen-per-watt efficacy compared with 8 to 15 lumens per watt of non-halogen incandescent. The compact fluorescent lamp life varies from lamp to lamp but the range is between 8000 hrs to 12000 hrs compared to the 750 hrs of line voltage general service lamps. The biggest difference between the lamp technologies is the consumer cost, which is as little as $0.25 for a general service lamp (with minimal profit margin) to $5.00 (with good profit margin) for a compact fluorescent lamp. Just think of how much money the lamp companies could make if every general service lamp were replaced.

Because the compact fluorescent lamp technology is more efficient producing light than incandescent technology, legislators in every country jumped onto this bandwagon as a "green" movement gesture. These legislators (not one lighting designer or lighting engineer) started promoting the elimination of all incandescent lamps without an understanding of the different incandescent families, or the application-specific functions of these diversified lamps.

In fact, I found out why the Hon. Turnbull announced when he did. Hon. Turnbull found out that in the week following his announcement, Philips was going to announce their intentions of ending production and supply of general service lamps globally. As Australia, New Zealand and Fiji are the only countries where the primary line voltage is 240 volt, the loss of the Philips incandescent lamps would make Osram the only supplier of 240-volt lamps. If Osram were to follow Philips, these three countries would be left without a major lamp provider. Better to quit than be fired – Hon. Turnbull beat Philips to the punch and got the headlines!

This was all good information that I thought my lighting designer colleagues should know. With Mr. Randy Sabedra (IES NY Section President) and Ms. Meg Smith (IES NY Section Chairperson for Programming and Education), we held six open seminars related to the impact of banning the incandescent lamps on lighting design. The three major lamp representatives spoke and confirmed the lamp companies' agenda. We also learned about high content of mercury in compact fluorescent lamps and difficulties disposing of these lamps; shortened lamp life due to greater on/off cycles due to residential use vs. commercial use; the inability of compact fluorescent lamps to dim. Most importantly, we learned the lamp companies do not have new technology lamps to replace all the other non-general service lamps – maybe they will in three to five years. The lamp companies are not able to provide us with lamping certainties regarding what lamps will be available in the coming years.

This puts the lighting designer-engineer-fixture/lamp specifier in a very difficult position with current projects. We cannot tell the owners not to build their projects because we do not know what light sources will be available when the project is built or re-lamped. The only real option left is for us to specify a fixture using an incandescent technology to achieve the desired performance based on application, even though there is no viable fixture/lamp alternative, nor is there certainty that any or all incandescent sources will be available for re-lamping in the future. This is a major dilemma!

Since my Australia trip, we have seen the emphasis on the current high efficacy source shifting from compact fluorescent lamps (in part due to concerns about mercury) to the "White LED"[1] technology. The improved performance, color rendering and beam control are making this source more applicable. It is clear this is a direction the lamp companies are pursuing. There is hope that it may be possible that a "White LED" can achieve the beam control and appropriate light output that require an incandescent to be used. However, as long as the "White LED" is purely phosphor-based it will never be able to color shift, and consequently, it cannot replace the incandescent source for 4- & 5-star hotels where dimming and color shift are critical.

When I got off the plane from Australia, I was embarrassed that I got caught off guard. I was whining about how this was going to make it impossible to satisfy our client designers, and I was generally pissed off at our industry as a whole for passively letting the possible loss of all incandescent sources get so far along without a whimper or comment. Two and a half years later, we know little more than what we learned during our seminars, other than that the banning of incandescent technology sources is closer to reality. It would be easy to be a dinosaur and lament the loss of incandescent. Instead, we changed our design approach for all projects starting with the Grand Hyatt Melbourne Public Spaces. We only use low voltage halogen lamps for all fixtures because we believe there is a chance these lamps will survive the longest of the incandescent lamps. This approach has significantly reduced the power usage of all of our decorative fixtures.

In addition, we are trying to become the Timothy Leary of lighting sources, actively experimenting and searching for alternative solutions to achieve the simultaneous dimming and color shifting – thanks to Hon. Malcolm Turnbull.

FOOTNOTE

1. These solid state sources are technically not a white LED but a blue LED source making phosphor produce white fluorescent light. This is one of the greatest marketing ploys ever, as this source would be less marketable if it were named correctly as a "Miniature Fluorescent" source.

Polo/Ralph Lauren, New York (Craig Roberts)

Photograph by Francois Halard

Polo/Ralph Lauren, New York (Craig Roberts)

Photograph by Francois Halard

CRAIG ROBERTS
CRAIG ROBERTS ASSOCIATES
DALLAS, TEXAS

Craig began his career in 1976. He's a graduate of Parsons School of Design and a real professional. My first contact with Craig was a little frustrating – he was rejecting my shop drawings for his projects. I got to meet him later after those bad days of rejections. He is a real perfectionist and one of the few who insists on quality at the correct cost. His firm name changed in 1986 when he added associates Stephanie King, Robert Mapes and Granville McAnear – all wonderful designers in their own right.

Craig's varied list of projects could fill a book, from hotels to casinos to retail venues all over the world. His firm was the first of its kind in the Southwest. Craig has done countless Polo stores, and his most challenging lighting project is that wonderful flagship Polo on Madison Avenue in NYC.

POLO/RALPH LAUREN NEW YORK
BY CRAIG ROBERTS

One of the most challenging and rewarding projects of my career was for Ralph Lauren. The Rhinelander mansion on Madison Avenue was to be converted into the flagship for Polo/Ralph Lauren and was a completely new design concept for the company. I had worked on many Polo stores prior to that, but the design of those stores was more contemporary and much simpler (and smaller). The Madison Avenue flagship was to convey a much more glamorous image appropriate to its setting in a grand Madison Avenue mansion.

The building, however, did not have a glamorous interior by any means. It had been used for office space, and the interior had to be completely redesigned to match the grandeur of the landmarked historic facade. The signature staircase, for example, was not there at all. This was, I believe, in 1984 (the store opened in 1986). The brilliant interior architectural designer was Naomi Leff, and I worked very closely with her team and the Polo design staff in an attempt to integrate lighting as unobtrusively as possible into the luxurious residential ambience that was the design goal for the project.

In the mid-1980s, lighting equipment was far less sophisticated than that available today. If the project had been designed more recently, the approach taken would have been quite different. Now, it is possible to use flangeless recessed lighting fixtures with very small apertures that blend seamlessly into the ceiling, but that was not possible at the time. While some trimless fixtures were available, they were larger than we wanted to see there.

Architectural historians typically believe that when making modifications to a historic building, what is old should appear old and what is new should appear new. While only the facade of the building was historic, the same approach seemed appropriate for the interior. The best solution for the recessed lighting, essential for the dramatic highlighting of all the merchandise and extensive displays, seemed to be what is commonly referred to as a "pinhole" adjustable fixture. This at least allowed one continuous flange the color of the ceiling without a trim retaining ring visible on the ceiling. It created something that was obviously modern but with as little impact as possible on the elaborate plaster ceilings. Where possible, indirect lighting was introduced to highlight the beautiful ceilings and to provide ambient light.

At the time, retail lighting was also far less sophisticated than today, and there were few beautifully lit stores. At Polo, the approach was to utilize for ambient lighting, in addition to the lighted ceilings where possible, the kind of traditional antique decorative lighting that would have been appropriate to the period when the house was built. Against that soft, warm residential ambience I introduced intense highlighting of every single merchandise display. That created a very dramatic environment in which the merchandise was the clear star. This may seem obvious today, but to the best of my knowledge there were no stores with this carefully orchestrated specific type of high contrast drama prior to the Polo flagship.

Of course, the Polo design staff created a new standard in store display with this project, and the displays were elaborate and extensive. All the cases that could possibly be lit were lit internally, and the merchandise was featured in a warm glow that gave it the quality of jewelry, imparting to the store the feel of a very luxurious house museum.

At the same time that the Madison Avenue store was being completed, the Polo/Ralph Lauren store on the Place de la Madeleine in Paris was about to open. I was in Paris supervising the final adjustment of all the lighting in that store when I received a frantic call from Jerry Robertson at Polo in New York requesting that I board the next Concorde to New York to organize the adjustment of that lighting for the opening. The Paris store came together well, as it was a much smaller project, so after working into the night to finish that, I left the next morning for New York.

The scale of the New York store with its vast quantity of focal lighting required a monumental effort to complete the adjustment in time for the opening. The union contractors in New York were not helpful and could not have completed the work in time given their union rules and restrictions. They would not even allow anyone from Polo or my office to get on a ladder and adjust lighting ourselves, so we could not help. It became obvious quickly that they were not going to meet the deadline, so Polo concluded their contract. I assembled a team of top quality residential electricians that I had often worked with in Texas and immediately flew them to New York to complete the lighting adjustment in time for the opening. They did manage to meet the deadline with help from the rest of us, and the store opened with lighting perfectly adjusted.

Polo does a great job of maintaining lighting, and lighting in that store remains almost exactly as it was designed 25 years ago.

University of Michigan Cook Legal Reading Room (Gary Steffy)

Photograph Courtesy of Curt Clayton Studio

University of Michigan Cook Legal Reading Room (Gary Steffy)

Photograph Courtesy of Curt Clayton Studio

University of Michigan Cook Legal Reading Room (Gary Steffy)

Photograph Courtesy of Curt Clayton Studio

GARY STEFFY
GARY STEFFY LIGHTING DESIGN INC.
ANN ARBOR, MICH.

This man is the "professor" of a great cadre of brilliant people, a firm founded in 1982. He is also the author of two great technical books about lighting, both of which I have given as presents to those who could benefit from his expertise. Gary is very succinct in regards to what he wants technically, and when he writes a specification you read every line because he means exactly what he says.

His portfolio is unique in that he has tackled some of the most difficult projects in the world: restoration of the Michigan state capitol; the Cathedral of the Most Blessed Sacrament in Detroit; the Michigan Hall of Justice, and on and on. Since three of my grandkids are University of Michigan Wolverines, we have lots in common with Gary. I have had the pleasure of working with him on many complex and rewarding projects, including lighting parts of Michigan's law library. His right-hand man and partner is also a Gary – Gary Woodhull.

Gary S. writes that his most interesting challenge is luminance. Read what this concept means to him – and Go Blue.

MY GREATEST LIGHTING PROJECT
CHALLENGE AND WHY
GARY STEFFY

There must be several interpretations of the title charge, "My Greatest Lighting Project Challenge and Why." If it means, "Which *project* was my greatest challenge," I'd say none stand as greater than others. Not to denigrate projects, far from it, but rather to attest to the breadth of projects and the depth of challenges on each one – none is greater than any of the others. There is no single project that stands as *the* ultimate challenge. Every project has an embedded challenge (or two, or three, or more). While these challenges are broadly categorized as budget, schedule, design aesthetic, efficiency, scale, or personalities, none are above the rest and none are beneath the rest. That is, on one project, budget may be the driver. On another, schedule may be the driver. On most all projects, design is a driver. Am I proud of the budget projects? Why yes. I'm also proud of those projects that are notably efficient. And those that look terrific. I'm most proud of the projects that meet clients' and/or users' vision needs on a daily basis – and since I endeavor to meet such needs on *all* projects, every project ranks as a unique and great challenge. It just wouldn't keep me going otherwise!

On the other hand, if the title means, "Which *aspect* of a project is my greatest challenge," I'd say luminance. No contest. Without luminance – speaking broadly of grayscale and chromatic luminances and their contrasts – there is no visual tangibility to a project. Architectural surfaces regress and lose contrast, and/or color, crispness, and vividness. They lose their ability to convey information and therefore lose meaning. Spaces become bland and sleepy voids, blending together with no uniqueness. Scale and character are nonexistent. People aren't engaged. All of the rich architectural detail in the world at one extreme and all of the simple, clean-lined modern detail at the other extreme are pointless without the right execution of luminance. Reflected and transmitted light make architecture. Oh, make no mistake, to see light one must have dark. It is this choreography of light and dark – luminance – that makes the world visual for the sighted population.

Another aspect of a project that runs a close second as my greatest challenge is the balancing act necessary to maintain focus on luminance while addressing all of the other criteria vying for attention. This decade and perhaps the next are filled with sustainability and efficiency "criteria" mandates that sap focus on luminance. So much so that we *do* risk losing visual tangibility of interior and exterior built settings. All the resources used to quarry the stone, grow and harvest the wood, make the chemicals less toxic and more friendly, mine and mill the aluminum, make the steel – and get all this stuff to the project site – are for naught if the lighting renders those materials in the dim bland haze of greige settings epitomized by living and working environments in the iron-curtained communal blocks of what many Americans must have hoped was a long past and foreign experience.

Some code writers bloat light levels purportedly in the name of safety and progress, but to values that rival those used for casual reading, writing, and conversation in the States. Do we really need 10 footcandles *minimum* at *all* elevator thresholds; do we really need 10 footcandles *average* in *all* occupiable spaces where no daylight is offered; do we really need 10 footcandles *minimum* on all new stair treads?

Other code writers whack allowable lighting loads purportedly in the name of energy reduction and progress, regardless of code require-ments let alone appropriate design requirements. Still others insist that all of humanity, regardless of geographic location and general intentional activity, shall be in bed by 10 p.m. and lights-out accordingly. Such tar-geted "criteria" have devolved to baseless, nearly-whimsical exercises in vanity for the constituents espousing them. It is ironic in 2010 that "10" is the new default value!

As exemplified in a recent renovation/restoration project at the University of Michigan Law School's Cook Legal Research Library Reading Room, luminance rules. A pre-restoration photograph (Figure 1) shows the extreme nature of background luminances. An issue common where daylight is a primary source of ambient lighting, sky luminance is extraordinarily great on many days. If room surfaces are finished darkly, like the ceiling here, the resulting contrasts exacerbate the problem – making the darks look even darker and the brights look even brighter. Combine these background luminance issues with dark table tops and intense task lighting and the onset of tired eyes and headaches is accelerated during long study sessions.

Figures 2 and 3 illustrate the Reading Room and ceiling after restoration work. Refinishing and/or cleaning surfaces helped to improve luminances. However, the task lights at tables were refitted with lower-wattage, high-color-rendering, 3000K T5 fluorescent lamps on 2-level stepped-dimming ballasts controlled by photocells. The refinished tables are lighted to lower levels, yet the better-color lamps offer significantly improved appearance – making the most of 80-year-old embodied energy.

The big story, however, is the ceiling. The reflectance of the ceiling before any work was estimated at 5 percent. Cleaning and restoration of the ceiling were estimated to result in a 10 percent reflectance. Significant, but not enough to better balance the bright windows and the nighttime cavern appearance.

Uplighting the ceiling was an obvious technique to employ. Modifying an RSA footlight with custom snoots further hand-trimmed on site by the electrical contractor and using 39-watt PAR20 ceramic metal halide spot lamps in a new valance-air-grille detail at the base of the windows brings the ceiling to life.

Ceiling luminance, though not technically balanced with other surface luminances, is better aligned with the periodic heads-up-thought-breaks of work study tasks. Reductions in task lighting wattage, permanently dimming historic chandeliers, zoning the space and lights into thirds and using photocells to step down or step up task lights and ceiling uplighting according to daylight availability all combine for an estimated minimum 30 percent annual energy reduction over the pre-restoration system of T12 task lights, screwbase CFL retrofitted stack lights, and incandescent chandeliers.

Up to the challenge,
I am Gary Steffy, LC, FIALD, IES, Hon. Aff. AIA/MI
President of Gary Steffy Lighting Design Inc.
Images copyright Curt Clayton

Orlando Hilton Lobby, Florida (Charles "Chip" Israel)

Photograph Courtesy of Lighting Design Alliance

Orlando Hilton Lobby, Florida (Charles "Chip" Israel)
Photograph Courtesy of Lighting Design Alliance

CHARLES (CHIP) ISRAEL
LIGHTING DESIGN ALLIANCE
LOS ANGELES, CHICAGO, DUBAI

Chip, who like Randy Burkett is a Penn State graduate, formed his company in 1992; before that he worked for Ray Grenald. When Ray decided to sell the Los Angeles practice, I gave Chip a little advice, and might have been some help. I am extremely proud of this man who has become a legend in a very short time. His projects are so varied and diverse that one wonders how he's been able to accomplish so much so quickly. (You should ask him to show you his Dubai calling card ….)

What I am most proud of on Chip's behalf, and I think he would tell you the same, is that he is a Fellow of the IALD – a huge honor for such a young man. I also thank him for getting me interested in the IALD Education Trust. His most interesting challenge was a Disney project; his story of it is wonderful from beginning to end.

DISNEY'S WILDERNESS LODGE
CHARLES (CHIP) ISRAEL

Over the past two decades of work in the field of lighting design, since my graduation in 1984 from Penn State's architectural engineering program and my first job at Lutron in Philadelphia, every single project I worked on has been a true challenge to my creativity, analytical capabilities and my management skills, not to mention my sanity – but if I were to choose the single most challenging project, it would most probably be Disney's Wilderness Lodge in Florida's Magic Kingdom.

This deluxe hotel was inspired by the Great American Northwest National Park lodges from the turn of the 20th century, honoring our history and paying homage to our heritage with architectural grandeur, craftsmanship and artistry, while celebrating the majesty of the unspoiled wilderness which was, and one hopes will always be, our national legacy and trust. The lodge turned out magnificently, better than anyone could have imagined during its chaotic birth.

I come from the old school (though at the time it was anything but) – my first taste of the lighting industry came from my student days, summer employment in an architectural office. Yes, we actually drafted with pencils and sliding parallel rules, and I can still calculate and sketch a job in the time it takes the current generation of lighting designers to boot up their computer. At Lutron I had bosses like Gary Dulanski, Dr. Dimmer, Jim Yorgey and Paul Trively – the best teachers a young designer could hope to learn from. I ended up learning much, including important life lessons – the need to be punctual, the need to be well dressed and professional. Well, at least I was professional. But most importantly, I learned a code to live by: Listen to the client and service the client, no matter what.

To set the stage: The Disney job began under the auspices of Grenald Associates, but four months into the three-year schedule, the contract and job transitioned to our new firm, Lighting Design Alliance. This came at the moment in the late '80s when I was branching away from my longtime partner, the incomparably creative Ray Grenald.

Originally the Lodge was conceived to be set adjacent to an authentic Old-West village where the working folks would dress in period fashion. The village was, sadly, never built, but the challenges on the lodge project alone were many and varied and daunting, to say the least. This was actually the first Auto-CADD project we had ever done and most of our design team was in the process of learning the program – file management, plotter pen settings, etc. We were in battle mode the whole three years of the project.

The continuing disasters challenged both my creativity and patience – it was a continual learning experience. Remember, this was the early '80s when computers were in their infancy: files were lost; ghost images appeared and then disappeared, and the files were massive and had to be sent by disks – pioneer days where my architectural training skills with a slide rule and pencil still came in handy (and always will, I might add). Our internal network was the sneaker network, where we were copying files and running them to the different computers in the offices. Ironically the CADD revolution was labeled as a time saver, but at the time it was anything but that. Decades later, that promise has been delivered – but back then it was a pipe dream.

The designer on the project was Peter Dominick of Urban Design Group. In our first meeting he gave his vision: a hotel lobby unlike any other – grand, magnificent, startling, oversized – inspired by the great public works and National Parks Lodges of the turn of the century, a tribute to the Teddy Roosevelt image of American greatness, the power and grandeur of our land and our history, the Native Americans and the Europeans that came after. It would evoke the complex, bloody, fascinating history of the times, the interaction between Native cultures and pioneer spirit, an immense and complex vision of the American West. The lobby would boast a great, 85-foot-tall fireplace that would make the entire room glow, a warm flickering pulsing light for the weary traveler, a mellow ambience for the exhausted hunter – a place for martinis, Scotch and steaks, talk of big bucks bagged, the fish that got away, or the one that didn't.

It would include a bubbling spring flowing into a creek, tumbling over a sparkling waterfall and emptying into the featured swimming pool, as well as Fire Rock Geyser, fashioned after Yellowstone National Park's Old Faithful, erupting on the hour with a plume of water jetting 120 feet into the air – not to mention the 727 guest rooms sporting themes of wildlife, nature and Native American designs, plus some very, very special honeymoon suites and a private club to pamper the high rollers.

The grounds were to be illuminated by flickering lanterns and washed by that greatest of all lighting designers, the golden setting sun.

Peter Dominick's passion for the authenticity of the design was infectious and inspiring. Every team member started and finished the project with the same high level of passion that Peter inspired in us.

Taking our cue from American pioneer and Native American cultures, a true sense of being in harmony with nature permeates Disney's Wilderness Lodge – inside and out. Authentic decor and genuine artifacts pay homage to ancient Native American cultures and the pioneering spirit of early American explorers.

You can imagine what a challenge it was. Every minute on every plane ride I was sketching alternative designs, racking my brain for a better way to elaborate our theme. When I returned to home base in LA, I would immediately run to one of several libraries to research period designs, always checking and double-checking that every possibility had been covered before choosing a direction and implementing it. Every fixture on the project was custom designed with the inspiration coming from artists – from Remington to Georgia O'Keefe to Native totem carvers, sand painters, and of course we exhausted the resource of vintage photographs: cowboys, Indians, cattle drovers, schoolmarms, etc. My vacations were filled with trips to many of the great lodges like the Ahwahnee and the Old Faithful Inn.

The story line developed and every design aspect of the project was coordinated around it. Peter continually pushed us to review every option, challenging our constitutions and our aesthetics, rather than settling for the easy solution.

The design elements for the lighting were echoed in the graphics and were introduced into the furniture. It was very much like a Frank Lloyd Wright project, for which he designed every element, but in our case, we were spread across the globe, coordinating with fax machines and telephone calls, aiming for the same perfection, the same level of harmony between elements. That passion for perfection carried us all well past our design fees. No one cared. We had to continue on with the quest. The designs were refined. Extensive mockups were made and then the designs were refined again. This included full-scale prototypes of the tepee-shaped chandeliers, which were originally designed to be 10 feet tall, then enlarged finally to 15 feet tall. The construction administration phase continued late into the nights with every fixture being aimed just right.

When the Lodge was opened there was great fanfare and celebration, everybody cheered and toasted our success, we danced the night away – it was the magnificent end to a fantastically complex and challenging project. It was a wonderful moment in time, working with that team – such dedication to the job, such passion for perfection. It was a rare and wonderful team which met every challenge and crunched every deadline and delivered a perfect and harmonious design that continues to please Lodge visitors day in and year out. And for me, it was the experience of a lifetime.

Carlsbad Caverns (Ray Grenald)

Image Courtesy of i stock photo

RAY GRENALD
GRENALD WALDRON ASSOCIATES
NARBETH, PA.

Ray Grenald was one of the first lighting designers I had the pleasure of knowing. His career and experiences are bigger than life-size, from the Carlsbad Caverns to lighting the White House. Ray has always been a great teacher, and along with his partner Lee Waldron – who has a background in theater, film and television lighting – has established one of the most innovative lighting design firms in the world. Ray was there the day they formed the IALD. His story is fascinating.

HOW I GOT STARTED IN LIGHTING
RAYMOND GRENALD

MY BEGINNING

One spring day back before World War I, my dad closed his eyes and stuck a pin into a map of the United States. He had decided that the lower east side of Manhattan was not a healthy place to raise a child. So placing my mother, pregnant with my older brother, in the sidecar of his motorcycle, the two of them set off on a 1600-mile journey over what were then mostly unpaved roads to Kentucky.

My professor of Human Geography once commented that there were two regions of the United States which time had passed by virtue of the terrain and any routes of travel such as roadways or railroads. Because of this the people in the area tended to develop their own unique sub-cultures, languages, customs and values. One was the Rogue River Valley of Oregon (What! You've never heard of it?). The other was the Bluegrass Region of Kentucky.

Living in the early 1930s in Kentucky was equivalent to living in Manhattan during the late 1800s. It meant that, among other things, I grew up in what could be considered as the Victorian Era, a time that much of the remainder of the country experienced some 60-70 years earlier!

Regardless, it may have been foreordained that I would end up in the practice of lighting! Some of my earliest memories from childhood clearly deal with an interest with light.

Several of our neighbors drove electric cars which were steered with a tiller-like handle similar to one found on the rear of a small sailboat. With a single seat running athwart the body and glass windows all around, they provided excellent visibility, sat high enough to easily ford any small stream and traversed the streets virtually soundlessly. Since I never saw them after dark, I cannot testify whether the lanterns on either side were electric or carbide.

But, growing up in Kentucky in this era, I was exposed to a surprising variety of light sources. These included natural gas, as there was a great deal of subterranean gas found lying in cavities near the surface of the earth. Some farmers drilling for water would discover such pockets. This required little more than a box of matches for ignition, and made for some pretty spectacular events.

Kerosene lamps were also commonly relied upon in the days before the formation of the Rural Electrification Administration in the early 1930s. Both coal and wood were readily available and necessary for cooking and heating. One free by-product was light. At night, streets were illuminated by gas lamps or the relatively new mercury lamps which emitted an ominous light quality. Some red, white or green globes lined the parkway streets in town. These lamps did little to illuminate the park or streets, but they were comfortingly pretty.

On those hot humid nights so common to the Ohio River valley we would climb into our giant touring car (a four-door convertible with large wood spoke wheels) and go look for a cool breeze along the river.

About dinnertime the sidewheelers and paddlewheelers would head into shore to discharge passengers and cargo. The Showboats were festooned with white electric lamps and gave off a magical light that glistened in the reflections off the water.

When the weather was good some people would picnic in their cars or horse-drawn wagons. After the sun had set and darkness slowly settled over the river, the Showboats would come to life. Outdoor lines of light would flicker on and the steam calliope would "clear its throat" beginning with a series of shrieks before bursting into formulaic melodies by John Philip Sousa and, of course, Stephen Foster.

For a treat on some hot nights young couples, and even not-so-young couples with young children, could go to the German Beer Gardens. The men drank beer and the women and children enjoyed their lemonade or iced tea and listened to the musicians trying to keep their stringed instruments in tune. Young couples danced under the strings of colored lamps which were festooned across the sky and were strung over the fenced enclosures. Ice cream parlors would also run a string of white lamps across the fronts of their stores.

But the most memorable of the colorful lighting effects were designed by real professionals. Sometime in the early 1930s an outdoor open theater was built in a natural bowl in one of our major parks. Groups of live professional actors, actresses and musicians performed in traveling road shows from Broadway. In lieu of proscenium-hung curtains, water fountains surrounded the stage. This curtained mist was illuminated by concealed colored floodlights. The effect was entrancing and, on occasion, better than the actual performance.

The South and the great Midwest finally emerged from the Great Depression primarily because of World War II. I believe I "grew up" because of the War, especially when I was selected by the President (and my draft board) to serve my country. I received a personal letter from the President of the United States – "Greetings," it began … !

With two years of Aeronautical Engineering schooling behind me, I was "fortunately," I initially thought, inducted into the Army Air Force and attached to an aviation engineering squadron. This has always reminded me of the prediction implicit in that great WWI song, "How are you going to keep them down on the farm after they've seen Paree?!" In my case it was great cosmopolitan centers like the Aviation Cadet Center in San Antonio, Texas, and airfields in northern Brazil, West Africa, Libya and Egypt. I really was in the "Big Time"! My squadron operationally tested new types of airplanes and related equipment – some of which failed. Luckily, I survived an unexpected plane crash and spent a year in a military hospital recovering from assorted injuries.

By the time I was released from the hospital, I had lost some of my romance with flying and I switched my college major to architecture. I decided to move out west to facilitate healing. That move, an open prescription for narcotics and an entirely new philosophy about life changed me – and, here I am!

From the first day of a student's architectural education, he or she was given an increasingly complex series of design problems which started as a sophomore with a short two-hour sketch problem and increased in duration and complexity until the final year with an extensive graduate thesis problem.

In my sophomore year I came to a major point in my understanding and approach to creative design. The criteria by which we would be judged on our first building design problem included:

- Zoning
- Circulation
- Orientation
- Flexibility

• Appropriateness

Each of these elements and its task in the design process were explained to the class. When we were invited to ask questions, I responded as innocently as one would in a Dickens novel, "What about the *people*?"

After a lengthy pause, the response by my teacher was, I suppose in retrospect, clear and to the point: "*What about* the people?!?"

There was obviously some kind of disconnect. After a moment's consideration I realized that the professor really didn't know to whom I was referring. So I explained, "The people who will be using the building."

After another long pause, "Well, *what* about them?"

"Aren't we concerned about who they are or what they do and their working environment?"

After another long pause, "What do you mean by environment?"

I will note that this was in 1948; and, believe it or not, the word "environment" was neither common nor popular.

The design critic was very polite and at that point asked whether I minded if we could carry on this side conversation later in the day so that members of the class who were not interested in my question could leave – which they did!

I, in turn, headed for the school's library and opened up a voluminous dictionary to find the word "environment." I remember the complete definition was short and succinct: "That which evokes a response."

As an architectural student I realized that I was disturbed by this (apparent to me anyway) lack of discussion about my belief about the environment. I pointed out to my professor that architecture failed to focus on the human issue of perception and the resultant behavior. In other words, what the architectural designer conceived was not necessarily what the client or public perceived.

Later, I met with my second-year design critic who thought the question significant enough to discuss it further with the Dean. He explained that no one had ever asked that type of question before but acknowledged that it represented a valid issue worth further study. Fortunately, the chairman of the architecture department supported my "unique philosophy" and helped me develop a new curriculum which included: Human Physiology, Human Geography (now called Ecology), Experimental and Behavioral Psychology, Environmental Studies, Industrial Design and Public Speaking.

At first I referred to my approach to design as Environmental Architecture. However, in less than 10 years the word "environment" had begun being usurped by engineers and scientists to describe physical factors in a quantitative manner. I had to find another word to more accurately discuss what I believed. The word I chose was "experiential," which I hoped would convey my belief that the world around us exists as we experience it. And, by changing what we experience, the outcome can alter both our perception and our resulting response. Today, I call what I do "experiential architecture," which, of course, includes architectural lighting design.

Let me elaborate about how I apply this to my work. People experience the world differently, and not just because of culture differences. I see two major reasons for this. First, think of the brain as a piece of hardware; then, accept the fact that we now definitively know that each mature brain is wired differently. In addition, our learning process shapes the brain connections differently for every imaginable aspect of the living experience, which would include heredity, diet, disease, culture. What is remarkable is not the diversity, but the similarity in spite of all the pressure for diversity.

Secondarily, perception is a relative experience. As an example, one can ask, "How sweet is a grapefruit?" If we eat a sugary sticky bun first, the grapefruit will taste sour. However, if we taste something sour first it will taste sweet. Likewise, we first can ask similar questions such as: how large is a room, how bright, and so on. And then ask, "What is the intended experience of the room in relation to what occurs visually and psychologically in the room before, and the room after?" Perception is relative. Ancient civilizations were quite aware of this, as demonstrated by the remains of their architecture. I applied this to my work as an architect.

A few years later, one of my first architectural designs came to the attention of the local electrical utility company. They convinced me to join the Illuminating Engineering Society and to submit a house that I designed in the annual lighting design competition. I was responsible for the design of the architecture, interiors, furniture and lighting. It went on to win the IES National Residential Lighting Award. The following year another project took first place in an international residential lighting competition.

I found myself in demand as a public speaker and considered an expert in a field in which I knew myself to be unqualified, although my instincts were pretty good.

But, I knew I had better set about learning before I made a fool of myself. General Electric copied much of the design intent of the first house at their teaching facility in Cleveland. The people at that company later became my friends and early mentors. I soon found myself working at two professions – as an architect and as a lighting designer. So, in 1966, I made the decision to limit my professional practice to architectural lighting design and cease the general practice of architecture.

In a career of over 50 years, first as an architect and later as an architectural lighting designer, there have been hundreds of projects varying in size and complexity – from individual homes to urban streetscapes. And yet with each, the lighting design has been conceived to evoke predetermined responses.

Several lessons to be learned regarding experiential spaces are:

1. Time is a major issue in the design of human experiences.
2. A good designer learns when "enough" may be too much.
3. The moment that an additional sense (of the five senses) is involved, the impact of the existing design elements must be

re-evaluated!

LIGHTING FOR THE EXPERIENCE OF DINING

If I were designing a dining space, my first task would not be to write a cookbook or a dissertation on the digestive process because it relates to eating. Yes, I would be interested in the anatomy of interior design, but much more. I would strive to understand what lies within the function and purpose of the space. What will the people be doing there?

People of different cultures do dress differently. They also act differently. As any Chinese or Japanese person will tell you, civilized people eat with chopsticks! People from India would disagree of course. In Mumbai, everyone knows that civilized people eat with their fingers. Though personally, I must admit that in the western civilizations of Europe and the Americas, well-mannered people eat with knives and forks, though wielding these utensils differently.

It is important to remember that humans are animals and as such subject to all the ills that are normal to that category. Observing other animal types you see elements of commonality to various sub-species; for instance, sensitivity to light and movement. Plants are sensitive to light, but not to movement. There are of course exceptions. In the evolutionary process, animals which did not respond to light and movement either did not eat or were eaten.

So, a major question to ask is what exists in common among these people of different cultures, places and times in history when analyzing their eating habits? Well, we can simplify the question by limiting those of whom we speak. Elements of commonality are followed through deductive reasoning:

1. We speak of animals.
2. These animals are specifically – People!
3. To quote Aristotle, "People are by nature social creatures."
4. Eating is the solitary process of ingesting food for survival. If

we were automobiles, it would be called "refueling."

5. There is a difference between eating and dining.

6. Dining is a social activity normally involving two or more people.

I recognize that in the broadest sense eating is an ablution. Eating in a fast food restaurant is "social refueling" – appealing to the most basic animal instinct. But dining is an act of social bonding. Dining in its highest sense can be one of the most civilized experiences in human gratification.

Additionally, tactile sensation must also be considered, to the point of representing a conscious or unconscious distraction. This latter issue represents an often overlooked task in casual dining. Imagine dining for a prolonged period such as one or more hours – even three or four hours. Our bodies' circulation system demands periodical stimulation – let's think of it as creative squirming.

For fine dining, all of this means "No" to a sensory-deprived area. And, "No" to an area with exaggerated stimulus. But, "Yes" to acoustics where sound is of a very low level and where the nature of any sound is unambiguously clear and familiar. Instead, what is the intended effect of the experience and what does the light need to do to make it happen? The senses of smell and taste we must leave in the hands of an artist of another kind – the chef. The best of them understand how to marry odors, flavors and visual appearances and match them to wines and other beverages in order to achieve one of the highest levels of gratification in civilized humans.

✧   ✧   ✧   ✧

And this is how we need to address the lighting. It isn't just how much light needs to occur at the tabletop. The lighting should be designed to enhance the physical appearance of everyone and to be "social petal" in nature – to bring people together in the same manner as being around a glowing campfire in a forest clearing. The spatial surrounding needs to be illuminated sufficiently so that what is threatening can clearly be seen as missing (comedian and humorist alike should clearly misunderstand that).

And now having said that, let us finish with an epicurean experience of lighting. Philosophically and fundamentally I believe that light is the one intangible element of architecture. And, it can be magical when it is anonymous, but adds to the visual delight of the space.

There are three basic issues to be satisfied by the lighting designer for good dining. The proper lighting for:

- Surround Space
- Faces
- Food

The surround must be illuminated unambiguously to characterize the setting and dispel any sense of real or implied threat. The lighting on feature elements should be coherently focused from one direction whenever possible while casting shadows in an attendant manner.

The faces of those who surround you should appear friendly and healthy. Young people want to appear attractive and people of achievement want to appear interesting. This is accomplished through the use of high color rendering lamp sources and reducing hard shadows from lighting that is badly placed.

Lastly, the food should be illuminated as one would a work of art – both beautiful and irresistible (even when reduced to crumbs).

In the case of one opulent dining space I designed only for use on "special occasions," the lighting proved so pleasant, attractive, irresistible and such a seductive sybaritic experience that the client and family began dining in the space nightly. Dining soon led to lingering and remaining seated for unreasonably long periods. And, as one might expect after a year dining in this fashion, the members of the family grew grotesquely fat and the client suffered a near fatal coronary!

USING LIGHT TO DIRECT MOVEMENT

Another more profound problem involved a particular President and his habit which disturbed members of the White House staff at daily morning meetings in the Roosevelt Room located across the hall from the current Oval Office. This room was the original Oval Office of President Theodore Roosevelt and now serves as the major conference room in the West Wing. Each morning, the Chief of Staff meets with the members of his staff to discuss the various tasks to be performed that day. During the morning meeting, the President will often drop in.

In this instance, President Reagan would attend the morning meetings – during which, he would stroll up and down along one side of the staff members seated at the table who turned or swiveled in their chairs in order to maintain eye contact and to show proper respect.

In meeting with staff members to familiarize myself with the functioning and needs of the space, one of the members jokingly asked whether I could use the new lighting design to get the President to stand still. This comment was greeted with amused laughter of everyone in attendance. There was an even bigger laugh when I responded, quite seriously – "Of course." They thought I was joking. I wasn't!

The Roosevelt Room was a depressing space devoid of windows and with a large square skylight which had been plastered over at the beginning of WWII out of concern that it would be an easy target for German bombers. I was told that the room was used around three hours a day. The existing lighting system was installed in the early '50s and was comprised of glaring fresnel lens downlights on switches and supplemented by an assortment of floor or tabletop lamps controlled by pull-chains – some three-way, some one-way, some inoperable.

The new lighting employed a central dimmer panel with a four scene preset and was designed for four distinct activities:

1. After-hour tours of the West Wing
2. Dining – lunch and coffee breaks
3. General conferences
4. General conferences – with the President in attendance

The lighting design consisted of refurbished table and floor lamps for the visual background, recessed halogen downlights for task lighting on the conference table, and cross-lighting for faces and wall-washers for artwork. The original skylight was reconstructed with dimmable fluorescent lighting above the white translucent lay-light to appear as "real" daylight. We added three low voltage adjustable accent fixtures as key-light, fill-light and back-light for a special purpose. These were carefully aimed and with a set intensity.

When the President entered the newly re-lighted room for the first time, the Chief of Staff pushed one button on his remote control. All halogen lamps as well as the skylight dimmed and executed a slow cross-fade with the three accent lights. The President intuitively understood both the intent and the mechanics of the lighting system. Later I was informed by the Chief of Staff that he walked to the "significant end of the table and sat down – and never again strolled the room." He dominated the room; someone said, "Not even Charlton Heston could have appeared more important!"

Incidentally, after the new lighting was completed, it became the most popular room in the West Wing, often being used as much as 12 hours a day.

LIGHTING THAT EMPLOYS ALL MY BELIEFS

The most complicated and most satisfying project that I have designed resembled a moonscape, only far more complex.

Carlsbad Caverns National Park is located in the southeastern corner of New Mexico. It would be lost if placed within a gigantic cave such as Mammoth Cave in Kentucky. But Carlsbad Caverns is considered by many to be the most beautiful cave in the world. While I have visited many caves in the world, I have yet to find any with comparable grandeur and innate beauty.

When I began this project in 1972, the estimated length of the cave was 18½ miles long. It is now known to be larger. The bottom of the cave is approximately 950 feet deep and the asphalt paved trail is 3½ miles long. The humidity within the cave is close to 99 percent and the temperature an even 55 degrees year round.

After descending 1½ miles from the surface through often breath-taking formations, the visitor finds a rest area with an underground fast-food restaurant and a large elevator to the surface. Or, if you wish to continue the journey, there is an additional two miles of trails through the "Big Room."

To enter the cave, the visitor descends a steep, zig-zag ramp hundreds of feet into what appears as a black hole. This long descent assists in the adaptation of the eye from the 10,000+ footcandles of a sunlit day at the surface into the near complete darkness of the cave. Projecting horizontal shelves of rock at one point provide necessary seating for resting stressed muscles and further eye adaptation.

In the summertime, the area beyond the seating area is occupied by sleeping bats, which upon awakening relieve themselves. The accumulated animal waste results in an odor that serves to encourage visitors to move on as quickly as they are able.

Following the trail further downward, the visitor passes an area called the auditorium. This is perhaps the size of a football field devoid of anything of real beauty. In a word it is "boring" with a marsh-like floor and plain drab walls and ceiling.

Several hundred feet beyond, the asphalt trail runs through a narrow stone divide with high cliff walls. It then extends 50 or 60 feet further where one officially enters the cavern.

Caves are considered "living things." The magic ingredient for sustaining life is water. In this particular cave, it drips down, flows through and oozes up. The system of stalagmites and stalactites grew with time. In 1974, someone in the National Park Service realized that Carlsbad Caverns was dying – it was drying out! After some study, it was determined that the culprit was the existing incandescent lighting system.

The previous attempts at lighting of the cave ignored the geological wonder and beauty of the caverns. By simply using one light source generally close to the trail, the entire experience became a dull monochromatic experience. The Park Service records had shown that the majority of the visitors left at the midpoint of the journey rather than continuing through the full extent of the cave.

After arranging a full-size mockup of six different lighting approaches, I was given approval to proceed with the work. The new lighting approach does not require a step-by-step discussion of cave lighting. What is of significance is the creation of an all-inclusive philosophy which took into consideration the issue of human perception resulting in a dramatic shift in response.

There is no accurate engineering survey of the cave because it is far too complex. So, in order to fully understand the layout of the cavern system and the visitor experience, I walked the cave top-to-bottom and bottom-to-top. I also walked along the one-way loop of the "Big Room" both backward and forward over two dozen times and memorized as much as I could of what I encountered and saw.

There were many human aspects that were important in the revolutionary changes to the lighting redesign. And, were I to do it again today, I am not certain that I could achieve the same result. Still, the principles remain the same. Some of these factors appear so irrelevant that to mention them should elicit a snort or even a chuckle or two:

1. Age – no, not the cave's – my age! Now more than 35 years later, I lack the physical stamina and much of my memory. As you can imagine it would be impossible to plan a series of sensory climaxes or to avoid boring repetition without the degree of knowledge and understanding gained from traversing the cavern system dozens of times to etch the experience in my mind.
2. Identification of the physiological issues which needed to be addressed.
3. Awareness of the physical challenges which had to be dealt with.
4. The potential for psychological arousal which could be exploited.
5. The need to simplify maintenance.
6. The need to reduce energy consumption.
7. The importance of education for the visitors.
8. The creation of a going-away gift of an enriched memory.

There are fewer contrasts in life greater than light versus darkness – each is enhanced by contrast with the other! This situation quite naturally exists in most every cave. Part of our task was to take this opportunity to exploit the extreme range of contrast, but do it in the context of safety in order to deal with the cave's often slippery-when-wet asphalt ramps, which generally require a higher level of illumination.

I used 14 different lamp sources to address the visual complexity of the cave. All sources were completely concealed. With only two location exceptions, all lamps were "white," although they included incandescent, fluorescent and mercury sources. Both these exceptions included single blue color fluorescent lamps which were heavily baffled and mounted so that the lamps were blocked from view. Each was located at the bottom of very deep "holes" (one was called the "Bottomless Pit"). The very slight blue light would evoke an image of infinity and people stopped throwing objects into these holes.

The slight range of lamp color temperatures helped me to add depth and dimension to the cave, much as an artist would with the hue of pigment, by using low color temperature fluorescent lamp sources for features that were closer in distance and more distinct and using a series of cooler higher color temperature fluorescent sources for distant features.

The issue of color fidelity was considered of prime importance. Samples of different rock or mineral formations were assembled, labeled and taken to the surface where color characteristics under natural daylight allowed for accurate description. Back in the darkness of the cave, I used the information to expose the formations to the spectrum of my selected lamp vocabulary that provided the most accurate color rendering.

The new lighting was conceived to address the human experience of the journey through the cave and to provide a greater appreciation for the natural wonder that was to be explored. At the bottom of the entrance, we illuminated the face of the walls and the entry gate – a visual terminus – by putting a definite "there" to the end of the long, slightly perilous journey. Moreover, the area at the stone shelf which served as a bench was more brightly lighted to serve as the defining place to rest – at a point further away from the stench of bat guano.

After this point, I dropped the illumination level more quickly and used indirect fluorescent lighting to wash out what little form existed at the "auditorium." By the time the cave visitor had reached the gateway to the narrow defile beyond the cavern entrance, the level of illumination was one hundredth of a footcandle. This was adequate for safe illumination because a white stone curb lined the sides of the black asphalt path and there was nothing to "step in" or "trip over" on the path. The existing exposed red flood lamps and fixtures were replaced by concealed narrow beam quartz lamps which were dimmed to achieve a warmer light and to extend lamp life. In addition, a small concealed 5000K fluorescent light was used to illuminate behind the formation.

Emerging at the end of the trail the visitor was stunned by a beautiful formation called the Devil's Spring. A slender red stone stalactite from above joined a slender stalagmite rising from a pool of water. As the visitor passed through the narrow divide, the reflected light off the stone became the sole source of illumination. Because it was the most striking and most colorful element encountered by the visitor up to this moment, the formation's impact was powerful, and made more significant by the lighting.

The Devil's Spring formation was pivotal in its position on the trail. Its character was to represent the first element, philosophically, in the manipulation of the balance of the cave's architectural lighting for the following reasons:

1. The formation sat in a pool of water. The entire cavern was carved out by water and I felt that the presence of water was so overtly obvious that it should be emphasized.
2. All of the lighting fixtures were concealed.
3. Though the area was small, light was used to both illuminate and model form. In that case, the incandescent accent lighting came from one direction, casting coherent shadows to express the form of the stalagmite and stalactite forms. The fluorescent lighting of the background wall exaggerated the depth of the space by the variation in color temperature.
4. The background "wall" was reflected in the pool and added the necessary separation of materials.

The cave visitors were given a false sense of security by the color and scale of the formation, because 35 feet beyond the Devil's Spring, space exploded into nothingness. A wooden railing prevented further movement ahead. This was necessary because the trail ended at a precipice where the cavern floor dropped away hundreds of feet below, and the ceiling appeared for the first time as a significant plane hundreds of feet above. The cave wall to the left fell back perhaps 80 feet and the far wall across the large cavity was perhaps 200 feet away. Unlike other surfaces, this wall was inconsistent in form, with large punctuations of the surface creating perceived balconies and large openings providing views of impenetrable blackness and interstitial trails below and beyond.

The impact upon the cave visitors was predictable. The response was to inspire a feeling of terror and to evoke a near universal desire to turn back.

While the cave was in truth a very dangerous place, it had been made safe courtesy of the United States Park Service Rangers stationed at the railing, whose task was to point out that returning to the cave entry at this point would necessitate a long, difficult hike back and upward; however, if they turned right and followed the handrail separating them from the abyss they could see the trail leading down to a very tangible floor of rock and some rather interesting formations at a well-defined end of the trail.

The lighting of this space is from concealed fluorescent lamps with very cool color temperatures of 5000K and 7500K. The lighting is placed to minimize form and shadows and to heighten the sense of depth. The lamps were the highest color rendering light sources available.

Something else of great importance came up at this point in the journey. How long can individual excitement be sustained? This is a significant question which is worthy of research either by the military or, more importantly, by Disney. Lacking such data but having closely observed my own children, I made certain assumptions:

1. The period of interest sustained by people varies with age.
2. If the participant is forced into a period of sensory deprivation prior to reaching a state of boredom, then interest can be sustained for prolonged periods.

Trial and error tended to validate this theory, which I call pacing. The process proved relatively simple and the pacing process in the cavern proceeded as follows: Periods of stimulation or excitement were followed by periods of relaxation, re-sensitization through sensory deprivation, or perhaps the best word would be boredom. Furthermore, periods of excitement became more intense and shorter in periods of experience. Periods of relaxation became longer and blander as the visitor proceeded.

Because it was impossible to move the various formations so as to juxtapose them for the greatest effect, compromises had to be made. A number of truly beautiful formations in the "wrong place" were virtually erased by allowing them to disappear into darkness, or by using light to create a level of misdirection.

Another important part of the lighting solution dealt with orientation. Walking through the cave over and over again, I noticed other subtleties in perception that were corrected. For example, one cluster of huge stalagmites, called the Hall of Giants, was experienced from the trail in which visitors meandered by moving through and around these forms. Each time I walked throughout these 85-foot-high forms I was left with a sense of uneasiness.

Finally I came to realize that the original lighting was aimed at the face of each of these "giants" in the direction of the person's movement. This is not the way we encounter forms in real life, whereby the sun and resulting shadows are coherent (i.e. they always come from only one direction). To test this, I placed temporary lighting according to my theory. It worked!

With the light coming from basically one direction the visitor had the feeling that the trail meandered through the formations rather than the sense that the formations rotated around the visitor. As a result, and whenever possible, groups of formations were illuminated from the same, or very close to the same, compass orientation.

With the lighting that was implemented, the cave took on an entirely new appearance that was experienced in a totally new way. Visitors, who previously left at the mid-point, now continued along the entire 3½-mile walk. Portions of the cave that were previously "unseen" came into existence and encouraged further exploration. Maintenance was reduced to the point that the Park Service "gained" an additional employee, through the money saved by simplified maintenance and by lamps with longer life. Also significant was that the dryness caused by the previous lighting had ceased being a problem.

CLOSING

Throughout my life I have pursued this quest of experiential architecture and how the experience of one space or a series of spaces can evoke a predetermined response. Of greatest importance, one must remember that Light can be Magic! That is a concept that I learned early on from another mentor and personal friend – Lesley Wheel. It has stayed with me all these years. Architecture is the art of expressing space and the science of enclosing it. Light is the medium by which it is perceived. We use light as architecture. We build with light.

SAVING THE BEST FOR LAST…
FAMILY, FRIENDS, AND FRIENDLY RIVALS

Family and friends … Without them, the road gets rocky. With them, you can go on forever.

Family first: I'm a lucky man. I met my dream girl early in life and now we're surrounded by our gifts – our children and grandchildren.

In May, 2009, Roz and I made a trans-Atlantic crossing on the Queen Mary II from New York to London. Each day of the six-day trip, the clock was set ahead one hour. We arrived with no jet lag, or even ocean-liner lag, and enjoyed our week in London.

What a metaphor for raising kids: enjoying each day of the journey and then having the pleasure of reaching the destination – in our case, our 12 grandchildren. It seems like just two weeks ago that we were having fun with our foursome, and before we knew it, we were delighted grandparents to a dozen!

Since we had our four children in six years in our 20s, we were young enough to have fun with them, and the gifts of grandparenthood have come while we still have our marbles and can count our grandchildren among our friends. How lucky we are – but I'm getting ahead of myself.

Marti made us parents at age 23, when kids today are still trying to figure out if and when they should grow up.

She was our little doll to play with, for Roz to have fun teaching and dressing up – that is, when I wasn't busy turning her into a tomboy. Before we knew it, she was in college, at Northwestern University in Evanston, Illinois, a beautiful campus on Lake Michigan.

The fact that she and our two oldest boys went there was poetic justice for Roz, who had applied there a generation before after an academically successful first year at the University of Illinois. She was not admitted because, at that time, Northwestern had a two-percent Jewish quota, unbelievable as it seems today to those who have forgotten the quota system. It was before Lester Crown had donated the Student Union there and before the 1963-64 Civil Rights Act. It was the first time Roz encountered the anti-Semitism I had grown up with.

Marti graduated from Northwestern Phi Beta Kappa, stayed on to get a Master's in teaching, and has had an illustrious career as an educator here in California, from Saratoga High School, teaching English and coaching swimming, to Harvard Boys Prep School in Studio City, where she not only taught social studies and English and was 7th grade counselor, but coached 7th and 8th grade boys in basketball and led them to two unbeaten seasons – to the amazement of all the fathers whose first reaction was, "A girl coach?"

She went on to get another Master's degree at UCLA in psychiatric social work, obtained her LCSW license and had a successful practice dealing with troubled adolescents until she decided to return to teaching. She is now dean of 7th grade and algebra teacher for 7th and 9th grades at Sierra Canyon, a private school in Chatsworth, where many of her students are offspring of big names in the entertainment industry.

Her marriage to Phil Artsis recently ended, but their children, our only local grandchildren, remain extremely close to us, geographically and emotionally. Our oldest granddaughter, Jamie Artsis, set the standard for the third generation of grandchildren. I watched her play organized soccer as a four-year-old, watched her develop into an athlete with a discipline I did not have as a young man. It was also my pleasure to see her become an unbelievable scholar, like her mother. We stood in the hot sun in Virginia during August, 2001 while her club team won the national soccer tournament. As a freshman at Harvard-Westlake High School, she played on the varsity soccer team as a starter from the first day. She was recruited by over 20 Division 1 schools, including Harvard and Yale. Michigan was her final choice and she was an All-American as a freshman. She enjoyed a full scholarship there and was one of only 6 athletes in the history of University of Michigan soccer to score three goals in one game against a Big Ten opponent. Do not get the feeling that she only excelled at soccer; when she graduated, she was also commended as a scholar, graduating Phi Beta Kappa like her mother.

After graduation, she was chosen by Nike to work in Oregon for a time. After the recession began, all jobs were frozen and she came back home. Jamie now enjoys working at Sony Pictures, in print advertising, for "a perfect boss."

Jamie and I have had a very special relationship since the day she was born. If I could write a recipe for a granddaughter, she would be the model. She is sweet, sensitive and caring.

Our oldest grandson, Max Artsis, was born two years after Jamie. He is one of those rare individuals who has everything -- personality, good looks, and the ability to talk to anyone on any subject. I am not saying this because he is my grandson, but this youngster has evolved into a mature, well-balanced man. While at Calabasas High School, he was the lead in most musical and theater events. In "The Music Man," he was outstanding. He not only was great as an actor, but as the quarterback for the high school, he could throw a football fifty yards in the air. He recently graduated from the University of Michigan. After graduation, he was selected to be an NBC/Universal page, a rare honor, where young men and women are trained to be television executives. Max currently works on "The Tonight Show with Jay Leno." He loves acting, and, if things go right, you will see his name on many billboards. I admire his work ethic, his self-discipline, and his ability to strive to achieve his goals. I am proud to say that he is not only my grandson, but my "sports buddy," and my friend.

✿   ✿   ✿   ✿

While in high school, our oldest son, Steve, "inherited" Marti's swimming school when she left for college. He joined Marti at Northwestern when she was a junior and immediately commenced working toward his premed major. When he was just two years old, Steve declared he wanted to be "just like Dr. Clark," our family pediatrician. While Steve also studied psychology, we believed he would choose to be "just like Dr. Clark," a pediatrician, since he always loved being around little ones. After medical school, his interests led him towards cardiology, and then to a fellowship in electrophysiology. Since finishing his training, Steve has been part of a large cardiology group covering two counties on the Jersey Shore, has lectured, and is an outstanding physician, but he is still the same sweet, unassuming person he was as a child.

His graduation from medical school was an emotional experience for us and for my mother, who accompanied us. To think that we'd raised a young man who would save generations of patients from illness and potential death was thrilling.

While at Northwestern, Steve met and married Cathy Daniels, with whose large, mostly medical family he remains close even though their marriage ended in 2004. With Cathy, a talented architect, he gave us three lovely granddaughters, each remarkable in her own right.

Steve and Cathy settled in New Jersey and we welcomed their first, Julia, into our family just ten months after her older cousin Jamie. Both Steve and Marti loved having daughters about the same age, and compared notes often.

Julia, who was an adorable little girl with her blonde hair and big brown eyes, has grown up to be a delightful, strong, independent young woman who makes circles of friends everywhere she goes. She graduated from the University of New Hampshire, then crossed the country to Eugene, Ore., where she taught pre-school, and has settled near Boulder, Colorado, to be near a dozen of her "best friends." After a summer working in organic gardening, she is spending the winter working and playing at a ski resort. She is a true Renaissance woman who knows how to enjoy her life.

Within 11 months of Julia's arrival, her sister Nicole was born, our first dark-haired kewpie doll! Together with Jamie and Max, they soon became the Big 4. Even though the cousins were bi-coastal, they spent many fun times (with their parents) at Disneyland on the West Coast, made trips to Vermont and New Jersey, and grew to be inseparable whenever possible. What fun they were!

Nicole, or Niki, was always sweet, task-oriented, serious, and breezed through academically. Like her sister, she graduated from Rumson, New Jersey, High School. With her long graceful legs, she was a natural for the track team and received many scholastic honors. Niki followed her parents to Northwestern but her interests were neither medicine nor architecture. She majored in economics and is now working with a hedge fund in Chicago. Niki loves living in the city where her "Grammy Roz" grew up. She calls us often and is a joy. We look to her to change the "culture" of Wall Street as she rises in her profession.

Four years after Niki, Steve and Cathy surprised us with yet another little brunette beauty, Marielle. She seems to have been born with a sense of style – even as a pre-teen, she could advise friends and family on how to create a "look." Marielle's fashion instincts are probably the outgrowth of her mom's aesthetic abilities in designing houses, and her dad's amazing eye in his hobby of photography. I've no doubt Marielle can have a future in some aspect of the retail or design world. She is charming, smart and beautiful, and will likely make her mark once she completes her training.

Our second son, Jeff, went to Northwestern two years after Steve. Jeff seems to have been destined to be an outstanding attorney and has always been an avid student of politics. As a child, he was obsessed with Bobby Kennedy's candidacy for president, and was heartsick when Kennedy was assassinated one day after Jeff's birthday, June 5, 1968. Years later, Jeff was a major fund-raiser for Hilary Clinton's presidential campaign at the behest of Senator Evan Bayh.

After graduating from Northwestern, Jeff went to law school in Washington, D.C. Living and studying in the nation's capital served to heighten his political interests. Jeff was on the Law Review, and when his brother Mike applied to the same law school two years later, Jeff wrote a letter of recommendation on Law Review stationery, extolling Mike's virtues as a writer. What a proud moment for Roz and me to read one brother praising another so eloquently.

After working in two outstanding law firms in D.C. and New York City, Jeff formed his own firm and is now a founding partner of Zukerman, Gore, Brandeis and Crossman, a boutique business law firm in Manhattan. As the song goes, "If you can make it there, you'll make it anywhere."

Jeff married Ruth Katzka, with whom he had twin girls, Kate and Rachel. Roz had always wanted twins, and now we had them, thanks to Jeff and Ruth. As New Yorkers, Kate and Rachel soon grew into streetsmart kids who knew their way around that amazing city.

Rachel graduated from Horace Mann High School, is now attending Northwestern (do you detect a theme here?) and is in the same sorority as her cousin Niki. Kate graduated from Hewitt High School, a fine girls' school, and is very happy at Tulane University in New Orleans – an interesting departure from the Big Ten schools her sister and most of her cousins attended.

When the girls were six years old, their parents' marriage also ended, and we did not get to see as much of them as we would have liked. One of the sad things about our mobile society is that everyone lives so far away, and it's hard to spend as much time with all 12 of our grandchildren as would have been possible if we all lived in closer proximity. Modern technology in many ways has prevented real intimacy, substituting electronic contact.

But Kate and Rachel's joint Bat Mitzvah was delightful; we were so proud of their accomplishments, and seeing them blossom into lovely young women. Their parents have done a wonderful job of nurturing their individual interests. Rachel loves writing and will likely make that part of her life's work. Kate, echoing her dad's interest in politics, spent a summer working with the "Hilary for President" campaign. Both girls are in the middle of their college years, and it will be interesting to see where their interests lead them.

Shortly after the millennium, Jeff married Kathy Bransford, a lovely young woman and talented Wall Street powerhouse. She is very family oriented and manages to bring her young family to visit us often. Kathy and Jeff have given us our two youngest grandchildren, Jake Joseph (named after Roz's father) and Molly Marie (named after Kathy's grandmother). With all the females in his life, I'm sure Jeff enjoys having a son to do "guy things" with and teach about dinosaurs, sports and U.S. presidents. Jake is a fun First Grade student at Horace Mann, loves his sisters, and lives too far away from us! Little Molly is a pre-schooler, also at Horace Mann, and a miniature Kathy, an interesting combination of tomboy and girly-girl who can play trucks with Jake and then head off to ballet class. Roz and I wish we could be more a part of their growing-up years instead of just seeing them intermittently, as was true of their big sisters.

As noted earlier, Mike is our youngest son and has the most fun sense of humor in our whole family. He went to UC Berkeley, the only school he applied to after graduating from Beverly Hills High. At the time, Roz asked him why he didn't apply to any other UC schools as back-ups in case he didn't get in. His comment was, "Why give them any options?"

Mike met Hilary Davis at Berkeley when they were both 20. They got married at 30 after they both went to different law schools. Mike went to the same law school as his brother in D.C. and worked in a law firm there which represented many financial institutions in the area. He passed the D.C. bar, as well as several surrounding states. This led to his being head-hunted to a San Francisco law firm when Wells Fargo acquired Crocker Bank. He and Hilary moved to the Bay Area and live in a quiet small town near Oakland called Piedmont.

Hilary went to Northwestern Law School – we had to like that – and worked at an environmental law firm in Spokane, Wash. Mike's and Hilary's lovely wedding in the Napa Valley produced three wonderful grandchildren.

Their oldest, Lynn, graduated from Piedmont High, where she excelled, was on the newspaper, and spent several spring breaks building homes in Mexico for Habitat for Humanity. She is attending U. of Michigan (could be another pattern building there), got into their Ross School of Business and is minoring in Mandarin. Given that combination, she has great employment chances with a financial or government agency. Lynn is independent, loves sports and music, and like her brother, played piano for many years. She calls us often with updates on her activities. We love hearing from her.

Our next oldest grandson, Brad, was born two years after Lynn. He loves art, briefly considered architecture as a career, studied acting, and is as enthusiastic as the rest of his family about the great outdoors. They have often gone as a family on camping trips, skiing, playing tennis and biking, and Brad even recently went spelunking. He spent a month after graduation traveling through Europe and showed his writing skills in a fun, fascinating travelogue. He was accepted at all of his choices for college, and is now at the University of Oregon enjoying their winning streak. (We all want our kids and grandkids to have it easier than we did, but it doesn't seem to be working out that way scholastically. When we applied to schools, we just showed up. There were no SATs or ACTs as requirements. Were those the "good old days"?

Mike and Hilary have really created a family unit that enjoys doing things together. To celebrate their 20th anniversary and both their 50th birthdays, they took their whole family to Eastern Europe and made an educational trip out of it, including hiking in the Alps. Their family motto appears to be "Carpe Diem," or "Seize the Day!"

Sara, their youngest child, is named after Roz's mother and is an adorable, bright 11-year-old. She seems to have inherited her father's sense of humor, and is cute, sweet and a very interesting young lady. Her mom is the coach of her soccer team. Sara also loves swimming, tennis, basketball and dance.

As their youngest, Sara has a very special place in their family. Since I had two older siblings who spoiled me, I can identify with her position in the batting order – not a bad place to be! As I write this, I know she is looking forward to getting her first cell phone as she enters sixth grade.

All of Mike and Hilary's children are polite, well-mannered and never forget to actually write thank-you notes – quite refreshing in this age of e-mails.

All our grandchildren have a very special place in our hearts and minds. We appreciate the opportunities we do get to see them, and even though they're farther away than we'd ideally like them to be, as Roz's father used to say, "I would rather hear good news from far than bad news up close."

But we still wish we all lived closer together and could be together more often. For now, Facebook and texting will have to do, supplemented by trips to see them.

They say you can pick your friends, but not your relatives. The Zukerman part of the family is very small, so the relatives we have become closest to are Roz's cousins. Many of her relatives are in Chicago, and we have "adopted" them as close extended family.

Doug and Sherry Gorin are our first cousins, but Doug has been more like a brother to me, and I cherish the Passovers and Thanksgivings we spend together. Sherry, a Barkan, epitomizes what Roz's sister Jeannie gaily observed one day – "We are such nice people!" That they are, and Sherry is a great mom and grandmother. Their daughter, Jenny, was recently married to Randy Scheingold and we could not be happier.

Josh is Sherry and Doug's son; he and his wife, Jennifer, moved here from Chicago – even though Doug and Sherry had a hard time with it – and they took to Los Angeles as if they were born here. Chase and Reid are their two sons and they are delightful, and it is a pleasure to watch them grow up. Sherry's sister, Paula, is another favorite cousin, married to Al Madasky, who was dean of the business school at the University of Chicago. We have always enjoyed our visits with them in Chicago.

On the other side of Roz's family is one of her closest cousins Betty Gaylin, who is married to Will Gaylin, M.D. I met them at our wedding, and we have always remained great friends. Will was a famous Manhattan psychoanalyst and is the author of many great books ... Betty, a woman who says what she means and means what she says. I love them both.

I met Jeannie Glasser, Roz's sister, when she was eight years old, the day I met her father. This beautiful, wonderful lady is a scholar in languages and has been teaching since the day she got out of college – a mission handed down from her father and mother. She and Roz are great friends, besides being sisters.

✧   ✧   ✧   ✧

It's been said that good friends are like stars – you can't always see them, but you know they're there. Friendship is a sanctuary in which we find solace when the rest of the world is inhospitable. And true friends are a blessing too often taken for granted.

A true friend is someone who does not expect too much from you and accepts you as you are – someone who is happy when you succeed, wants the best for you, and is not critical when you fall down. A friend extends a helping hand.

Some people seek friends; some have the ability to attract them. Either way, having good friends around to exert a positive influence on your life is very important.

Friendship doesn't require constant shoring up, and words aren't always required; comfortable silence can equal more than a thousand words. Just being there counts.

But like other enduring relationships, it does require commitment. Sustaining a friendship isn't always easy; it's a responsibility. When someone chooses you as a friend, they have chosen you as one to trust, one in whom they can confide, one to whom they turn for support. In your lifetime, if you can count five good friends, then in my opinion you are a success.

What's a good friend? Someone you can call in the middle of the night and say, "I need you here right now because I need a blood transfusion or a kidney transplant to save my life." If you sent out such an SOS, how many people would come running? One, two? Maybe you could find five – five friends who would bail you out with a kidney or a suitcase full of dollars. In my life, I think I've had five who would.

My old college roommate, Dr. Harry Graff, is a remarkable man and friend. Harry is a psychiatrist who listens to people's problems and then charges them two hundred bucks for listening. Harry has always been my friend and I love him like a brother. In fact, he is my fraternity brother. Harry lives in Miami with his wonderful wife, Ruth. I could always call on Harry in an emergency.

Dr. Selwyn Shkolnik, my other roommate and my doctor, was another such friend. Smart, considerate, kind, Selwyn was one of those rare individuals God gives us for a while, to do wonderful things on earth, and then takes back much sooner than we would wish. I loved this man and I miss him every day. His wife Dee and I have been friends since our first day at the University of Illinois.

Joseph Taback, one of Los Angeles's best lawyers, tough and smart, with a wonderful sense of humor, was one of my first friends in Los Angeles, a man who stood up when I needed him and a man everyone respected. His sense of humor may have been dry, but his wit was keen. I loved him like a brother also. I miss him and always will. Natalie, his wonderful wife, is still one of our dearest friends.

My protégé, Mr. Loren Kessel, is one of the brightest men I have ever known. He is so highly respected in our industry that I like to think I taught him some things, but I suspect it's the other way around. Loren is, and always will be, one of my best pals. He has risen to be a vice president of Cooper, and his work ethics are the best I have ever seen. His wife, Alison, is sweet, bright, a talented writer, and a great mother. Loren will always be a son to me.

The last, but far from least, of the five is my very best friend, Roz – my wife, my pal, my wonderful soulmate, family and friend both. She has been my inspiration in whatever I undertook, never criticized me (wink wink) and my crazy ideas. She was always there when I needed her and is the most wonderful mother – and grandmother – any kids ever had. She never forgets a birthday or anniversary. And all the grandkids admire her for going to law school and becoming a lawyer at the age of 49.

Will Rogers was quoted as saying he never met a man he didn't like. In my business career, I tried to give everyone the benefit of the doubt. My competitors have rarely if ever given me that benefit. I guess I deserved it, because I've always wanted to win at whatever I did.

It has always been my belief that if you work harder than your competitors and give the customer what he wants when he wants it, at a fair price, you will succeed. That philosophy has worked, and it will continue to. It's a constant in this business world, even when the cast of characters changes.

In my time on the business stage, I've gotten to know a lot of people. There are friends, there are acquaintances, and there are colleagues I wish to acknowledge, who have been very important in my life.

Short of calling for that kidney transplant, I've trusted them in life-and-death career situations, and they've never let me down.

Of course there is my old pal from AZA basketball days, Bill Brown, the CEO and owner of Bill Brown Sales and other companies too numerous to mention. Bill and I have remained great friends since we met at 13, and he has always been a stand-up man and a gentleman. He is a leading manufacturer of components for the lighting industry. His wife, Norma, was a bridesmaid at our wedding and has been a friend of Roz since they were 15. Bill is, and will always be, my friend.

Stuart Ingwersen, pal of my youth, is still close to me. He always brings me news from our hometown, keeping me up-to-date as to who died. Kidding aside, Stuart and I will always be friends. His brother, Noel, is also a wonderful friend whom I don't see often enough.

Kirk Nix is a wonderful, kind and sensitive human being who has more talent in his little finger than most interior designers in this world. His firm, KNA, has fast become one of the most successful in this world of design, and Kirk is a close, valued friend for whom I have great admiration.

Pete Thornton, CEO and founder of Focal Point Lighting – when I was down, he was there for me, offering a helping hand. I like to think I helped Pete start his wonderful company when we went to Hanover, Germany, and picked out his future products. He operates a company the old-fashioned way, the correct way.

Frank Conti is head of one of the most successful lighting agencies in America, Enterprise Lighting in NYC. Whatever I had to offer him, he said yes, sight unseen. He is fair, honest and a credit to our industry. I admire this wonderful man and am proud to call him my friend. Frank has inspired and taught me a great deal about respect and what it means to be a good friend.

Bill Warren, the "Professor" – from back in the day at Holophane – was always so much smarter than the rest of us and shared many of my hair-raising adventures in the lighting industry. I admire Bill. His greatest asset is his unbelievable vision. He is still going strong and seeing clearly, an amazing man and great friend.

Simon Atkinson ... When your biggest customer is also your friend, you've arrived. Simon, head of lighting for Capitol Light & Supply, is the fairest, most honest customer I have ever known. Simon was there for me long before I had it made. I will always cherish this friendship.

Bobby Freedman, my partner in Johnson Mercedes, saved my life many times. Without him I could never have made my company successful. I will always love this diamond in the rough. If he likes you he will go to hell and back for you. I never met a man like him. His word is his bond. Sheril, his lovely wife, is a doll and a wonderful lady in the truest sense of the word.

Ken Chyten, my lawyer and man of steel ... always there when I've needed counsel and also the hardest-working and smartest man I have ever known; I admire and respect his brains. We introduced him to his wife, Marci, the daughter of one of my best friends, Joe Taback.

For over 20 years I have had the pleasure of watching the remarkable Keith Johnson develop into the brightest graphic genius on the planet. He has made all our companies better than they were. His friendship will always be an important part of my life.

Drew Andries and Justin Weaver, my two whiz kids, together personified what a company can evolve into when people of vision are on board. Both of these young men are very near and dear to me, engineers who never say "I can't" because they always can.

David Baron, my rabbi, teacher and friend, is a true intellect whose insight amazes me. He has been a close friend for a long time. Adrienne, his beautiful wife, is just as lovely as David and sings like an angel.

Chris Oliva is truly the brightest lady in the lighting business. Even if we almost never have agreed on anything, I respect her diligence and hard work. My company could never have been as good without Chris.

Sean O'Connor is as sweet and sensitive as any man I have ever known, a good and loyal friend and of course a lighting designer of amazing grace, range and brilliance.

Abe Bolsky was a wonderful man who tutored me from day one as head of Tishman Los Angeles and was always there whenever I yelled, "Help!" He will always be in my heart; he is now one of God's helpers.

Joel and Nancy Winter are my New York pals who mean everything to me. They are always considerate and caring and forever my iPod gurus, without whom I would not have any music to listen to. Nancy and I shared so many laughs my stomach still hurts.

Richard Stellar, a big talented teddy bear, a wonderful human being, is as talented and creative with words and graphics as anyone I've ever met. Nuala, his Irish lass, is always there to pick up the pieces.

Stanley and Joyce Black, my first friends in Los Angeles, are the most charitable, wonderful people in this city; they never say no to the needs of others. Joyce should have been a stand-up comic, and Stanley has more friends around the world than Bill Clinton and Ronald McDonald combined.

When you get to be my age, health becomes a concern. Dr. Michael Duffy has been there since the day he took over my former roommate's medical practice, and I admire and respect him not only as a doctor, but a man with real heart.

Dr. David Cossman .... This brilliant and dedicated M.D. saved my life on two different occasions. He is considered one of the best vascular surgeons in this country, and I shall always be grateful for his dedication and perseverance .... Tom Sokol, M.D., who recently had the pleasure of taking out part of my colon, gave me the gift of renewed life. I shall always admire this man of wit and wisdom .... Dr. Carey Strom is a Chicago native who not only is a brilliant physician but could have an evening job as a stand-up comedian.

Greg Skalaski, Billy Pisani and Les Hiscoe, three men from Boston, are great people who live by their word. They run different factions of Shawmut Construction, the most honest and honorable company I have had the pleasure of doing business with. We tried to pull the Patriots through in their Super Bowl game in Phoenix, but to no avail.

Tom Sica .... After knowing this man as a rep and as a friend, I have so much respect and admiration for his ability to stand up and be counted when it matters.

Jerry Feig ... Most of you would not have known him, but he was very instrumental in teaching me about the lighting business. He was bigger than life, an icon who started Marco Lighting, one of the first real recessed lines of products. He later sold to Lighting Corporation of America and became its president. He knew how to run a company the old-fashioned way: the customers came first.

Jerry's son Steve Feig and I have been friends for over 40 years. He is the founder and CEO of Del Ray Lighting, a fantastic company which is recognized as one of the leaders in its field. Steve continues to be an icon in his own right, dazzling the lighting industry with his innovations. I like to think I helped him get started when I took him to Hanover to find the products which later became his core product line.

My Canadian friend, Joey Sadofsky, has built a wonderful lighting company. Joey is one of the old-time friends, always there, and always can be counted on.

Steve O'Bryant is one of my closest friends. His company, O'Bryant Electrical, is one of the three major electric contractors in Los Angeles. We have been together for over 35 years, and he has always been there through thick and thin. I will always treasure his friendship, and his lovely wife, Cathy, is so bright, she keeps everything humming at home and in the office. Steve is currently the president of Los Angeles NECA (National Electric Contractors Association) and I am so proud of him.

Barry and Linda Evanchick, two of our most interesting friends, who live in New Jersey, have been our friends for many years. Barry was the former Lieutenant Governor of New Jersey, and prosecutor of many of New Jersey's worst criminals. His wife, Linda, works for Senator Lautenberg, and Roz loves discussing the political wars going on in Washinton. Wenever we go east, we always catch up with these delightful people.

Ken Walker, competitor and friend, is one in a million, and even though he does not take my advice, I love him as a friend who can always be counted on no matter where you are – in business or a barroom brawl.

There are so many representative organizations I have enjoyed working with, I would like to thank those who were most outstanding. In Los Angeles: Prudential Lighting Products, Jeff Ellis....... New York: Enterprise Lighting Sales, Frank Conti..... Electric Lighting Agency, Tom Sica..... Arizona: Wild West Lighting Sam Kramer..... Redlands, CA: Kirk Sommers Sales Inc., Kirk Sommers...... San Francisco, CA: Cal Lighting, Mike

Butala..... San Diego, CA: Western Light Source , Andy Fisher..... Las Vegas, NV: Alsco, Inc., Art Sloan....... Philadelphia, PA: Marty Berman Associates, Larry Berman ...... Miami, FL: Lighting Dynamics, Inc., Sandy Langer...... Washington, DC: New Design Light, Tom Albert...... Chicago, Ill: Pilipuf and Grist Associates, Nick Pilipuf....... Little Rock, AR: Malmstrom White, Doug Malmstrom.... Denver, CO: Illumination Systems, Jack English.... Orlando, FL: Lighting Partners of Central Florida, Shane Rawleigh....... Tampa, FL: Tampa Bay Lighting, Jeff Buchanan....... Albany, NY: Quality Lighting, Bruce Ballderston.......

Charlotte, NC: Bodwell & Associates, Ken Bodwell..... Detroit, MI: Resource Lighting, Jeff Chaney...... Minneapolis, MN: Pulse Products, Jon Kirkhoff... St Louis, MO: Lighting Associates, Paul Warner and David Jockenhofer....... Spokane, WA: Ambient Lighting, Mike Peters .... Seattle, WA: Pacific Lighting, Mike Thomas......

Dallas, TX: Texas Lighting Sales, Jim Weathers ... Hawaii: Sunburst Design, Peter Dawson..... Boston, MA: Reflex Lighting, Paul Mustone..... Last but not least an old friend in Miami, FL.. Stuart Yageroff

Bruce Belfer of Belfer Lighting is not a close pal, but I want to compliment a competitor who took a company that was in shambles and built it up to national prominence. I'm proud of Bruce and his hard work ....

Today Zia Eftikar is head of Phillips Lightolier Lighting, something he has always wanted. I admire him and am proud to call this competitor an old friend.

I respect the competition Rick Spaulding, CEO of Lightlab Corporation, has given me over the years; he is one tough competitor.

Tim O'Brien, CEO of Zumtobel, has the toughest job in America – to sell his products west of the Mississippi, but if I know Tim, he will get it done. A great guy with whom we loved to travel through Europe ... Mark Eubanks, the new head of Cooper Lighting, is bright, educated and a delightful individual who deserves great respect and admiration. I wish him well in the world of lighting ... After working with Dean Dal Ponte for two years, I am proud to call this delightful man my friend.

Well, that's about it, although I'm sure I'm leaving someone out. Did I say I had five true friends? After looking over this final chapter, I feel more like George Bailey in *It's a Wonderful Life* – the richest man in town.

It has been a wonderful life – and it's not over yet. I've had my share of battles since my childhood ones, and I haven't won every one, but it definitely hasn't been dull. It's been said that the ancient Greeks never wrote a man's obituary. They asked only one question: "Did he have passion?" If the answer was yes, the man had lived a full life. By that standard, my life's been a success – and there's enough passion left in the tank to keep going.

Jack Zukerman

My Wife: Roz Zukerman

My Four Children: Mike, Jeff, Marti & Steve

My Grandsons: Brad Zukerman, Jake Zukerman & Max Artsis

My Granddaughters:
Sara Zukerman, Lynn Zukerman, Kate Zukerman, Nicole Zukerman,
Jamie Artsis, Julia Zukerman & Molly Zukerman
Note: Rachel and Marielle Zukerman were not present
when the photo was taken.

My Granddaughter, Jamie Artsis, playing soccer at University of Michigan
Picture courtesy of University of Michigan Athletic Department

INDEX

ABOUT THE AUTHOR

Jack Zukerman is an entrepreneur, an American industrialist, and manufacturer who carved a niche for himself and his companies in an industry that demanded innovation. J. Paul Getty's formula for success is to rise early, work hard and strike oil.

In the case of Jack Zukerman, oil took the form of a small halogen lamp that revolutionized lighting. Zukerman's duality as a well respected and judicious captain of industry is often pitted against his "roll the dice" flair for creating out-of-the-box marketing campaigns that firmly cemented a popular lighting trend into modern day architecture. If taking chances in life is your thing, then Zukerman is your type of man. Jack's journey was punctuated by giants of industry, monarchs and mobsters. Zukerman's business accomplishments were tempered by his commitment to family and friends.

Jack Zukerman lives in Los Angeles with his wife, Roz, an accomplished attorney.